Step-by-Step Cooking

Gary Rhodes

Step-by-Step Cooking

Gary Rhodes

**Over 100 easy-to-follow recipes
and essential techniques**

EBURY PRESS
LONDON

First published in Great Britain in 2001

3 5 7 9 10 8 6 4

First published by Ebury Press
Random House, 20 Vauxhall Bridge Road,
London SW1V 2SA

Random House Australia (Pty) Limited
20 Alfred Street, Milsons Point, Sydney, New South Wales 2061, Australia

Random House New Zealand Limited
18 Poland Road, Glenfield, Auckland 10, New Zealand

Random House South Africa (Pty) Limited
Endulini, 5A Jubilee Road, Parktown 2193, South Africa

The Random House Group Limited Reg. No. 954009

www.randomhouse.co.uk

A CIP catalogue record for this book is available
from the British Library.

ISBN 0 09 188085 8

This book was designed, edited and produced by
Eaglemoss Publications Ltd, based on the partwork
Good Cooking with Gary Rhodes

Printed and bound in Italy by De Agostini

contents

introduction

Nothing beats a home-made meal cooked to perfection. But if you thought good food meant using unusual ingredients and complicated techniques, then think again. In *Step-by-step Cooking* you'll find all the kitchen know-how you need to prepare mouth-watering meals – quickly and with the minimum of fuss – with ingredients that are easily obtainable.

Step-by-step Cooking is a collection of over 100 delicious recipes for light meals, main meals and desserts, each illustrated with full-colour step-by-step photographs that show you exactly what to do from start to finish. Since good cooking depends on mastering the essential techniques, all the basic skills are clearly explained and I've also added some of my favourite top tips to give you extra advice whenever you need it.

In addition to each main dish, I've added variations and serving suggestions to give a twist to traditional recipes so that you can adapt them to cater for all tastes and occasions.

Here's wishing you many years of happy cooking.

essential information

kitchen safety

- **Always wash your hands before preparing or handling food.**
- **Wash fresh produce before preparation.**
- **Prepare and store raw and cooked food separately.**
- **Clean work surfaces, chopping boards and utensils between preparing food which is to be cooked and food which is not.**
- **Put chilled and frozen foods into your fridge or freezer as soon as possible after purchase.**
- **Keep raw meat and fish at the bottom of your fridge.**
- **Keep the coldest part of your fridge at 0-5°C.**
- **If you are pregnant or elderly, avoid food that contains raw eggs.**
- **Check _use by_ dates on packaging and keep to them.**
- **If re-heating food, make sure that it's piping hot.**
- **Keep pets away from worktops and food dishes.**

notes on the recipes

- **Measurements are given in both metric and imperial: do not mix the two.**
- **Spoon measurements are level.**
- **Tbsp and tsp are used for table spoon and teaspoon: tbsp means 15ml, tsp means 5ml. An accurate set of measuring spoons helps to avoid mistakes.**
- **Season, unless otherwise stated, means seasoning with salt and freshly ground black pepper.**
- **Eggs are size 2 (large).**
- **Ingredients are listed with the most important first, then other ingredients in the order of use.**

oven temperatures			
Celsius	**Fahrenheit**	**Gas**	**Description**
110°C	250°F	$^1/_4$	Cool
120°C	250°F	$^1/_2$	Cool
140°C	275°F	1	Very low
150°C	300°F	2	Very low
160°C	325°F	3	Low
170°C	325°F	3	Moderate
180°C	350°F	4	Moderate
190°C	375°F	5	Moderately hot
200°C	400°F	6	Hot
220°C	425°F	7	Hot
230°C	450°F	8	Very hot

stocks

Stocks are must-have ingredients for successful cooking. It's well worth making a batch of stock once a month and freezing it in the amounts needed for your favourite recipes. Stocks keep for two months in the freezer. However, if you haven't the time or have run out, you can buy ready-made meat, fish or vegetable stocks in the chill cabinets of most large supermarkets – these have authentic colours and flavours. Alternatively, use stock cubes – choose either the salt-free variety or dissolve them in slightly more water than recommended (twice the amount for fish cubes) to reduce the saltiness.

Meat stock

Traditionally, rich brown meat stocks were made from beef or veal bones. But a relatively inexpensive cut of beef, such as shin, makes great stock too. Browning the onions and vegetables first will ensure the stock has a richer colour.

beef stock

makes about 1.7 litres (3 pints)
pre-heat oven 200°C /400°F/ gas 6

ingredients
1.8kg (4lb) shin of beef,
cut into large pieces
2 large carrots, coarsely chopped
3 celery sticks, coarsely chopped
2 large onions, unpeeled and quartered
2 tbsp olive oil
1 leek, chopped
6 peppercorns
1 sprig of fresh thyme
1 bay leaf

equipment
large saucepan – about 4.5 litres (8 pints) capacity or larger

1 Roast the carrots and celery in the oven for 20 minutes until lightly browned.
2 While the vegetables are roasting, in a large saucepan, sweat the onions in oil for 30 minutes, stirring occasionally, until richly browned.
3 Transfer roasted vegetables to the saucepan. Lay all the remaining ingredients on top and fill the pan to within 2.5cm (1in) of the rim with cold water.
4 Bring to the boil slowly, removing any scum which floats to the top with a large metal spoon. Turn down the heat and simmer for 4 hours. Occasionally remove any more scum which rises to the surface.
5 To strain the stock, ladle the liquid, vegetables and meat into a sieve or colander over a large bowl, jug or saucepan. For the clearest stock, line the sieve with clean muslin first.

chicken stock

makes about 1.2 litres (2 pints)

ingredients
0.9kg (2lb) raw chicken carcasses or joints
25g (1oz) unsalted butter
1 onion, peeled and chopped
1 celery stick, chopped
1 leek, roughly chopped
3 black peppercorns
1 bay leaf
1 sprig of fresh thyme
1.5-2 litres (3-3½ pints) cold water

1 In a large saucepan, melt the butter and lightly soften the onion, celery and leek, without letting them get browned.
2 Add the chicken, peppercorns, bay leaf and thyme to the pot.
3 Cover with the water and bring slowly to the boil. With a metal spoon, remove any scum that rises to the surface.
4 Reduce the heat and simmer for 2-3 hours, de-scumming occasionally.
5 Strain the stock through a sieve or colander set over a large bowl, jug or clean saucepan, and throw away the bones, herbs and vegetables.

For white stock, you can use a raw chicken carcass, bony chicken joints – wings or drumsticks are best – or a whole chicken, which you can eat as well.

fish stock

**makes 2 litres
(3½ pints)**

preparation time
10 minutes

cooking time *30 minutes*

ingredients
55g (2oz) unsalted butter
1 large onion, sliced
1 leek, sliced
2 celery sticks, sliced
a few stalks of fresh parsley
1 bay leaf
6 black peppercorns
900g (2lb) turbot, sole or plaice bones
*300ml (10fl oz) dry
white wine*
2.25 litres (4 pints) water

1 Melt the butter in a large pan over a low heat. Add the onion, leek and celery and stir well.
2 Cook slowly for 3-4 minutes, or until the vegetables are softening but not coloured. Then add the fresh parsley, bay leaf and black peppercorns.
3 Meanwhile, chop the bones with scissors and rinse under cold water. Add to the pan and cook for a few more minutes.
4 Pour in the wine. Boil vigorously for 2-3 minutes until almost dry. Add the water, bring to the boil and simmer for 20 minutes, removing any scum with a large metal spoon.
5 Ladle the stock into a sieve set over a bowl. Discard all the bones and vegetables.

Turbot and sole bones produce the best-flavoured stock, although you can also use plaice, cod, haddock, whiting, coley and salmon bones. Avoid mackerel and herring bones because these produce an oily stock with a distinctive flavour.

For all types of fish stock you can either use bones and trimmings from fish you have filleted yourself, or ask your fishmonger to do the filleting for you. Always remove the eyes and gills from any fish heads, since these will impair the stock's flavour and appearance.

pastry

Making your own pastry adds a personal touch to pies, tarts and quiches. So if you have the time, try out the recipes below. Otherwise, you can buy several types of ready-made or partly-made pastry in most supermarkets. Look for fresh pastry in the chill cabinets and frozen pastry in the freezer section.

Shortcrust pastry

Melt-in-the-mouth shortcrust pastry is the quickest and easiest pastry to make at home. Simply follow a few tricks of the trade and featherlight shortcrust pastry is very straight-forward to make.

shortcrust pastry

makes 350g (12oz)

preparation time *10 minutes*

resting time *20 minutes after binding, 15 minutes after lining dish*

for **cooking times** *and* **oven temperatures** *follow individual recipes*

ingredients
225g (8oz) plain flour
150g (5oz) chilled unsalted butter, chopped
1 egg, beaten (an extra egg yolk can be added for a richer flavour)

equipment
large mixing bowl
metal sieve
rolling pin, at least 30cm (12in) long
large marble slab or cool, smooth surface for rolling

1 Sift the flour into a bowl. Using your hands, rub the butter into the flour, lifting the mixture above bowl level to introduce air, until the mixture resembles coarse breadcrumbs.
2 Add the beaten egg and mix it into the pastry crumbs with a round-bladed knife until they start to bind together. Then, using one hand, lightly gather the mixture together to form a soft, but not sticky ball of dough.
3 Wrap the ball of dough in a sheet of plastic wrap and chill in the fridge for 20 minutes before starting to roll it out.

rolling the dough

1 Lightly flour the rolling pin and surface. Starting from the centre, roll outwards, working in one direction only – generally away from you – using short strokes.
2 Regularly give the dough a quarter turn to prevent it from sticking and lift it occasionally to re-flour underneath.
3 Roll the dough out until it is about 3mm (⅛in) thick and forms a circle at least 5cm (2in) in diameter larger than the dish being lined.

lining the dish

1 Grease the dish before lining it. Wrap the pastry around the rolling pin, taking care not to stretch it, and unwind it over the dish. Let the surplus pastry hang over the edge.
2 Press the sheet of dough gently down into the angle between the sides and the base.
3 Roll the rolling pin over the top of the dish to cut off the surplus dough or trim off excess with a small knife.
4 With a fork, prick small holes across the base to let any steam that forms during baking escape.

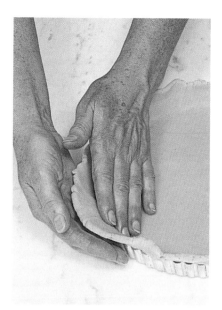

variations

It's easy to make delicious pastry variations. All you need to do is add extra ingredients to the flour or use a different type of flour.

pepper pastry
Add 2 tbsp freshly ground black pepper.
nutty pastry
Add 1 tbsp finely chopped roast hazelnuts or almonds.

wholemeal pastry
Substitute 115g (4oz) plain wholemeal flour for half the quantity of plain flour.

Puff pastry
Traditional puff pastry is the flakiest, and perhaps the trickiest, pastry of all to make. The recipe below describes a much simpler and quicker method. The result is almost as rich and light as the traditional version, and makes an excellent substitute in all but the most elaborate recipes.

puff pastry

makes about 675g (1½lb)
450g (1lb) plain flour, chilled
1 tsp salt
275g (10oz) butter, chilled until very hard and sliced into small pieces
300ml (10fl oz) iced water

1 Sieve the flour with the salt into a chilled mixing bowl.
2 Add the butter and water to the flour and salt in the bowl. Using two blunt knives, slice and fold the ingredients together, making sure you do not chop up the butter too finely.
3 Gather the dough into a ball. Work quickly, to avoid overhandling the dough and softening the butter. Cover with plastic wrap and refrigerate for 30 minutes.

rolling the dough

1 On a lightly floured surface, roll out the dough to a neat rectangle, 45cm (18in) long and 15cm (6in) wide, with square corners. Roll the dough away from you, making sure it doesn't stick.
2 With a short side of the dough towards you, fold the top one-third into the middle. Then fold the bottom third over it to form a square of dough.
3 Turn the dough through 90° to bring the top seam to the left.
4 Gently press all the seams with the rolling pin to seal them. Leave to rest for 20 minutes in the fridge.
5 Repeat the rolling, folding and turning cycle three times. Let the dough rest for 20 minutes between each cycle.

chapter one
light meals

fish & shellfish

Fish soups 13-16

Fish tarts 17-20

Fish quenelles 21-24

meat & poultry

Tortillas 25-28

Meat pasties 29-32

Meat terrines 33-36

vegetarian

Omelettes 37-40

Savoury egg tarts 41-44

Savoury tartes tatin 45-48

fish soups

You can make fish soup with most kinds of fish but red mullet gives one of the best flavours for this tasty meal in a bowl

There are many interpretations of fish soup – ranging from a stew-like bouillabaisse from the South of France to the creamy chowders of New England.

Colourful broth

Here versatile red mullet is used to make a chunky broth and an equally flavoursome smooth soup. Red mullet is an ideal ingredient for soup making – it's wonderful sweet flavour makes a tasty stock for both of these soups. The vibrant colour of the red mullet fillets makes an attractive garnish for the broth – with crisp air-dried ham adding a splendid final flourish.

However, fish broths and soups like these are very adaptable and you get equally good results using a variety of other white fish, such as tilapia or sea bass, instead of the red mullet. In practice, it's best to opt for the freshest fish available on the day from your fishmonger. Just avoid salmon and trout, herring or mackerel, which are rather oily.

Rich smoothie

If you prefer a silky smooth soup, try the variation recipe. For a continental touch, serve it with spicy sun-dried tomato mayon-naise on toasted French bread.

Gary's special touch

I love the savoury taste of Bayonne and Parma ham. They are both air-dried hams which go almost brittle when grilled. This texture and their cured flavours work very well with the red mullet and add an extra dimension to the soup. If you can't get hold of either ham, use thinly cut, lean streaky smoked bacon.

making red mullet broth

You will need

serves 4

preparation time
1 hour

cooking time
1 hour 5 minutes

for the stock
450g (1lb) whole red mullet
knob of unsalted butter
1 onion, roughly chopped
1 carrot, roughly chopped
1 leek, roughly chopped
2-3 celery sticks, roughly chopped
1 fennel bulb, roughly chopped
1 garlic clove, crushed
½ bunch fresh tarragon
1 star anise

pinch of saffron
4 tomatoes, quartered
2 glasses white wine, about 300ml (10fl oz)
1.2 litres (2 pints) water

for the broth
4 small fillets of red mullet, scaled and boned
1 tbsp olive oil
1 large carrot, cut into 5mm (¼in) dice
1 large onion, cut into 5mm (¼in) dice
2 celery sticks, cut into 5mm (¼in) dice
1 small fennel bulb, cut into 5mm (¼in) dice
55g (2oz) Bayonne or

Parma ham
2 tomatoes, skinned, deseeded and diced
25g (1oz) unsalted butter
a few tarragon leaves to garnish
salt and pepper

for the rouille
1 red pepper, deseeded and chopped
1 small red chilli, deseeded and chopped
2 garlic cloves, crushed
55g (2oz) fresh white breadcrumbs
1 egg yolk
150ml (5fl oz) extra virgin olive oil

1 To make the stock, melt a knob of butter in a large saucepan and cook the onion, carrot, leek, celery, fennel, garlic, tarragon and star anise for 6-8 minutes until softened.

The quality of the fish stock you use is crucial to the final flavour of both soups. It's best to make your own but, failing that, a good bought fresh fish stock from the chill cabinet is fine.

To make your own stock, sweat as much flavour from the vegetables as possible to add depth to the soup. Then make sure that the whole red mullet is washed and gutted before you cut it into pieces. You can throw in the head and bones as they are strained out later. When straining the stock, use the back of a ladle to press the fish and vegetable mixture gently to extract maximum flavour.

Smart finish
When you buy the red mullet fillets for the broth, ask your fishmonger to scale them for you or do it yourself. Simply run the blade of a knife against the scales under cold running water to remove them.

For an attractive-looking broth, dice the vegetables as neatly as possible. To garnish the finished broth in the bowls, grill the Parma or Bayonne ham before you grill the fish as it doesn't have to be hot when you serve it.

Making rouille
The rouille is made in much the same way as home-made mayonnaise. Once all the other ingredients have been blitzed in the food processor, add the oil in a slow trickle. Continue until all of it is incorporated and the rouille is thick, glossy and smooth. Passing it through a sieve makes it even smoother.

5 Cut the ham into strips, then grill for 1-2 minutes until crisp. Butter a baking tray, put the red mullet fillets on top and grill for 3-4 minutes.

2 Add the saffron and tomatoes and cook for 1-2 more minutes. Chop up the fish and add the pieces, including the head and bones, to the pan. Cook for a further 3 minutes.

3 Add white wine and reduce by three-quarters. Add the water and cook for 20-30 minutes. Strain through a sieve, pressing the mixture very lightly with the back of a ladle.

4 To make the broth, heat the olive oil in a large saucepan, add the diced vegetables and cook for 6-8 minutes until softened. Add the mullet stock and simmer for 10 minutes.

6 For the rouille, blitz all the ingredients, except the oil, in a food processor. Add a little oil, replace the lid, and drizzle in the rest of the oil. Sieve, then chill.

7 Stir the tomato and butter into the broth and season well. Add the tarragon leaves. Ladle the broth into the bowls and arrange a mullet fillet on top. Top with the crispy ham strips, garnish with a few more tarragon leaves and serve with dollops of rouille.

Variations on a theme

red mullet soup

This smooth rich soup has a bisque-like texture. It is served with a hot spicy mayonnaise on toasted French bread.

serves 4

preparation time
15 minutes

cooking time
50 minutes

for the soup
450g (1lb) red mullet fillets, scaled and sliced
2 tbsp olive oil
225g (8oz) tomatoes, chopped
1 fennel bulb, chopped
1 large onion, chopped
2 carrots, chopped
1 leek, chopped
2 celery sticks, chopped
1 garlic clove, crushed
300ml (10fl oz) Noilly
Prat or dry vermouth
300ml (10fl oz) white wine
a pinch of saffron
1.2 litres (2 pints) fish stock (see page 9)
2 tsp tomato purée
small bunch fresh basil
small bunch fresh tarragon
salt and pepper

for the rouille
1 tsp sun-dried tomato paste
1 tsp harissa (chilli paste)
2 garlic cloves, crushed
150ml (5fl oz) ready-made mayonnaise
4 thick slices French bread
basil leaves, to garnish

1 Heat the oil in a pan and sweat the tomatoes, vegetables and garlic for 2-3 minutes.
2 Add the red mullet fillets, Noilly Prat and white wine. Bring to the boil, then simmer for 5-6 minutes.
3 Add the saffron, stock and tomato purée. Simmer for 40 minutes. Add the herbs and season.
4 Process the soup in batches in a food processor. Pass through a sieve into a clean saucepan. Heat gently.
5 For the rouille, stir the sun-dried tomato paste, harissa and garlic into the mayonnaise. Spoon on to the toasted bread.
6 Ladle the soup into bowls, float the rouille toasts on top. Garnish with the basil leaves.

why not try...

fish by any other name
The red mullet broth is just as good made with snapper, John Dory or sea bass.

in a seashell
For a real treat, add cooked, shellfish, such as mussels, clams, prawns, crabs, scallops and razorshells, in or out of their shells, to the finished broth.

white fish
For the variation, most white fish – including plaice or lemon sole – blitzes well to give you a smooth soup.

spicy
Add some spice to the soup by sprinkling a large pinch of chilli flakes into the vegetables when you sweat them off, or use a fresh deseeded and chopped chilli.

creamy
You can swirl a little double cream into the smooth red mullet soup at the last moment for extra richness.

eats well with...

As these soups are quite rich, fresh crusty bread is the only accompaniment they need. For a more substantial meal in a bowl, you could serve boiled new potatoes with the red mullet broth.

fish tarts

Delicate, flavourful and good hot or cold, fish tarts are delicious served with a piquant dressing

Fish, which combines delicacy of texture with a rich taste, tastes particularly good when it's baked in a tart. This is especially true of smoked fish, which has an extra depth of savoury flavour. Combined with cream and eggs, smoked haddock and salmon produce tarts which are a sophisticated delight.

Fish tarts are excellent as lunch dishes or, made in individual tins, perfect for dinner party starters. They eat well hot or cold so are also ideal for picnics.

Smoky flavour
The salty-sweet flavour of smoked haddock, mellowed by cream and eggs, makes a sensational tart. The fish is poached in cream, which is then cooled, whisked with eggs and poured over the flaked haddock in the tart cases. Here the individual tarts are served with a spicy tomato dressing which you can make in a couple of minutes, while you are waiting for the tarts to bake.

Salmon tart
In the variation recipe, smoked salmon is combined with white wine, dill, onion, cream and eggs to produce a luxurious dish. You can accompany it with a simple leaf salad.

Gary's special touch

This is an old favourite of mine. The taste of smoked haddock permeating the whole tart is just sensational and the creamy filling, pepped up with parmesan, is a treat. I do recommend you use smoked haddock which hasn't been dyed bright yellow – the uncoloured version is so much better.

making smoked haddock tart

You will need

serves 6

preparation time *15 minutes, plus 20 minutes for chilling pastry*

cooking time *15-20 minutes for pastry; 10-15 minutes for tarts*

pre-heat oven *200°C/400°F/gas 6*

ingredients

225g (8oz) puff or shortcrust pastry (see pages 9-10)

280-350g (10-12oz) smoked haddock fillet

300ml (10fl oz) double cream

a knob of butter

2 onions, finely sliced

2 eggs, beaten

1 tbsp freshly grated parmesan

for the dressing (makes 500ml/18fl oz)

9 tbsp tomato ketchup

125ml (4fl oz) white wine vinegar

3 tbsp Worcestershire sauce

a few drops of Tabasco sauce

150ml (5fl oz) extra virgin olive oil

150ml (5fl oz) olive oil

3 shallots, finely chopped

4 tomatoes, skinned, deseeded and diced

2 tbsp chopped fresh basil or tarragon

salt and pepper

equipment

6 x 10cm (4in) tart tins, buttered; baking sheet

When making this dish, it's important to bear in mind that smoked haddock is already quite salty. Much of this salt will pass into the cream in which the fish is poached, so there is no need to add more salt. Add a little pepper to taste as you make up the cream and egg mixture – but go easy on this.

The smoked haddock is poached for 2 minutes in the cream. You can tell whether it is cooked by trying to separate the flakes with the point of a knife. The flakes should start to come away quite easily. They will also look opaque and white when cooked – if they aren't quite cooked, they appear transparent. As you flake the cooked haddock, keep a look out for bones – remove and discard any that you come across. Tweezers are particularly handy for removing tiny bones. Discard the fish skin as well.

Big tart

If you prefer to make the smoked haddock tart in one large pastry case, remember that you will need to bake it for 25-30 minutes – 10-15 minutes longer than the individual tarts.

Spice it up

A smoked haddock tart is excellent served with a spicy tomato dressing. You get the best flavour for the dressing if you use half extra virgin olive oil, mixed with a less deeply-flavoured oil – in this case, standard olive oil. The dressing is intensely flavoured and piquant so you only need a small quantity on the plate. Serve more on the table in a jug, and refrigerate any left over. It will keep well for several days and tastes wonderful with other smoked fish dishes or chicken. Serve lemon wedges with the tart too.

1 Make pastry and line tins. Chill for 20 minutes, then line with greaseproof paper and baking beans, and bake blind for 15-20 minutes. Remove paper and beans. Leave oven on.

5 Break the haddock into flakes, discarding the skin and any bones. Distribute the onions between the pastry cases, then top with the fish.

2 Poach the smoked haddock. Put the fillet in a sauté pan, add the cream, bring to a simmer, then cook for 2 minutes. Remove the haddock and set aside. Save the cream.

3 Melt butter in a frying-pan and add the onions. Cook for a few minutes until soft and golden. Remove onions, squeezing out as much butter as possible with a spoon.

4 Add half the cooled, fish-infused cream (discard the rest) to the beaten egg. Whisk to combine thoroughly, then stir in the freshly grated parmesan.

6 Pour the egg, cream and parmesan mix into the pastry cases. Sit tarts on baking sheet and bake for 15 minutes until filling is set and golden.

7 Make dressing. Mix ketchup, vinegar, Worcestershire sauce and Tabasco. Then whisk in olive oils. Add shallots, tomatoes and herbs; taste and season. Serve with warm haddock tarts.

Variations on a theme

smoked salmon tart

To make this tasty dish, you can use smoked salmon trimmings which are less expensive than whole pieces. To lower the fat content, use crème fraîche in place of cream.

serves 6-8

preparation time
15 minutes, plus
20 minutes chilling pastry

cooking time
15-20 minutes for pastry;
25-30 minutes for tart

pre-heat oven
190°C/375°F/gas 5

ingredients
225g (8oz) shortcrust pastry (see pages 9-10)
300ml (10fl oz) white wine
10 peppercorns
a knob of butter
1 large onion, finely chopped
300ml (10fl oz) single or double cream
2 eggs, beaten
salt and pepper
225g (8oz) smoked salmon trimmings, chopped into 2.5cm (1in) pieces
1 tbsp chopped fresh dill
2 tbsp grated cheddar

equipment
23cm (9in) fluted tin, about 4cm (1½in) deep, buttered; baking sheet

1 Make pastry, then roll out and line the flan tin. Refrigerate for 20 minutes, then line with greaseproof paper and baking beans and bake blind for 15-20 minutes. Remove paper and beans. Leave oven on.
2 Put wine and peppercorns in a pan and boil to reduce to 2-3 tbsp. Remove and discard peppercorns.
3 Melt butter in a frying-pan and add onion. Cook for a few minutes until soft but not browned. Then squeeze out as much butter as possible with a spatula.
4 Add cream to the beaten eggs with the cooled reduced wine and whisk. Season to taste with pepper and a little salt.
5 Arrange the onions evenly over the base of the pastry case. Cover them with the smoked salmon and sprinkle fresh dill on top.
6 Top the fish with grated cheese then pour the egg, cream and wine mixture carefully into the pastry case. Then sit tart on the baking sheet and bake in the oven for 25-30 minutes until filling is set and top is golden-brown. Serve warm or cold with a crisp cucumber salad.

why not try...

different fish
Replace the smoked haddock or salmon with skinned fillets of trout, lightly poached in milk. Add some just-wilted spinach, roughly chopped, to the tart filling. Alternatively, use flaked smoked mackerel in place of salmon in the variation recipe – serve with a bold mustard sauce and lots of green salad.

wholemeal
For a nuttier flavour and richer colour, make the fish tart with wholemeal pastry. For home-made pastry, simply replace half the plain flour with wholemeal (see page 10).

eats well with...

Serve smoky-flavoured fish tarts with simple accompaniments such as mixed salads, new potatoes, lightly boiled or steamed carrots, cauliflower or broccoli. An exception to this rule is tomatoes – their slight acidity is the perfect foil to the creamy tart fillings. Slice them, roast them or stuff with a herby filling and serve alongside the tarts.

fish quenelles

Quenelles are little dumplings of puréed fish, perfect for a light lunch or an elegant dinner party starter

Definitely the aristocrats of the dumplings, quenelles are light, delicate combinations of very finely puréed fish made into a mousse with egg whites and cream. (The name *quenelle* comes from the German word for dumpling – *knödel*). The aim is to make the puréed fish absorb the cream – the egg whites help with this, as does the addition of salt. The quenelles are shaped between two spoons, then briefly poached in water or stock, drained and served with a well-flavoured, creamy sauce.

Fine texture

It's possible to make quenelles with a very light mousse consisting solely of fish, egg white, cream, salt and pepper. However, in these recipes, the basic fish purée is strengthened with breadcrumbs and, in the variation recipe, milk and butter. The main recipe uses fresh crab meat and the quenelles are served with a fish *beurre blanc*.

Whiting quenelles

Whiting is a favourite fish for quenelles – its firm but fine white flesh is ideal for puréeing. In the variation recipe, whiting quenelles are served with a rich, buttery hollandaise sauce.

Gary's special touch

Crab is quite an unusual choice for tender little quenelles but the flavour is sweet and delicious. Like most shellfish, crab is more moist than ordinary fish so the breadcrumbs are important for creating a firm, mouldable texture. Use a mixture of white and dark crab meat – the dark meat alone would be too wet.

making crab quenelles

You will need

serves 4	shellfish stock (see page 24)
preparation time 20-30 minutes	
cooking time 10-15 minutes	**for the beurre blanc**
	1 shallot, peeled and finely chopped
for the quenelles	5 tbsp fish stock (see page 9) or
675g (1½lb) crab meat – brown and	shellfish stock, using your crab shells
white mixed	(see page 24)
salt and pepper	1 tbsp white wine vinegar
2 egg whites	225g (8oz) unsalted butter, cut into
150ml (5fl oz) double cream	thin slices and chilled
175g (6oz) stale white breadcrumbs	salt and freshly ground white pepper
300ml (10fl oz) fish stock (see	a squeeze of lemon juice
page 9) or court-bouillon or	

You'll need 1 very large crab or 2 smaller ones to produce 675g (1½lb) meat. Reserve the shells and use to make shellfish stock. You could substitute canned crab for fresh, but the flavour won't be as good.

A food processor is very useful for making the purée, although you can pound the crab with a pestle and mortar, then sieve it. Keep everything cold to help stop the mix from splitting. A further precaution is to refrigerate the mix after the egg whites have been added but before the cream and breadcrumbs go in.

Use tablespoons to mould the quenelles, dipping the spoons into hot water between each quenelle to make it easier to get a smooth shape.

Flavour bath

The quenelle poaching liquor is important for flavour. You can use salted water, but court-bouillon, fish stock or shellfish stock give more depth. When ready, the quenelles should be just firm to the touch and creamy inside. This should take about

Cook's notes

Fish stock
Home-made fish stock is the best poaching liquid for these quenelles. If you don't have time to make your own, use a carton of fresh stock from the supermarket. Avoid stock cubes, as they are generally over-salty and have a less delicate flavour.

12 minutes but times may vary. If the tops of the quenelles are still wet, flip them over and poach for a little longer.

Butter up

Make the *beurre blanc* while the quenelles are poaching. The sauce consists largely of butter, flavoured with an intense reduction of shallots, vinegar and fish stock. It's important that you keep the stock mixture hot but not boiling while you whisk in the butter – too much heat and the sauce will separate.

Put the crab into a food processor or liquidizer and blitz to a purée. Season with salt. Put the mixture in a large bowl, sitting in another bowl full of ice, and beat until smooth.

5 Poach quenelles very gently for 10-15 minutes until firm. Remove with a slotted spoon, drain on kitchen paper and keep them warm.

2 Beat the egg white very briefly with a fork to break it down slightly, then gradually add it to the crab purée in the bowl. Beat the mix until thoroughly combined.

3 Keeping the bowl on ice, beat in the cream a little at a time, making sure the mixture remains fairly firm. Stir in the breadcrumbs and season well with salt and pepper.

4 Heat the fish stock in a sauté pan. Beat the crab mix hard, then, using 2 wet tablespoons, mould the crab mix into egg shapes and slide them into the hot stock.

6 For the sauce, boil shallot, stock and vinegar until reduced to 2 tbsp. Strain, return to pan. Keeping stock hot, whisk in butter until sauce is thick.

7 Season sauce with salt, pepper and lemon juice. Flood the plates with the sauce, then arrange 3 quenelles on each plate.

Variations on a theme

whiting quenelles

These delicious quenelles are made with a fluffy, delicate whiting mousse. Serve them with hollandaise sauce for a rich and impressive starter.

serves 4

preparation time
20-30 minutes

cooking time
10-15 minutes, plus 2-3 minutes grilling

for the quenelles
55g (2oz) stale white breadcrumbs
2 tbsp milk
15g (½oz) butter, melted
hollandaise sauce (see page 172, at double quantity)
350g (12oz) whiting fillet, skinned, boned and chopped
pinch of grated nutmeg
juice of half a lemon
2 egg whites
125ml (4fl oz) double cream
salt

for the garnish
115g (4oz) cooked shelled prawns
fresh dill, finely chopped

1 Put the breadcrumbs into a bowl and pour milk over them. Add the melted butter. Mix to a coarse paste, then chill for at least 1 hour.

2 Make the hollandaise sauce (see page 172) and keep it warm by sitting it in a bowl over hot water while you cook the quenelles.

3 Put the breadcrumb paste, fish, nutmeg, lemon juice and egg whites into a food processor. Blitz to a smooth purée.

4 With processor still running, pour in cream, taking no more than 10 seconds to add it.

5 Fill a sauté pan with salted water, to a depth of about 5cm (2in). Bring to the boil, then reduce to a slow simmer.

6 Mould the whiting mousse into quenelles with 2 tablespoons dipped in hot water. Slide each quenelle into the poaching liquid and poach gently for 10-15 minutes until firm when pressed.

7 Remove quenelles from the liquid with a slotted spoon and drain on kitchen paper. Place them in a warm, buttered dish.

8 Pre-heat grill to high. Pour warm hollandaise sauce over quenelles, then place gratin dish under grill and cook until golden. Garnish with cooked prawns and fresh dill.

why not try...

court-bouillon
A court-bouillon is an alternative to stock for poaching quenelles. Put 1.1 litres (2 pints) water into a large saucepan with 150ml (5fl oz) white wine vinegar, 1 peeled, sliced carrot, 1 peeled, sliced onion, 1 stick of celery, 12 black peppercorns, 2 bay leaves and a little salt. Bring to the boil and simmer for 20 minutes. Cool, then strain and use as required.

shellfish stock
Yet another alternative is to poach the quenelles in shellfish stock – or use shellfish stock for making the *beurre blanc*. Put 1 peeled, sliced onion, 1 peeled, sliced carrot, 1 sliced stick of celery, a selection of shells (prawns, mussel shells, lobster or crab cases), 1 bouquet garni and 6 black peppercorns into a saucepan, cover with water and bring to the boil. Reduce heat and simmer for 30 minutes, skimming from time to time. Strain, then boil to reduce by one-third. Use as required.

tortillas

Essentially pancakes made with wheat or corn flour, tortillas are surprisingly simple to make and very versatile

Tortillas are the daily bread of Mexico – they can be wrapped around various fillings to make a tasty meal or served to accompany other food. There are basically two types – the traditional Mexican golden corn tortillas made from maize flour, and the no-less authentic but more convenient ones made from wheat flour.

In this age of fast food, tortillas have come into their own as a perfect modern ingredient – flexible enough to team with any meat, vegetables and even fish. Bring a stack to the table with a variety of fillings and you have the makings of a delightfully relaxed meal.

Under wraps
Tortillas are very much an extendable feast. Making them is just the tip of the iceberg. You can choose to prepare any one or more of a wide variety of fillings – hot or cold meats, poultry and sausage or beans. Chicken is used in the main recipe and a spicy combination of chorizo and chilli in the variation recipe.

The basic fillings are just the start of more to come. Traditional tortillas are also filled with salsa, soured cream, grated cheese and guacamole (avocado dip).

Gary's special touch

I'm told that Mexicans think that home-made tortillas are far softer and superior to bought ones – so who am I to argue? They are certainly fun – to make and to eat. You simply roll them around a traditional mix of fillings, such as spicy guacamole, crunchy salsa and refried beans and then . . . just enjoy them!

making and filling tortillas

You will need

makes 12-14
12 x 15cm (6in) tortillas

for the tortillas

225g (8oz) plain flour
1 tsp salt
1 tbsp lard or vegetable fat
125ml (4fl oz) warm water

for the filling

3 chicken breasts, poached, cooled and shredded
½ crisp lettuce, finely shredded
salsa (see Recipe tip below)
soured cream (optional)
grated cheese (optional)

Making tortillas with wheat flour is like making pastry – you rub the fat into the flour to form a fine crumb, add water to bind the mixture together, then let the dough rest before rolling it out.

Corn tortillas are even simpler, except that you need to buy some yellow maize (corn) flour – *masa harina* – from a delicatessen or large supermarket. You just mix the corn flour with water to form a dough. This a little stickier than the wheat-flour dough but don't let that put you off – corn tortillas are delicious.

It is easier to press the soft corn dough flat in a special tortilla press but you can produce perfectly good flat discs by rolling small balls of the dough between sheets of plastic wrap.

On the griddle
Watch tortillas carefully while they are cooking – you want them to be lightly browned and speckled on each side but not over cooked as they become dry and brittle.

Keep cooked tortillas warm by wrapping them up in a stack as they come off the griddle. Cover them first in a clean napkin or tea-towel, then in foil and put them in a warm place.

Always keep freshly made tortillas warm – or warm up stored or bought tortillas – before using them.

Tasty side dishes
Serve the tortillas with their traditional accompanying dishes – rice, refried beans and guacamole, as well as cheese, soured cream and salsa – and you will provide an enjoyable and well-balanced meal.

Recipe tip

Fresh salsa
A spicy salsa makes a crunchy contrast to other tortilla fillings.

450g (1lb) tomatoes, chopped
½ red onion, finely chopped
2-4 tbsp chopped coriander
3 garlic cloves, finely chopped
1 green chilli, finely chopped
pinch of salt
juice of ½ lime

Mix all the ingredients in a bowl, cover and leave in the fridge until ready to serve.

1 Sift the flour and salt into a large mixing bowl. Rub in the lard or vegetable fat lightly with your fingertips until the mixture resembles coarse breadcrumbs.

4 Warm an ungreased griddle over a moderate heat. Cook the tortillas, one at a time, for 1½-2 minutes on each side until speckled brown.

2 Gradually add the water and mix to a soft dough with a palette knife or fingers. Knead lightly, form into a ball, cover the bowl with a cloth and leave to rest for 15 minutes.

3 Divide the dough into 12-14 portions and form into balls. Roll out each ball of dough on a lightly floured board to a round measuring about 15cm (6in). Neaten the rounds if necessary.

Cook's notes

Folding or cutting tortillas
A taco, in Mexico, is a soft fresh tortilla rolled around fillings. In Tex-Mex speak, however, a taco is a crisp, deep-fried open turnover – a pocket for filling.
An enchilada is a fresh tortilla which is fried before rolling it up around a filling like a Mexican taco and serving with tomato sauce.
A burrito is a Mexican taco, with the ends of the roll folded under to form a neat parcel.
A quesadilla can be a turnover or a sandwich. A tortilla is either folded over the filling or another one is laid on top, then it's fried.
Nachos are tortilla wedges, fried until crisp, with melted cheese.

5 Put 1 tbsp chicken in the centre of a warm tortilla with a little lettuce and salsa – soured cream and cheese too. Fold in two sides to create a roll.

6 Then fold in the ends to create a parcel – on a Tex-Mex menu this is a *burrito*. Lay it, flap side down, on the plate. Serve with refried beans, rice and guacamole and the rest of the salsa.

Variations on a theme

corn enchiladas

Corn tortillas are very easy to make but it is important to get the texture of the dough right. If it is too dry and crumbly, add a little water; if it is too wet, add more masa harina. While it's easier to flatten the dough into neat rounds with a special tortilla press, you can also roll it out.

makes about 14

for the tortillas
275g (10oz) masa harina (maize flour)
250-350ml (9-12fl oz) water

for filling and topping
4 tbsp olive oil
1 large red onion, finely chopped
2 garlic cloves, crushed
1 green fresh chilli, deseeded and chopped
450g (1lb) fresh tomatoes, chopped
½-1 tsp mild chilli powder
pinch of caster sugar
pinch of salt
4 chorizo sausages, cut in 5mm (¼in) discs
85g (3oz) grated strong cheddar cheese

1 Put the masa harina into a bowl and stir in 250ml (8fl oz) of the water, mixing to a soft dough, adding a little more water if necessary. Cover the bowl with a cloth and set aside for 15 minutes.

2 Pre-heat a griddle.

3 Knead the dough lightly and shape it into 14 balls. Roll out each ball into a thin disc 14cm (5½in) in diameter.

4 Cook the first tortilla on the hot griddle for about 1 minute on each side. Griddle the others in the same way.

5 Pre-heat the oven to 180°C/350°F/gas 4.

6 Heat 2 tbsp olive oil and fry the onion, garlic and chilli for 2-3 minutes. Add the tomatoes, chilli powder, sugar and salt, then simmer for 15 minutes.

7 Meanwhile fry the chorizo for 3-4 minutes until browned.

8 Fry each tortilla briefly in the remaining olive oil. Fill each warm enchilada with a spoonful of the chorizo, then roll up and pack tightly together in an ovenproof dish. Cover with the tomato sauce and top with grated cheese. Put in the oven and cook for 20 minutes until browned and bubbling.

9 Serve accompanied by a lettuce and avocado salad, refried beans, soured cream and guacamole.

eats well with...

guacamole
Roughly mash 2 avocados. Add ½ finely chopped onion, 3 chopped tomatoes, 1 finely chopped green chilli, the juice of 1 lime, 3 tbsp chopped coriander and ½ tsp salt and mix well. Season to taste.

refried beans (*frijoles refritos*)
Fry 1 finely chopped medium onion in 1 tbsp olive oil for 3-4 minutes until softened. Drain and rinse 2 cans kidney beans, then fry the beans for about 5 minutes until they start breaking up. Stir in 2 tsp cider vinegar and serve.

any left?

Wrap leftover tortillas in foil and store them in the freezer.

Fry them whole until crisp and top them with meat or vegetables – these are known as *tostadas*.

Cut stale corn tortillas into triangular pieces and bake or fry them to make crisp tortilla chips (*tostaditas*). Turn these chips into nachos by sprinkling them with grated cheddar and baking them until the cheese has melted. Dust with chilli powder to taste.

meat pasties

Pasties – meat and vegetables in pastry cases – are invaluable standbys for lunches, snacks and picnics

Traditional Cornish pasties are made with beef, but almost any meat can be used. In the main recipe it's lamb, herbs and vegetables. The puff pastry is light and crisp and the filling is given a lift with a dash of Worcestershire sauce. The meat and vegetables are cooked in advance, then enveloped in pastry when cold.

Maximum moisture

No less than four root vegetables go into the pasty filling – carrots, swedes, parsnips and potatoes, which can soak up quite a lot of liquid. The main recipe calls for 850ml (1½ pints) of chicken stock (reduced to intensify the flavour) plus 600ml (1 pint) of concentrated beef stock or con-sommé. Not only do these give plenty of moisture to the filling – they provide a tasty gravy as well.

Cornish pasty

In a traditional Cornish pasty the beef and vegetables are not cooked in advance. The pasty is baked for a full hour, rather than the 30 minutes for the lamb version here. The Cornish pasty is made in the alternative shape, the sides pulled up over the centre of the filling and pinched together in a scalloped crest.

Gary's special touch

My lamb pasty recipe is a bit of a build-up assembly job. Each vegetable is added to the filling mixture separately, for example the potatoes (left), and cooked for the appropriate time. It may seem a lot of bother, but care taken at this stage is worth it when you eventually come to taste the end result.

making lamb pasties

You will need

makes 8

preparation time *30 minutes, plus 20 minutes for resting pasties in fridge*

cooking time *1 hour for lamb and vegetables; 30 minutes for baking*

pre-heat oven *200°C/400°F/gas 6*

ingredients

25g (1oz) oil or beef dripping
450g (1lb) lean lamb, chopped to 1cm (½in) dice or coarsely minced
1 garlic clove, crushed
115g (4oz) onions, finely chopped
115g (4oz) carrots, peeled and cut into 1cm (½in) dice
115g (4oz) celery, diced
½ tsp chopped fresh thyme
½ tsp chopped fresh sage
salt and pepper

25g (1oz) plain flour
850ml (1½ pints) chicken stock (see page 8) reduced to 300ml (10fl oz)
115g (4oz) swede, peeled and cut into 1cm (½in) dice
115g (4oz) parsnip, peeled and cut into 1cm (½in) dice
600ml (1 pint) concentrated beef stock (see page 8) or consommé – 150ml (5fl oz) for filling and optional 450ml (15fl oz) for gravy
2 potatoes, cooked in their skins, then peeled and cut into 1cm (½in) dice
dash of Worcestershire sauce
800g (1¾lb) puff pastry (see page 10)
1 egg, beaten

equipment
baking sheet

1 Heat oil or beef dripping in a pan, add lamb and fry, colouring on all sides. Add the garlic, onions, carrots, celery and herbs, cover and cook for about 10 minutes.

Don't roll out your pastry too thin. It has to support a considerable weight of filling without tearing apart – indeed, it should be possible to hold the pasty comfortably in the hand while you eat it. The ideal pasty is firm and full, but not so juicy that it drips when you bite into it or so dry that it clogs in the mouth.

Super stocks

This recipe calls for both chicken stock and beef stock – they give vital extra flavour to the pasty, as does the reduction of the chicken stock before adding it to the filling mix. The vegetables are added at different times to the pasty filling, each time with a little stock, gradually building up flavour and moisture. This allows for the different amount of time each

vegetable takes to cook and it means that each retains its distinct character in the filling. Serve the remaining hot stock or consommé as a gravy with the pasty – if you wish, thicken it with a little cornflour, and add a few drops of Tabasco, brown sauce or HP sauce to give a bit of a flavour fillip.

Super snacks

You can serve your pasties either hot or cold. They make a delicious meal served on their own as a quick snack or light lunch. They are also interesting additions to picnics and buffets. For a more substantial dinner you can serve them hot with vegetables such as broccoli, peas or green beans, preferably vegetables which are not already included in the pasty.

5 Roll out puff pastry and cut into 6-8 x 15cm (6in) squares. Spoon some filling on to each square, slightly off-centre. Brush around edges with beaten egg.

2 After 10 minutes, season meat and vegetables, then add flour and cook for a few minutes. Add ⅓ of the reduced chicken stock and cook for 10-15 minutes.

3 Add swede and parsnips and another ⅓ of the stock and cook for 10 minutes. Check seasoning, then add remaining stock and 150ml (5fl oz) of beef stock or consommé.

4 Add potatoes to pan and cook for 5-6 minutes. Check the seasoning again and add 2-3 drops of Worcestershire sauce for a spicy flavour. Leave to cool down completely.

6 Fold pastry over filling to make triangles. Trim to half-moons, then pinch all around to seal edges. Brush with egg. Rest in fridge for 20 minutes.

7 Dampen baking sheet, sit pasties on it and bake in pre-heated oven for 30 minutes until crisp and golden. Eat as they are, or with the rest of the hot stock or consommé as a gravy.

Variations on a theme

traditional Cornish pasty

There are probably as many 'genuine' Cornish pasty recipes as there are Cornish households. People remember the pasties of their childhood, made by mum or grandma – and can't be persuaded that any other version is authentic. The point is, of course, that the ingredients for the traditional Cornish pasty varied according to the state of the family's finances – if times were hard, then the amount of meat would diminish, until eventually only vegetables would go in! The main difference between this recipe and the lamb pasty on the previous page is that the ingredients here are not cooked before being wrapped in the pastry. And in this version the pastry is pinched together at the top to make a crest, rather than being folded over to a half-moon shape.

makes 2
preparation time
10 minutes for pastry plus 20 minutes resting it in fridge; 15 minutes for meat and vegetables
cooking time *1 hour*
pre-heat oven
200°C/400°F/gas 6

ingredients
350g (12oz) shortcrust pastry (see pages 9-10)
450g (1lb) chuck steak
140g (5oz) onion, chopped
85g (3oz) turnip, chopped
225g (8oz) potato, diced
salt and pepper
pinch of thyme
1 egg, beaten

equipment
baking tray

1 Make shortcrust pastry. Rest in fridge for 20 minutes.
2 Cut off skin, fat and gristle from meat, then chop the meat with a sharp, heavy knife.
3 Mix meat with vegetables in a bowl, season, then add thyme.
4 Roll out pastry and cut into two dessert-plate sized circles. Spread steak mixture down middle of each circle.
5 Brush rim of pastry with beaten egg. Then bring up the two sides of the pastry to meet over the top of the filling and pinch together into a scalloped crest. Make 2 holes on top so that steam can escape.
6 Place pasties on baking sheet and brush with beaten egg. Bake for 20 minutes, then lower heat to 180°C/350°F/gas 4 and bake for 40 minutes.

why not try...

lard pastry
A Cornish pasty was often made with shortcrust pastry using lard – not butter and egg. For this you need 225g (8oz) flour and 115g (4oz) lard and a little water. Rub the lard into the flour in the usual way, add water as needed, then work into a dough and wrap in plastic and rest in the fridge for about 1 hour before continuing with the recipe.

bacon and egg pasty
If beefsteak was scarce – or too expensive – a Cornish pasty could be made with leeks, bacon and hard-boiled egg. Use shortcrust pastry as before, and make the filling with leeks cut into 2.5cm (1in) long chunks, cooked in boiling salted water then drained thoroughly, bacon cut into small pieces then fried, and at least 1 whole hard-boiled egg per pasty. Tuck the whole egg into the centre of the filling.

eats well with...

Traditionally, a Cornish pasty was always eaten on its own – with all the vegetables in the filling, it made a meal all by itself. But it can be served with boiled potatoes, vegetables or a mixed salad.

meat terrines

Every slice of this succulent terrine is packed with delicious flavours and textures

This simple terrine is ideal as a light lunch or a starter. As with any meat terrine, it should be made at least 2 days in advance. This allows plenty of time for the flavours to blend and strengthen. Once cooked, the terrine is refrigerated, ready to be served at the last minute.

This pork and duck terrine is infinitely adaptable. The duck meat can be replaced with goose or you could simply double the quantity of pork. When making terrines, it's best to plan ahead. It pays to pre-order all the meats that you will be using ready-minced from the butcher – request a fine or coarse mince, according to your preference.

Salad extras
Included here is a simple salad accompaniment and two different dressings. Quick and easy to make, these give a fresh, tangy touch to the rich meat. All you need serve with the terrine and salad are lightly toasted slices of baguette.

Pork and pistachio terrine
The variation recipe is a fine combination of pork with pistachio nuts. As in the main recipe, the terrine is weighted overnight to compress the cooked meat so it unmoulds easily and can be neatly sliced.

Gary's special touch

I like my terrines to be quite chunky so I mince the pork and other meats coarsely. This gives a good firm texture and the finished terrine slices like a dream into neat, sharp-edged portions with no sloppiness or sagging. **Do try my cranberry dressing – it's great with the flavours of pork and duck.**

making pork and duck terrine

You will need

serves 12-14

preparation time *20 minutes plus 2-3 hours standing and 24 hours weighting*

cooking time *1¼-1½ hours*

pre-heat oven *180°C/350°F/gas 4*

ingredients
500g (1lb 2oz) minced belly of pork, including 55-85g (2-3oz) pork fat
2 large duck breasts, minced
225g (8oz) duck or chicken livers, minced or blitzed in a food processor
half a glass of white wine

2 measures brandy
2 cloves garlic, crushed
12 juniper berries, chopped
6-8 black peppercorns, coarsely crushed or 20 green peppercorns, coarsely chopped
1 tsp salt
½ tsp ground mace
1 tsp chopped sage
16 rashers streaky bacon

equipment
1.2 litre (2 pint) terrine mould

I Mix all the ingredients except the bacon. Cover and leave in the fridge for 2-3 hours so the minced meats can absorb the flavours of the spices and herbs.

While cooking in its mould, the terrine is held together by rashers of bacon, which also contribute fat and moisture. The finished texture is quite chunky. If you want a finer finish, ask the butcher to mince the meat finely.

Think ahead

The flavour of the terrine is well developed because the meat, wine, brandy and other flavourings are left to stand in the refrigerator for 2-3 hours. After this, the assembly and cooking of the terrine is very simple.

After cooking, the terrine needs to be weighted overnight to press the meats together. Ideally, you should use a second heavy terrine mould that fits exactly over the first. Failing this, use a loaf tin weighted down with at least 2 large cans of beans. The terrine also benefits from being left to mature in the fridge for a couple of days after cooking. All in all, plan to make the dish 2-3 days before you actually want to serve it.

Recipe tip

Cranberry orange sauce
Boil 1 wine glass of port with 1 tsp chopped shallots until reduced by half. Add juice of 2 oranges and reduce by half. Add 450g (1lb) cranberries and 115g (4oz) sugar. Simmer until cranberries are soft. Cool, then chill until required.

Spinach and orange salad
Peel and segment 3 large oranges. Arrange on plates with 225g (8oz) baby spinach.

Green peppercorn dressing
Mix 4-6 tbsp walnut oil, 1-2 tbsp red wine vinegar, 1 large finely chopped shallot, 1 tsp chopped tarragon and 12 chopped green peppercorns. Season to taste.

5 After 1¼ hours, insert a metal skewer for 10 seconds, then gingerly press it on to your lower lip – it should feel hot. If not, cook for 15 minutes more.

2 Stretch the bacon rashers with a knife, then use to line the terrine mould, leaving the ends overhanging so there is enough to cover the top of the filled mould.

3 Spoon the terrine mix into the mould, pressing it down firmly and evenly. Then fold the bacon rashers over the top, so the terrine mix is completely covered.

4 Cover the terrine with a lid or with buttered foil. Place it in a roasting tin and pour in hot water to come ½-¾ of the way up the terrine. Place in the pre-heated oven.

6 Leave terrine to cool. When almost cold, cover with plastic wrap, top with a similar mould and apply weights. Chill for at least 24 hours.

7 Scoop out and discard congealed fat, slide knife round sides, then put mould in hot water for a few seconds. Turn out on to plate and slice thickly. Serve with cranberry sauce and spinach and orange salad, dressed with the peppercorn dressing (see Recipe tip).

Variations on a theme

pork and pistachio terrine

Here is a quick and easy terrine made with pork and pistachio nuts, marinated overnight with cognac and seasonings. The finished terrine looks very attractive with pieces of green pistachio scattered through it. Serve a few slices with a potato salad or a green salad if you like, along with a piquant dressing.

serves 8

preparation time
30 minutes plus marinating overnight and 24 hours weighting

cooking time *1 hour*

pre-heat oven
180°C/350°F/gas 4

ingredients
25-55g (1-2oz) shelled pistachios
2 tbsp cognac
1 tbsp salt
½ tsp freshly ground black pepper
¼ tsp freshly grated nutmeg
1kg (2lb 4oz) lean, boneless pork shoulder
300g (10½oz) hard pork back fat

equipment
1.5 litre (2¾ pint) terrine mould, lightly buttered

1 Put the pistachios in a bowl and mix with the cognac, salt, pepper and nutmeg.

2 Cut the meat and fat as finely as you can by hand (don't use a food processor – it will mince the meat too finely) and combine with the pistachio mixture. Cover the mix and leave it to stand overnight in the fridge.

3 On the following day, pack the pork and pistachio mixture into the prepared terrine mould and cover the terrine with a lid or kitchen foil. Stand it in a roasting tin and pour in boiling water to come half-way up the sides of the mould.

4 Bake the terrine in the pre-heated oven for 1 hour. Insert a skewer and squeeze out some juices. If the juices run clear, the terrine is cooked.

5 Allow the terrine to cool for 1 hour, then weight it down with another mould and some cans of beans to press the meat together. Leave to set overnight.

6 Scoop out any congealed fat and slide a knife around the sides of the terrine, then put the mould in hot water for a few seconds. Turn out on to a serving dish and slice fairly thinly. Serve with a potato salad and a green salad.

why not try...

sherry pork terrine
Cut 900g (2lb) belly pork into small cubes. Trim and slice 450g (1lb) pig's liver, then chop finely. Fry 1 large chopped onion in 25g (1oz) butter over a low heat for 5 minutes until soft but not brown. Add to pork and liver with 2 eggs, 1 tbsp dried mixed herbs, 2 tbsp medium sherry and 3 tsp salt. Season with pepper. Trim 225g (8oz) streaky bacon, stretch with a knife, then line a 1.2 litre (2 pint) terrine mould. Spoon in meat mixture and level off. Top with 2 rashers of bacon and 2 bay leaves, cover with lid and put in a roasting tin ¼-½ full with boiling water. Cook at 160°C/325°F/gas 3 for 2½ hours. Cool overnight, pressed down with weights. Serve cut into slices.

chicken and spinach terrine
This is an 'instant' terrine which requires no standing or weighting. Pre-heat oven to 180°C/350°F/gas 4. Slice 2 chicken breasts horizontally. In a small non-stick loaf tin, layer chicken with 900g (2lb) cooked chopped spinach. Pour in a little chicken stock. Place tin in a roasting tin half-filled with hot water, cover with damp greaseproof paper and bake for 1 hour. Cool for 30 minutes. Drain thoroughly, then serve cut into slices.

omelettes

Looking for the definitive omelette? Try this foolproof recipe with some exotic additions

An omelette is made from lightly set eggs, folded around a filling of your choice. You can serve it at any time of the day – as a breakfast to set you up for work, a tasty lunch with crusty bread, or a light supper with a glass of wine.

Here the omelette is filled with shredded spring onion and red chillies to add a kick to the mild flavour of the eggs. Blanching the onions and chillies beforehand softens them slightly and removes much of their spicy heat.

Generous portion

Each recipe makes one generously sized omelette. You can split the omelette in half to serve two people, but it is good to have your own neatly folded omelette on the plate. For a smaller serving, reduce the number of eggs you use and, if possible, make it in a small pan to keep it nice and thick. It also makes it easier to fold than if made in a large pan.

Great for leftovers

To transform a simple omelette into a hearty pizza-style meal, leave it flat and top it with lightly cooked colourful vegetables and grated cheese. For a good Italian feel, sauté the vegetables first in olive oil and flavour them with a teaspoon of pesto to add a super basil twist.

Gary's special touch

Opinions vary about the consistency of the perfect omelette. I prefer to keep mine pale on the outside and a little soft on the inside. If you like a firmer texture, cook the omelette longer to achieve a golden outside and a fully cooked interior. Do not be tempted to turn up the heat or the eggs will go hard and watery.

making the chilli-onion omelette

You will need

serves 1-2	4 eggs
preparation time 10 minutes	knob of unsalted butter
cooking time 10 minutes	salt and black or white pepper
ingredients	**equipment**
3 spring onions	18cm (7in) omelette pan or
½-1 small red chilli	non-stick frying-pan

As the spring onions and chilli are only briefly blanched before being added to the omelette, it is important to slice them very thinly with a sharp knife. For a hotter flavour, leave the chilli and spring onions completely raw.

Beating the eggs
Check there are no bits of shell in the eggs before you mix them. Beat the eggs with a fork or a balloon whisk until all the whites and yolks have broken down and are fully blended. Do not over-whisk the eggs or they will turn frothy and make the omelette watery.

Do not season the eggs until just before they go in the pan, otherwise the salt breaks down the beaten egg, turning it thin and dull looking. Go easy on the pepper as chilli adds plenty of heat to the overall flavour. Black pepper gives the omelette a lightly speckled surface. If you prefer a paler finish, use white pepper which you can't see in the finished omelette.

Heating the butter
Warm the butter until it is just melted and bubbling. Do not allow it to brown or the omelette will be over-coloured on the outside. You can always add a dash of vegetable oil to prevent the butter burning. If the omelette starts to stick, just slip another knob of butter or a drop of oil into the pan under the setting egg.

Just cooked
The eggs in an omelette are not really cooked in the conventional sense. They are merely warmed gently over a low heat until thickened and set softly. If the eggs are heated too quickly, they turn hard and release water. It is important to keep the heat low under the omelette pan and not rush the setting process.

Cook's notes

A traditional omelette pan is a heavy-based iron frying-pan with gently sloping slides. In time, the omelette pan develops its own non-stick surface as repeated layers of butter or oil coat and seal the inside – this is known as seasoning the pan. Don't wash your pan, simply wipe it with kitchen roll after use. If you don't have a special omelette pan, use a standard non-stick frying-pan instead.

1 Trim the spring onions. Cut into 2.5cm (1in) lengths, then into very thin strips. Remove the pith and seeds from the chilli. Cut into 2.5cm (1in) lengths, then in thin strips.

4 Add the butter to the hot pan and allow it to melt. Season the eggs, then pour into the pan. Cook gently for 3-4 minutes, stirring the eggs with a fork until lightly scrambled.

Watchpoint!

When handling chillies, it is advisable to wear rubber gloves to protect your fingers from the burning chemicals in the chilli juices. If you don't have any gloves, wash your hands very well, and do not under any circumstances touch your eyes, nose or mouth.

Remember, if serving omelettes to young children, to pregnant women, the elderly or infirm, make sure the eggs are fully cooked and firm inside. The easiest way to do this is to leave the omelette unfolded, and whizz it under the grill to cook the topside through.

2 Put the chilli and onions into a pan of boiling water. Leave for 30 seconds, then refresh in a bowl of chilled water. Remove from the water and dry on kitchen paper.

3 Set the pan over a low heat to warm. Meanwhile, crack the eggs into a large bowl and whisk lightly with a balloon whisk or fork until the whites and yolks are just mixed.

5 Sprinkle the onions and chilli over the eggs. Cook gently for a further 5 minutes, then lift the edge of the omelette to check that the base is set. Leave the top a little soft.

6 Tilting the pan over the plate, use a fish slice to slide the omelette gently on to the plate, folding it in half as it slips out.

Variations on a theme

quick pizza omelette

Omelettes do not have to be folded. You can leave them flat, scattered with pizza-style toppings. Simply slide them out of the pan on to the plate.

This recipe is a great way to use up little bits of pepper, a few tomatoes, some mushrooms, onions, olives, ham or cheese – use whatever you have to hand. In keeping with the Italian theme, the vegetables are fried in olive oil. Serve with crusty ciabatta bread.

serves 1-2

preparation time
10 minutes

cooking time
10 minutes

equipment
18cm (7in) omelette pan or non-stick frying-pan

ingredients
2 tbsp olive oil
½ onion, diced
½ red pepper, diced
½ green pepper, diced
5 mushrooms, quartered
salt and pepper
3 tomatoes, skinned, seeded and finely diced
1 tsp pesto
4 eggs
knob of butter
2 tbsp grated cheddar cheese
2 tbsp parmesan cheese, grated
basil leaves to garnish

1 Heat the pan, then the oil over a medium heat. Add the onions, peppers and mushrooms. Season with salt and pepper. Fry gently until softened.
2 Stir in the tomatoes and pesto. Fry for a further 2 minutes, or until softened. Transfer to a bowl and cover to keep warm.
3 Lightly beat the eggs. Melt the butter in the pan over a low heat until it bubbles. Season the eggs with salt and pepper, then pour into the pan. Stir occasionally with a fork until the base sets. Pre-heat the grill.
4 Remove the pan from the heat and scatter over the vegetables and cheese. Place the pan under the grill until the cheese melts and bubbles. (Cover the pan handle with foil if it is not heatproof.)
5 Slide the omelette, unfolded, on to a warmed plate. Garnish with a sprig of basil, then serve at once.

why not try...

You can add many things to an omelette. No rules apply, so mix and match flavours to suit your taste. Here are a few ideas.

morning glory
For weekend treats, flavour a plain omelette with traditional breakfast ingredients, such as bacon, black pudding, field or wild mushrooms, flaked kipper or smoked salmon.

fresh herbs
Chopped fresh herbs are the perfect complement to a plain omelette as the eggs do not mask their natural flavours. Parsley, chives, chervil, mint and tarragon are all ideal.

cheese selection
Most cheeses work well in omelettes. Grated hard cheeses, such as mature cheddar, taste grand.

Spanish omelette
Heat diced cooked potato in the pan before adding the egg mixture. Cook as before and finish off under the grill. You can also stir in some chopped anchovies and sliced peppers.

creamy mushroom filling
Lightly sauté 55g (2oz) thinly sliced button mushrooms in 1 tbsp butter for 2-3 minutes. Stir in 3 tbsp crème fraîche or mascarpone cheese. Spoon on to the cooked omelette and fold on to a warm plate.

savoury egg tarts

A good quiche simply melts in the mouth. This one, creamy rich and delicately flavoured with onion and herbs, is truly a quiche royale

Although French in name and origin, quiche has become a general staple, a favourite in pubs and restaurants, for formal parties and casual picnics. Its usual basis of eggs, cream and cheese, like the tomato and mozzarella basis of a pizza, combines well with a wide range of other ingredients – fish, meat, vegetables and other cheeses.

The difference between a good quiche and an excellent one – a quiche royale – lies in proper handling of the pastry in order to get a light, crisp finish, and in getting the texture of the filling exactly right. It should be firm enough to hold its shape when cut, but soft enough to retain its succulence.

A princely quiche
For the quiche royale, the normal quiche mix of eggs and cream is enriched by using extra eggs, double cream and gruyère cheese. The main recipe quiche royale gets its special lift from finely sliced onion and lots of mixed fresh herbs, while the variation has sweet peppers inside and a peppery pastry crust.

Gary's special touch

The flavour of this dish is based on the traditional French *fines herbes* blend of tarragon, chervil, parsley and chives – but the chives are replaced with finely sliced onion, and basil (with its lemony overtones) is added. Chervil can be hard to find, but if you are successful, use some and freeze the rest.

If you can't find chervil, add more of the other herbs.

making the herby quiche royale

You will need

serves 6

preparation time 1 hour	
pre-heat oven 220°C/425°F/gas 7	
cooking time 35-45 minutes	

ingredients

350g (12oz) shortcrust pastry (see pages 9-10)

40g (1½oz) butter

1½ tbsp groundnut or vegetable oil

2 large onions, thinly sliced

2 eggs and 1 egg yolk

150ml (5fl oz) double cream

115g (4oz) gruyère or cheddar, grated

1 tbsp each finely chopped fresh herbs – basil, parsley, tarragon and chervil

salt and pepper

equipment

20cm wide, 40mm deep (8in wide, 1½ in deep) loose-bottomed flan tin

Make your own shortcrust pastry, following the instructions on pages 9-10. If you are using bought pastry, you will need about 350g (12oz) to cover a 20cm (8in) flan tin.

Making the custard

It is important to slice the onions finely so that you get a delicate overall texture. Then cook them very gently until they are virtually transparent.

Do not let them brown, or their caramelized flavour may over-whelm the subtle tastes of the herbs and the quiche's pale filling will be a unattractive brown colour.

The extra egg yolk and the double cream make this a rich filling, but if you want a lighter mix, replace it with a half and half mix of milk and cream.

Baking the shell

The technique of blind baking the pastry in a hot oven, before adding the filling, ensures a crisp base. Here, it's more important than usual, as the quiche filling is cooked at a very low temperature in order to keep the texture creamy. (If you don't have the specially-made ceramic baking beans used here, you can use dried beans or peas which work just as well.)

When the filled tart is baking, check that the top is not colouring too much. It should be only lightly coloured; if it starts to get too brown, cover it loosely with foil and continue cooking.

Starters for 6

If you would rather serve individual quiches as an elegant starter, divide the pastry into 6 equal quantities and roll out. Line 6 x 10cm (4in) tart tins with pastry, and blind bake them as before.

Cook the mini quiches for approximately 8-10 minutes at 220°C/425°F/gas 7. Then pour in the egg and cream mixture. Lower the heat to 160°C/325°F/gas 3 and cook for about 15-20 minutes, or until the filling is just set.

1 Roll out pastry and line flan tin. Line the pastry with crumpled greaseproof paper and fill with beans. Bake for 15-20 minutes. Cool, then carefully remove baking beans and paper.

4 Mix the grated cheese with the eggs and cream and fold in the onions, herbs and butter and oil mixture. Season with salt and pepper.

Recipe tip

Warm pepper salsa

I large red pepper,
deseeded and quartered

I large tomato,
deseeded and finely diced

2 tsp chopped basil

juice of ½ orange

dash of lemon juice

salt and pepper

Place red pepper, skin
side up, under a hot grill
until the skin blisters.
Allow to cool and remove
the skin. Dice the flesh
finely and mix with the
other ingredients. Season
to taste. To serve, heat
through until just warm.

2 Reduce oven temperature to 160°C/325°F/gas 3. Melt together half the butter and 1 tbsp of oil in a frying-pan and cook onions until soft and transparent. Leave to cool.

3 Beat eggs and egg yolk together, add the cream and leave to one side. Melt the rest of the butter and oil together and leave to cool.

5 Spoon the filling into the pastry base and bake for 35-45 minutes until the flan is just set. Leave to rest for 20-30 minutes.

6 Serve the quiche just warm or at room temperature with a warm salsa of tomato and red peppers (see Recipe tip).

Variations on a theme

hot and sweet quiche royale

The sweet peppers and onions in this variation contrast with the hot peppery pastry to create a delicious trio of flavours. The spicy pastry works well with the savoury taste of the cheese and is a must for all black pepper lovers.

serves 6
preparation time _1 hour_
cooking time _35-45 mins_

pre-heat oven
220°C/425°F/gas 7

ingredients
350g (12 oz) shortcrust peppered pastry (see pages 9-10)
1 red pepper, deseeded and quartered
1 yellow pepper, deseeded and quartered
2 large onions, thinly sliced
40g (1½oz) butter
1½ tbsp groundnut or
vegetable oil
2 eggs and 1 egg yolk
50ml (5fl oz) double cream
115g (4oz) gruyère or cheddar, grated
salt and pepper

equipment
20cm (8in) flan tin as on page 42

1 Blind bake the peppery pastry shell as in step 1 on page 42.
2 Heat the grill to maximum, then grill the peppers skin-side up until the skins blister. Cool slightly, then peel off the skins, and cut peppers into strips.
3 Follow steps 2 and 3 on page 43.
4 Add cheese, cooled butter and oil to the egg mixture, then carefully stir in the pepper strips. Season with salt and pepper.
5 Lower oven temperature to 160°C/325°F/gas 3. Pour tart mixture into pastry case and bake for 35-45 minutes. Then gently feel the centre – the tart should be just firm to the touch and slightly browned. Rest for about 30 minutes before serving. Serve warm or at room temperature.

why not try...

quiche Lorraine
For the original tart from Lorraine in France, slice 3 or 4 rashers of cooked bacon or ham into small pieces and scatter them over the blind-baked shell. Then pour in the egg mixture. Use fresh parsley instead of the mixed herbs. Bake as before.

prawn quiche royale
Make the herby quiche royale as before, omitting the basil, tarragon, chervil and cheese. Scatter 225g (8oz) cooked shelled prawns over the part-cooked pastry. Pour in the egg mixture and bake as before.

quattro formaggio royale
Make up the quiche mixture using half gruyère and half cheddar cheese, and bake as before. Ten minutes before the end of cooking, lay 55g (2oz) of thinly sliced mozzarella on top of the filling. Grill 25g (1oz) fresh parmesan shavings on a non-stick surface until golden and leave to cool. Scatter over the finished tart.

eats well with...

A tomato salad dressed simply with good olive oil, salt and pepper is good with all of these quiches. For a sharper taste to complement the quattro formaggio royale, try a grainy mustard and chopped chive vinaigrette for the tomatoes.

savoury tartes tatin

Flavourful green tomatoes are caramelized, topped with puff pastry, then baked and turned over to make a delicious savoury upside-down tart

Tarte tatin is a classic French dessert, usually made with apples. The apples are caramelized in butter and sugar in a special pan, then topped with pastry. This is baked and then turned over on to a plate to serve. It looks stunning, and the flavour is immense. In this unconventional recipe, the tart is made with green tomatoes and is served as a light meal.

Green tomatoes

Green tomatoes are available to order from some greengrocers and are the best to use for this recipe. Their tart flavour contrasts well with the sweetness of the caramel. If you can't find green tomatoes easily in your area, you may have to wait for supplies from friends or neighbours who are growing their own. The alternative is to use very firm red tomatoes – in this case, cut down on the cooking time by 5-10 minutes.

Red onion tarte tatin

Red onions make a sweet and mellow upside-down tart – they are caramelized with balsamic vinegar and teamed with a peppery shortcrust pastry.

Gary's special touch

I love the slightly burnt flavour that you get when you caramelize food. That is why I give my green tomato tarte tatin a quick browning under the grill after it has come out of the oven and has been turned upside down. The end result is an even richer, darker, more caramelized version which tastes wonderful.

making green tomato tarte tatin

You will need

serves 4	2 tbsp balsamic vinegar
preparation time *10 minutes*	salt and pepper
cooking time *25 minutes*	8 dessertspoons soured cream
pre-heat oven *200°C/400°F/gas 6*	juice of half a lemon or lime

ingredients	**for the garnish (optional)**
dash of olive oil	a few fresh basil leaves, shredded
8 green tomatoes, halved widthways	1 small red onion, peeled and
salt and pepper	finely sliced
a knob of butter	shavings of fresh parmesan
2 tsp demerara sugar	coarse sea salt and coarsely ground
225-280g (8-10oz) quick puff pastry	black pepper (optional)
(see page 10)	
	equipment
for the dressing (optional)	25cm (10in) tarte tatin tin or
8 tbsp olive oil	ovenproof frying-pan

1 Heat pan and add a trickle of olive oil. Place tomato halves, cut-side down in pan in a circular pattern and season. Increase heat so tomatoes are frying, not stewing.

It's important to have the right size of tarte tatin pan, frying-pan or flame-proof, ovenproof dish – the tomatoes must fit exactly inside it. It's definitely worth investing in a special tarte tatin pan if you're going to make the recipe often. The special pan avoids the problem of the hot frying-pan handle. You can buy it from kitchen shops.

Hot handling

Ensure that your oven is very hot to help the tomatoes caramelize. To turn the tart out, put a plate over the pan, then quickly flick it upside down in one neat movement. If a few bits of tomato stick, simply scrape them off the pan and put them back in place.

If you want to brown the tart under the grill, be careful not to burn the edges of the pastry – cover the edges with a little collar of foil before placing under the grill or use a blowtorch for a more precise control.

Any place, any time

This savoury tarte tatin can be served at almost any time. It's great for lunch, perhaps served with a green salad and some new potatoes, and it's equally good as a starter for dinner, with the dressings and garnishes recommended here. It's also ideal for a quick supper. And, of course, there's nothing nicer than one of these for a picnic – the tart is every bit as good cold as hot.

Inside info

Tarte tatin is named after the Tatin sisters, who ran a restaurant in France at the beginning of this century and became famous for making the upside-down apple tart – although the recipe itself is very much older than this.

5 For an even richer, darker caramelized look, brush with more butter and sprinkle with more sugar. Flash under the grill until it begins to bubble.

2 After 1 minute, add butter and sprinkle with sugar. Fry for 1-2 minutes, shaking pan so tomatoes are coated and start to caramelize. Remove pan from stove and cool.

3 Roll out pastry to a 25cm (10in) circle. Place on top of tomatoes. Press lightly to help it take on the shape of the tomatoes and tuck in the edges neatly all round.

4 Bake tart for 25 minutes in oven until pastry is crisp and golden. Leave to cool for a few minutes. Turn tart out on to a serving plate (remember the frying-pan handle will be hot).

6 Mix oil and vinegar. Season. Then season soured cream and add lime or lemon juice. Spoon threads of sour cream and vinegar dressing across plates.

7 Sit a slice of tarte on top of the dressings and sprinkle with basil leaves, red onion slices and parmesan shavings. Sprinkle with a little sea salt and pepper. Serve with a salad.

Variations on a theme

red onion tarte tatin

Again, you need a tarte tatin pan – or a frying-pan that will move happily from hob to oven. This tarte turns a deep, rich, dark red colour and has a really luscious flavour.

serves 4-6

preparation time
10 minutes for pastry, plus 30 minutes refrigeration

cooking time *1½ hours*

pre-heat oven
180°C/350°F/gas 4 for onions; 200°C/400°F/gas 6 for pastry

ingredients
25g (1oz) butter
1 tsp caster sugar
6 small thyme sprigs
1.15kg (2½lb) red onions, halved lengthways
salt and pepper
1 tbsp chopped fresh thyme
1 tbsp balsamic vinegar

for shortcrust pastry
140g (5oz) plain flour
85g (3oz) butter, softened
1 tbsp black pepper
1 small egg, beaten
1 tsp chopped fresh thyme

equipment
as on page 46

1 Heat pan over medium heat, then add butter and sugar. As soon as butter starts sizzling, add thyme sprigs, then arrange onions in base of pan, cut side down. Fill gaps with remaining onions cut into wedges. Aim for a tight fit, with no gaps.

2 Season onions to taste, scatter chopped thyme over, then sprinkle vinegar on top. Turn heat down and cook onions gently for 10 minutes. Cover pan with foil, place in oven and bake for 50-60 minutes.

3 Meanwhile, make pastry (see pages 9-10) using the amounts here, adding pepper and thyme, and refrigerate for 30 minutes to rest.

4 Remove onions from oven and bring back to hob. Raise oven to 200°C/400°F/gas 6. Reduce buttery onion juices over a medium heat for 10 minutes, until there is just a little syrupy juice left in the pan.

5 Roll out pastry to a circle 25cm (10in) in diameter. Take pan off heat, then fit pastry circle over onions, tucking in edges around inside of pan. Bake for 25 minutes until pastry is crisp and golden.

6 Remove tart from oven and leave to cool a little. Place a flat plate over pan, turn it upside down and give it a quick shake to turn it out. If some onion sticks to the pan, scrape off with a palette knife and slip back into the space. Serve warm with a mixed salad.

why not try...

types of tomato
Instead of green tomatoes, use firm red tomatoes such as beef tomatoes, or try yellow tomatoes.

know your onions
Ordinary yellow onions are fine to use in the variation recipe. Also try sweet Vidalia onions.

take a leek
Slice leeks into rounds about 2.5cm (1in) high, arrange in tarte tatin pan and proceed as for red onion tarte tatin.

sweet shallots
Peel 30-40 shallots and 10 whole garlic cloves. Fry for 5 minutes in 55g (2oz) butter. Add 600ml (1 pint) vegetable stock. Simmer for 5 minutes. Drain and cool. Spread 85g (3oz) butter over base of tarte tatin pan and sprinkle with 55g (2oz) caster sugar. Cook over medium heat for 6-7 minutes until mix caramelizes. Remove from heat. Pile shallots and garlic into pan. Sprinkle with 1 tbsp balsamic vinegar and season. Roll out 250g (9oz) puff pastry in a circle and lay on top of shallots. Bake tarte in oven at 200°C/400°F/gas 6 for 25 minutes. Cool slightly, then turn out. Garnish with sprigs of thyme or marjoram.

chapter two
main meals

roasted fish fillets

Shallow-fried then quickly oven-roasted, cod fillets become incredibly crisp and tasty – the skin alone is good enough to eat by itself

Roasting in the oven is a particularly good way to cook fillets of firm, almost steak-like fish. It gives the fish extra depth of flavour and a wonderfully crisp skin. As with most fish cooking, this method is quick and easy – the cod fillets spend 3-4 minutes in the frying-pan and then go in the oven for no more than 5-8 minutes! This is a great recipe for cod – the firm white fillets of fish are served on top of potatoes and salad leaves, accompanied by deep-fried anchovies and a tasty sauce.

Plan in advance
For the complete dish you need to be organized. The vierge dressing is made a week in advance to give time for the flavours to infuse – and then there are the potatoes, anchovies and salad to think about. The deep-fried anchovies take a very short time to cook.

Get your skates on
The same method also works surprisingly well with more fragile fish, such as skate. The fish is quickly pan-fried, transferred to a baking tray and roasted, then served with mustard seed butter and toasted crumbs.

Gary's special touch

Cod is one of my favourite fish. Here I'm cooking cod fillets. Make sure you buy the right cut. A lot of cod is sold as steaks cut through the bone. It looks nice but can be difficult to handle when eating. And cutting straight through breaks down the texture of the fish, damaging those lovely large flakes I like so much.

making roast cod with anchovies

You will need

serves 4	1 tsp self-raising flour
preparation time 15 minutes	¼ tsp cayenne
cooking time 45 minutes	2-3 tbsp milk
pre-heat oven 200°C/400°F/gas 6	oil for deep-frying
	1 tbsp chopped capers
ingredients	2 shallots or ½ onion, finely chopped
4 x 175-225g (6-8oz) cod fillets	½ tsp chopped fresh parsley
450g (1lb) new potatoes	1 tsp chopped fresh coriander leaves
salt and freshly ground white pepper	1 tsp chopped fresh tarragon
150ml (5fl oz) vierge dressing (see	1 tsp chopped fresh basil
Recipe tip, far right) or olive oil	a few green salad leaves (optional)
juice of 1 lemon	
25g (1oz) unsalted butter	**equipment**
2 tsp cooking oil	frying-pan; baking tray, greased;
12 marinated anchovies	deep-fat fryer

Boil potatoes until tender, then peel. Cut into 5mm (¼in) slices while still warm, then season. Add 1-2 tbsp dressing or olive oil and half the lemon juice. Adjust seasoning. Keep warm.

This is a really scrumptious dish because all the elements complement each other perfectly. The bed of potatoes is spiced up with piquant vierge dressing, made a week in advance. (Don't skimp on the time for the dressing – it really does improve for every day all the ingredients spend infusing.) The dressing also enlivens the salad leaves.

The cod itself is quickly pan-fried, then put into the oven to cook briefly so it gains that gorgeous, distinctive roast flavour. Because it's cooked so quickly, the fish retains its texture – large white flakes with a juicy, almost transparent centre.

Serving the roast cod sitting on top of the sliced potatoes and salad leaves looks very professional – it's just how you might expect to see it presented in a restaurant. Before serving, drizzle a little more of the vierge dressing all around so you can dip forkfuls of flaky fish into it.

Advice on anchovies

Salty little anchovies, deep-fried until crisp, are delicious with cod. Use marinated anchovies (which are sold loose in delicatessens) rather than the tinned variety. They're very salty, so soak them in milk for an hour before cooking. Rinse them thoroughly in cold water, drain well and pat dry with kitchen towel. If you haven't got a deep-fat fryer, cook the anchovies in a frying-pan. Use about 5mm (¼in) of hot oil, but don't let it get so hot it smokes – and keep turning the little fish in the pan until they are crispy.

Tip-top timing

The potatoes and anchovies – and, of course, the dressing – can all be made in advance, but don't cook the fish too soon. Fish is a bit like a soufflé – it's much better to keep your guests waiting a little, so you can serve the fish as soon as it's ready, when it is at its best.

4 Deep-fry the coated anchovies in hot oil until very crispy. Lift out of oil, then turn out on to kitchen towel and keep warm.

Recipe tip

**Vierge dressing
makes 600ml (1 pint)**
Make this a week in advance.
Warm 600ml (1 pint) extra-
virgin olive oil with 15g (½oz)
coriander seeds. Then place
1 bunch fresh tarragon,
12 crushed black peppercorns,
4 chopped shallots, 2 crushed
garlic cloves and a pinch of sea
salt in a screw-top jar. Pour the
oil and coriander on top, screw
on the lid and leave to marinate
for 1 week, shaking the bottle
daily to help the flavours infuse.
Dressing left over from the
roast cod recipe can be kept in
the fridge for up to 1 week.

2 Melt butter and oil in a hot
frying-pan. Lay seasoned
fish in pan, skin-side down. Fry
until golden, turn over and fry
for 1-2 minutes more. Transfer
to oven, roast for 5-8 minutes.

3 Split anchovies through the
centre. Mix flour with
cayenne and a pinch of salt. Dip
anchovies in milk, then roll in
the cayenne flour, coating them
thoroughly all over.

5 Warm remaining dressing or
oil, add capers and shallots
or onion with a squeeze of
lemon juice and all the herbs.
Season with salt and pepper.

6 Arrange potatoes on plate, with green salad leaves. Spoon
dressing all around, with anchovy fillets. Top with the roasted
cod, with the crispy (skin) side showing. Brush with melted butter.

Variations on a theme

roast skate with mustard seed butter

Skate is almost always cooked on the 'bone' (actually cartilage, not bone, with this fish). This way the fillets keep all their flavour and juices. Once cooked, the fillets more or less slide off, making them very easy to eat. Here a glass of red wine adds body and strength to the cooking juices and the mustard seed butter.

serves 4

preparation time
10 minutes

cooking time
20 minutes

pre-heat oven
200°C/400°F/gas 6

ingredients
4 x 350g (12oz) skate wings
salt and pepper
2 tbsp plain flour
knob of unsalted butter
55g (2oz) fresh white breadcrumbs
1 glass of red wine
1 tbsp chopped fresh parsley

for mustard butter
55g (2oz) unsalted butter, softened
55g (2oz) grain mustard

equipment
frying-pan; baking tray

1 Season the skate wings with salt and pepper and lightly dust with flour on the pale (presentation) side. Heat a large frying-pan and add the butter. Colour the presentation side first, then turn in the pan before transferring the fish to the greased baking tray. Roast in the oven for 10-12 minutes.
2 Make mustard seed butter. Mix butter and the grain mustard, then set aside until you are ready to use it.
3 Toast the breadcrumbs under the grill, turning them occasionally until evenly golden, with a slightly crunchy texture.
4 A minute or so before the fish has finished cooking, take it out of the oven, place 1 tbsp mustard butter on each skate wing and spread evenly, then return to oven to finish cooking. Remove fish from oven and sprinkle toasted crumbs on top.
5 Sit fish on plates. In a pan, heat butter and juices left on baking tray and add red wine. Bring to boil and check seasoning. If sauce is too thin, add more mustard butter for a smoother finish. Add parsley and spoon sauce around fish. Serve with salad and new potatoes.

why not try...

Most other round fish can be roasted in the same way as cod. Try fillets of monkfish, haddock, hake or salmon. In all cases, take care not to overcook the fish or it will start to break up.

nut-brown butter

As an alternative to the wine and parsley for the skate, heat a frying-pan, add butter and cook until golden brown with a nutty aroma, adding a squeeze of lemon juice at the end. Adding capers to the nut-brown butter or to the wine sauce works well.

mustardy mushrooms

Instead of sitting your fish on a bed of potatoes, try mushrooms. Slice 450g (1lb) large button mushrooms thinly, then sauté them in butter with 1-2 tbsp Dijon mustard, seasoning with salt and pepper to taste. Lift the mushrooms out of the pan, draining them well, then arrange on a warmed plate. Deglaze the pan with a splash of white wine, stirring in all the butter, mustard and any bits of mushroom. Add a little flour, stirring it in well, then cook for 1-2 minutes until the sauce thickens. Finally stir in 2-3 tbsp single or double cream. Sit the roasted fish on the mushrooms, spoon a little sauce around and serve, with the rest of the sauce in a small sauceboat.

pan-fried flatfish

Quick pan-frying in hot oil or clarified butter makes the delicate, tender flesh of flatfish, such as Dover sole, meltingly moist and succulent

A favourite way of cooking flatfish such as sole is à la meunière – 'in the style of the miller's wife'. The name refers to the flour the fish is coated in before pan-frying. The method is excellent for all firm-fleshed white fish such as Dover sole, plaice, flounder, dab and lemon sole. Because it's cooked so simply, very fresh fish is vital for success.

Dover sole à la meunière

A classic restaurant dish using the finest-flavoured of all the flatfishes, Dover sole à la meunière is simplicity itself to make at home – and very quick. The fish is pan-fried in very hot oil or clarified butter (the golden pure fat taken off the top of melted butter). The coating of flour forms a crisp, golden crust around the moist, tender flesh.

The dish is finished with a luscious, foaming beurre noisette (nut-brown butter sauce). The flavour of the fish is so fine that it needs only the simplest accompaniments – serve with a few new potatoes or fresh buttered spinach, lemon wedges and parsley.

Gary's special touch

The classic method for cooking sole à la meunière is to fry the fish in clarified butter, but I prefer to use oil. To retain some of the essential lovely buttery **flavour, I brush the presentation side of the floured fish with softened butter, then fry it in the oil. I find this gives a consistent golden-brown finish every time.**

making Dover sole à la meunière

You will need

serves 4	salt and pepper
preparation time	1 lemon, cut into quarters, to garnish
10 minutes	
cooking time	**for the beurre noisette**
20 minutes	115g (4oz) butter
	1 tbsp lemon juice
ingredients	1 tbsp chopped fresh
4 x 350g (12oz) whole Dover sole,	parsley(optional)
skinned on both sides	salt and pepper
1-2 tbsp olive oil for each fish plus	
25g (1oz) softened butter or 25g	**equipment**
(1oz) clarified butter for each fish	one large heavy-bottomed frying-pan
2 tbsp flour	or oval fish pan

Season the first fish, then dip it in the flour, coating both sides. If the flesh is dry, first moisten with a little milk so the flour adheres. Repeat for the other 3 fish.

You can fry flatfish whole or in fillets (see the chart below for frying times). For small whole fish, fry over a high heat so the flour coating sets firmly, locking in all the juices. Start large whole fish and thick fillets over a high heat until the coating has sealed, then reduce the heat and continue frying gently until done.

Skinning the fish
The dark skin on the top side of the Dover sole is quite thick and tough, and doesn't make good eating. For the sake of appearances, and for easy filleting at the table (see panel on the opposite page), it's better to remove at least the dark upper skin before cooking. Make a cut across the fish just above the tail; ease the skin away with a pointed knife, then pull it off whole (you have to tug quite hard but it does come away). Repeat for the other side. Alternatively, ask your fishmonger to skin the fish for you.

Don't hang about
Speed is of the essence – both in the cooking of the fish and in serving it. The unclarified butter used for the beurre noisette is prepared in the same pan used for frying the fish and must be poured over the fish just seconds before serving. If the fish is left to stand with the sauce already poured on top, the coating – which should remain crisp and light – turns soggy and limp.

4 Lay the first fish into the pan (butter side down) and fry for 3-5 minutes until golden brown. Turn the fish over and fry the other side. Lift on to a hot serving dish and keep warm. Repeat for the other 3 fish.

Frying times
The time it takes to pan-fry fish over a medium heat varies according to the size of the fish and whether it is cooked whole or in fillets.

whole flatfish	**fillets of flatfish**
450-675g (1-1½lb) plaice, sole, flounder, dabs etc	plaice, sole, flounder, dabs etc
5-6 minutes on each side	1-2 minutes on each side

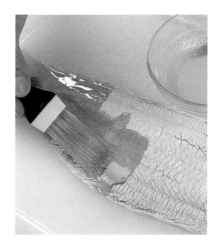

Filleting cooked flatfish

If you don't want to cope with the bones, the cooked Dover sole is easy to fillet at the table. This method makes 4 neat fillets.

2 Brush the presentation side (the side served upwards) of each fish with clarified or softened butter. Lay aside for 1-2 minutes to dry – this helps the fish to brown when fried.

3 Heat 1-2 tbsp olive oil in the frying-pan. To test if it's hot enough, dip one corner of the first fish in – it sizzles when the oil has reached the right temperature.

1 Hold the fish steady on a plate with the back of a fork. Then, using a sharp kitchen knife, slice all around the fish just inside the fins, cutting through to the plate. Work quickly so the fish doesn't get cold.

5 When all 4 fish are done, pour out the oil from the frying-pan. Add the unclarified butter to the pan and cook over a medium-high heat until it takes on a nutty brown colour and begins to froth.

6 Add the lemon juice, the seasoning and parsley (if using), then pour the beurre noisette over the fish and serve immediately with lemon wedges, fresh spinach and some new potatoes.

2 Slice down the centre of the fish to the backbone. Insert the fork under one fillet, then slide the knife under to free both top fillets.

3 Pull off the backbone and discard, then lift up the lower two fillets.

Variations on a theme

lemon sole with crispy shrimps

Crispy little fried shrimps are scrumptious as a topping on any pan-fried fish – and they give a real lift to lemon sole, which has a very mild flavour. Small brown shrimps are best – they need to be trimmed, leaving just the tails, still encased in the shell. Frying them in beurre noisette makes them extra tasty. If you can't find brown shrimps, go for shelled shrimps or little prawns.

serves 4

preparation time
10 minutes

cooking time
20 minutes

ingredients
4 x 350g (12oz) lemon sole, skinned
1-2 tbsp olive oil for each fish plus 25g (1oz) softened butter
2 tbsp flour
salt and pepper
beurre noisette (see page 56, replacing parsley with a squeeze of lemon juice)
115-175g (4-6oz) brown shrimps

1 Season the fish and coat with flour on both sides. Brush with butter, then set aside to dry for a couple of minutes.
2 Heat the oil in the frying-pan. When hot enough add the first fish. Fry for 3-5 minutes until crisp and golden brown, then turn over and fry the other side. When done, lift the fish out of the pan on to a hot plate and keep warm. Repeat for the other 3 fish.
3 Tip out remaining oil, then add the butter for the beurre noisette. Cook until the butter turns brown and frothy, then add the shrimps. Fry for about 1 minute until shrimps are crisp.
4 Add lemon juice and seasoning.
5 Pour the shrimps and beurre noisette over the lemon sole and serve with fresh peas.

why not try...

There are lots of different toppings to try with pan-fried flatfish, especially lemon sole, dabs, plaice and flounders – none of which has the superb flavour of Dover sole.

flaked almonds
Fry 85-115g (3-4oz) flaked almonds in the beurre noisette until they turn golden brown.

mushrooms
Slice 225g (8oz) mushrooms, add to the beurre noisette and fry for 2-3 minutes.

caramelized cucumber
Peel and slice half a cucumber. Sprinkle with salt and leave to drain for at least 1 hour. Rinse, then squeeze dry. Fry in the beurre noisette with a sprinkle of sugar to caramelize the cucumber slightly.

orange butter
Instead of making the beurre noisette, lay a line of trimmed orange slices down the length of each sole. Serve with pats of orange butter: soften 55g (2oz) unsalted butter, then beat in 2 tsp orange juice with 2 tsp grated orange peel and 1 tsp concentrated tomato purée; form into a roll in greaseproof paper and store in the fridge. Cut neat round slices to serve. Or try lime butter made in the same way, but replacing the tomato with 1 tsp chopped chives, a pinch of powdered thyme and a tiny pinch of grated fresh ginger.

deep-fried fish

Reminiscent of seaside holidays, deep-fried fish and chips are a treat. Here it's fresh cod fillet – the best battered fish ever

Just about any fish in the world can be fried – and a good covering of batter holds in the flavour and keeps the flesh moist. Served with crisp, golden chips, it's a great combination. A deep-fat fryer isn't essential – a heavy-based chip pan will do. All you need do is bring the oil to the right temperature and watch the pan.

On the side

Tartare sauce blends well with cod and is a perfect dip for chips. Ketchup or brown sauces are good alternative sauces, and lemon wedges or vinegar cut through the richness of the batter. Garden or mushy peas are traditional with fish and chips, but a crisp green salad or tomato and onion salad make a refreshing contrast.

Spicy fingers

Smaller pieces of fish deep-fry well. Thin slivers of herring or mackerel coated in cayenne have a real kick. And as the fish is cut so small, you can fry it in a shallow frying-pan in only 2-3 minutes. The chips in the variation are made with the potato skins. They are only fried once, not twice like regular chips, so are quick and easy. Serve with a salad and a soured cream dip.

Gary's special touch

Traditional batters need resting before cooking, but my version can be used at once. It's a frothing mix of beer and self-raising flour. I normally use lager, but a bitter works well and adds a touch of colour. The secret is to make sure the batter is very thick – keep adding lager until it seems almost too thick.

deep-frying cod and chips

You will need

serves 4

preparation time
15 minutes

cooking time
5-6 minutes pre-cooking the chips;
5-10 minutes per batch frying the
fish; 2-3 minutes to finish the chips
pre-heat oven 140°C/275°F/gas 1

ingredients
4 x 175-225g (6-8oz) cod fillets
225g (8oz) self-raising flour
salt and pepper

sunflower or corn oil for deep-frying
300ml (10fl oz) lager or bitter beer
lemon wedges and tartare sauce
to serve

for the chips
500-700g (1lb 2oz-1lb 9oz)
chip potatoes, peeled

equipment
deep-fat fryer or chip pan

There are a few things to remember when deep-frying. All the action comes at the end so you need to have everything ready before you start cooking. Don't be mean with the oil – change it if it gets dirty, burnt or speckled, otherwise the batter and the chips will turn out bitter and blackened.

If the oil is still clean after frying, cool it completely, then strain it and keep it in a sealed container in the fridge. Don't let it stand for days in the pan on top of the cooker – it will turn rancid and unusable.

Do not overcrowd the pan while frying as this reduces the temperature of the oil and makes the food soggy. Cook the fish pieces one at a time and cook the chips in batches. Don't overfill the pan.

It is important to dry the fish pieces and dip them in flour. This helps the batter to stick to the fish.

Frying the chips
The chips are cooked in two stages, which ensure they come out really crisp. First they are fried at a medium heat, which cooks the potato without colouring it and guarantees that the chips are cooked right through before serving. Secondly, they are fried again at a higher heat until crisp and golden. You can blanch the chips up to a day in advance and keep them covered in the fridge until required.

Cook's notes

If you don't have a deep-fat fryer or a cooking thermometer, cook the fish and both stages of the chips at the same oil temperature and increase or decrease the cooking time as necessary.

To test the temperature of the oil, lower a chip or a drop of batter into the pan. If the chip or batter sinks, the oil is too cold; if the chip or batter floats and the oil bubbles quickly around it, the oil is hot enough to start frying.

1 Cut the potatoes lengthways into 1cm (½in) thick slices. Then cut each slice into 1cm (½in) wide chips. Soak the chips in cold water for 10 minutes to remove any starch.

4 Whisk half the lager into the remaining flour until smooth. Gradually whisk in as much of the lager as needed to make a very thick batter.

2 Drain chips and pat dry. Heat oil to 190°C/375°F. Fry chips for 5-6 minutes until soft but not coloured. Stir chips or shake basket for even cooking. Drain on kitchen paper and set aside.

3 On a plate, season 1 tbsp flour with salt and pepper. Pat dry each piece of cod, then dip in the flour. Set aside. Heat the oil in the chip pan or fryer to 180°C/350°F.

Watchpoint!

Here are some safety tips:
- **Never leave the hot oil unattended.**
- **Do not let the oil get smoking hot – it may burst into flames.**
- **Do not allow any liquid to drop into the oil since it will spit out and may splash you.**
- **Lower the fish and chips into the oil slowly, taking care not to splash the oil. Use tongs or a fish slice to keep your hand well away from the oil or wear an oven glove. Use a metal basket to lower the chips into the pan and remove them.**
- **After cooking, let the oil cool in the pan.**

5 Dip a piece of cod in the batter, lower it into hot oil and fry for 5-6 minutes until crisp. Drain and keep warm in oven while you cook the rest.

6 Change the oil if necessary and heat to 200°C/400°F. Fry the part-cooked chips for 2-3 minutes until golden. Drain on kitchen paper, then serve with the cod, lemon wedges and tartare sauce.

Variations on a theme

devilled fried fish, crispy potato skins and soured cream dip

These small strips of fish can be cooked in 1cm (½in) oil in a shallow frying-pan, rather than a deep fryer or chip pan. The crispy potato skins are a way of using skins from peeled potatoes. Use a sharp knife, not a peeler, and leave a little flesh on the skins. Serve with soured cream for a refreshing alternative.

serves 4 as a starter
preparation time
20 minutes
cooking time *6-10 minutes frying potato skins; 5 minutes frying fish*
equipment *deep-fat fryer, chip pan or frying-pan*

ingredients
450g (1lb) skinless fish fillets: herring, mackerel, plaice or sole
vegetable oil for frying
3 tsp cayenne pepper
½ tsp salt
8 tbsp plain flour
8 tbsp milk

for the potato skins
skins from 1.3kg (3lb) potatoes, with 3mm (⅛in) flesh left on

for soured cream dip
200ml (7fl oz) soured cream or crème fraîche
2 tbsp fresh chives
2 tbsp lemon juice
salt and pepper

1 Cut fish into 1cm (½in) wide strips. Heat the oil.
2 Mix the cayenne, salt and flour. Dip the fish into the milk, then coat evenly in flour.
3 Drop half the fish strips into the hot oil and fry for 1½-2 minutes, or until crisp. Drain on kitchen paper. Fry the rest of the fish in the oil.
4 Cut the potato skins into even strips. Fry in batches for 3-5 minutes, or until golden and tender. Drain well.
5 Mix the soured cream with the chives, lemon juice, salt and pepper. Serve with the fish and potato skins.

why not try...

coating shellfish
Use the batter for coating king prawns, squid or other seafood.

other fish
Replace the cod with other white fish, such as haddock or whiting. If the fillets are thin, reduce the frying time to 5-6 minutes.

matchstick chips
For skinny-cut French fries, cut the chips into 5mm (¼in) thick pieces. Halve cooking times for both frying stages.

sweet chips
Make parsnip and sweet potato chips and serve the two together. (See page 98 for making sweet potato chips – make the parsnip chips in the same way.)

goes well with...

Make a refreshing salsa to fill the crispy fried potato skins. Finely dice ripe avocado, tomatoes, red and green peppers and a little fresh chilli. Toss with lime juice, chopped fresh coriander and salt to taste.

sauces for courses
Serve the deep fried cod with ketchup, brown or curry sauce in place of tartare sauce. Cod also goes well with the soured cream dip made for the fish strips.

baked fish

Baking gives fish a rich, deep taste – especially when it's stuffed with a spicy butter that flavours the whole fish

Whole mackerel is stuffed with a spicy garam masala butter, briefly pan-fried to brown and seal it, and then baked – while it's cooking, the butter melts, giving the fish a rich, spicy taste. Garam masala is a mix of spices used in Indian curries. You can buy it ready-made, but it's even better to make it yourself. A red onion and tomato salad cake complements the oily fish and the spicy butter.

All wrapped up
To keep all the spicy butter inside, you need to wrap the fish. Buttered foil works perfectly well – you pan-fry the fish through the foil to brown it a little before putting it in the oven. Or you can use pigs' caul, an edible fatty wrapping bought from the butcher – see Gary's special touch (below right). The fish is transferred straight from hob to oven, so use a frying-pan that can be put in the oven or a flameproof baking tray.

Small is beautiful
Using exactly the same method, substitute large fresh sardines for mackerel. You don't need to fillet them first because their bones are soft. Just slit them along the belly to gut them, pack in a basil butter filling and cook.

Gary's special touch

I wrap my mackerel in pigs' caul, a thin lacy net of a membrane veined with fat from around a pig's stomach. It keeps the food moist and is great for holding stuffings in too. And it's edible! If you use a caul, add a little oil or butter to the pan before frying the fish. But you'll find that foil protects the fish just as well.

making baked mackerel

You will need

serves 2

preparation time *20 minutes plus 30 minutes chilling in fridge; salad needs overnight chilling in the fridge*

cooking time *6 minutes in the frying-pan, 12-15 minutes in the oven*

pre-heat oven *200°C/400°F/gas 6*

ingredients

2 whole mackerel, head and backbone removed

55g (2oz) butter

1 tbsp finely chopped shallot or onion

pigs' caul (optional)

for the garam masala

2 tbsp coriander seeds

2 tbsp cumin seeds

1 tsp cardamom pods

2 bay leaves

1 tbsp black peppercorns

2 tsp cloves

½ tsp grated nutmeg

¼ tsp ground mace

¼ tsp ground ginger

for red onion and tomato cakes

4 plum or salad tomatoes

1 red onion, sliced

1 tbsp olive oil

1 tbsp groundnut oil

½ tsp balsamic vinegar

a squeeze of lemon juice

salt and pepper

a pinch of ground cumin (optional)

½ tbsp water

½ tbsp chopped fresh coriander

equipment

kitchen foil (if using)

flameproof baking tray or frying-pan

2 x 8cm (3in) diameter, 5cm (2in) deep ring moulds for tomato and onion salad

coffee grinder, blender or food processor for grinding garam masala

1 To make cakes, skin and deseed tomatoes and slice in rings. Make dressing: mix oils with vinegar, lemon juice and seasoning. Add cumin if using. Loosen dressing with water.

Ask your fishmonger to remove the mackerel backbones ('butterfly' filleted from the back). You end up with a deep flap in the fish, which is filled with garam masala butter in the main recipe, or with basil butter in the variation. You can ask your fishmonger to leave the head on the mackerel, if you prefer.

Prepare in advance

Prepare the garam masala mixture first – you can do this weeks in advance, if you wish – and store in a jar with a screw-on lid. Then make the butter and generously stuff the ready-boned fish with it. Wrap the fish tightly in buttered foil (or pigs' caul) and refrigerate for half an hour before baking – this sets the butter and helps hold the fish together. To cook, the fish are briefly pan-fried in the foil wrapping, allowing them to colour a little, then baked for 12-15 minutes in the oven. Make the red onion and tomato cakes the day before, to ensure that they are properly set.

Plan your portions

One mackerel per person is plenty – the fish are fairly rich. Allow two sardines per portion for the variation recipe because the fish are small.

5 Stuff mackerel: spread spicy butter evenly on both fish. Season and fold the 2 sides together. Wrap tightly in buttered foil. Chill for 30 minutes.

2 Season tomato and onion and build up cakes in layers in the rings. Put dressing and coriander between each layer. Refrigerate overnight in rings, then unmould to serve.

3 Dry roast all garam masala ingredients except mace, nutmeg and ginger in a frying-pan until they colour and smell aromatic. Cool, add other spices and grind to powder.

4 Make spicy butter. Melt 15g (½oz) butter. Add shallots with 2 heaped tsp garam masala and cook, without colouring the shallots, for 3-4 minutes. Cool. Soften rest of butter and mix in.

6 Fry the fish (in foil) in a flameproof baking tray or frying-pan for 2-3 minutes each side. Transfer fish to oven and bake for 12-15 minutes.

7 Remove mackerel from oven, unwrap and put on plates. Pour cooking juices over and serve with tomato cakes and lime wedges.

Variations on a theme

baked sardines with basil butter

Fresh sardines are much smaller than mackerel, but have a similar slightly oily texture and respond well to this method of quick pan-frying, then baking in the oven. Basil butter gives a beautiful, herby flavour. Serve with a tomato, basil and spring onion salad.

Preparing the sardines
Buy the fish ready-gutted – or gut them yourself. To do this, simply slit the sardines along the belly between the head and tail, open out the fish and pull away the innards in one piece. Rinse well and pat dry.

serves 2
preparation time
15 minutes for fish,
10 minutes for salad
cooking time *5-6 minutes*
pan-frying, 10 minutes
oven-baking
pre-heat oven
200°C/400°F/gas 6

ingredients
4 fresh sardines, gutted,
rinsed and patted dry
55g (2oz) butter, softened
1 tbsp chopped fresh basil
1 tbsp snipped chives
salt and pepper

for the salad
4 large ripe salad tomatoes

16 large basil leaves, washed
and patted dry
1 small bunch spring onions,
chopped
salt and pepper
130ml (4fl oz) classic French
vinaigrette (see below)

equipment
kitchen foil, buttered
flameproof baking tray or
frying-pan

1 Make basil butter. Put butter into bowl, add basil and chives and beat well.
2 Spread butter in the cavity of each fish, season well and wrap in foil. Put in fridge for 30 minutes to set.
3 Pan-fry fish for 2-3 minutes each side, allowing them to colour.
4 Transfer fish to oven and bake for 10 minutes.
5 While fish are baking, make salad. Slice tomatoes into rings and arrange in concentric circles on a serving plate. Tuck a large basil leaf between each slice of tomato. Sprinkle chopped spring onions on top and season. Make vinaigrette, then pour a little over the salad.
6 Remove sardines from foil and serve immediately, with some of the basil butter spooned around. Serve with tomato salad, the remainder of the vinaigrette and some crusty bread to mop up juices.

why not try...

baked herrings with onion butter
Prepare 2 herrings as in mackerel recipe. Then simmer 1 chopped medium onion with 30ml (1fl oz) balsamic vinegar, a pinch of salt and 75ml (2½fl oz) fish stock for 30-40 minutes, until onion is very soft and liquid has almost boiled away. Stir in 55g (2oz) unsalted butter. Remove from heat and add ½ tbsp Dijon mustard. Cool, then use to stuff herrings. Refrigerate for 30 minutes, then cook as for mackerel recipe.

herby variations
Any herb butter goes well with baked fish – parsley, chives, thyme, coriander or marjoram are all good. Also try curry powder instead of garam masala.

citrus slices
Add slices of lemon, lime or orange with the fish in the foil parcel.

classic French vinaigrette
Blitz 6 tbsp extra virgin olive oil, 2tbsp white or red vinegar, 2tsp Dijon mustard and salt and pepper with a hand blender.

open-steamed fish fillets

Gentle open steaming is perfect for fish fillets, keeping the flesh moist and flaky with no risk of overcooking, and leaving it with that lovely 'just-set' look

Steaming ensures that all the food's natural flavours and nutrients are retained, providing you with a wholesome meal. Open steaming (steaming without a lid) is ideal for delicate fish such as salmon, as it cooks gently from the bottom up, leaving it a delicate pink below and a rich orange on top.

The Scandinavian touch
Open-steamed salmon is delicious as it is, but here its taste is subtly enhanced by marinating. The flavours are based on Scandinavian gravadlax – a delicacy made by pickling salmon in salt, sugar, brandy and dill. Unlike the authentic version, which is eaten raw, this 'gravadlax' salmon is only partly cured before cooking.

Ringing the changes
White fish fillets, such as halibut or cod, can also be partly cured using aromatic spices and herbs; or they can be simply steamed with a little white wine, and dressed with a rich herb-filled butter sauce.

Gary's special touch

The long curing process for true gravadlax draws the moisture out of the fish, giving it a smoked salmon texture. My trick is to halve the salt and sugar in the marinade, and reduce the time marinating to 2-3 hours so that the fish retains its natural moisture, but still takes on those smoky-sweet tastes of gravadlax.
For a more intense flavour increase marinating time to 24 hours.

making the 'gravadlax' salmon

You will need

serves 4

preparation time
10 minutes plus a minimum of 2-3 hours for marinating

cooking time *10 minutes*

ingredients
900g (2lb) fillet of salmon, any remaining bones removed with tweezers (ask the fishmonger to fillet the fish for you)

for the marinade
25g (1oz) coarse sea salt
25g (1oz) caster sugar
2 tbsp brandy

for the sauce
2 tbsp brandy
¼ tsp demerara sugar
6 tbsp mayonnaise
2 tsp chopped fresh dill
2 level tsp Dijon mustard
salt and pepper
lemon wedges to serve

equipment
perforated pizza baking tray to fit in a wok, or a wire rack to fit in a baking tin

1 Mix salt, sugar and brandy to a paste and rub it on to the fish. Wrap the fillet in plastic wrap and refrigerate. Leave to marinate for a minimum of 2-3 hours – 24 will do no harm.

Marinating raw salmon in a mixture of salt, sugar and brandy for at least two or three hours before steaming adds flavour to the fish. In slightly different proportions, and with the addition of dill, the same marinating ingredients are used for curing (preserving) fish.

Open steaming
Open steaming is literally that – there's no lid! This gentle cooking method just sets the salmon, leaving all the flavours locked inside until you cut into it to eat.

Steaming method
You don't need any special equipment for open steaming. Here the pieces of fish, placed on individual squares of greaseproof paper, are cooked on a perforated pizza baking tray fitted into a wok over boiling water. The

water comes to just below the level of the baking tray. A wire rack in a baking tin also works well. You can use a proprietary steamer pan or bamboo steaming basket, but these are usually only large enough to fit two or at most three fillets at a time, so you would need to work in two batches, keeping the first batch warm.

Delicate dill
Authentic gravadlax is cured in a marinade with dill and is eaten with a mustard dressing. Here the dill and mustard flavourings are in the mayonnaise dressing which is served cold with the fish.

Potatoes are an ideal accompaniment for this dish. Serve them boiled or as a salad with some crisp fresh green leaves, tossed in a light vinaigrette dressing. (See page 66 for making the dressing.)

5 Set the baking tray in the wok and bring water back to the boil. Cook with no lid for about 8-10 minutes, depending on the thickness of the fillets.

2 For the sauce, bring the brandy and demerara sugar to the boil and reduce by two-thirds.

3 Leave the reduction to cool then mix well with the mayonnaise, dill and mustard and season lightly with salt and pepper.

4 Wipe excess salt from the fillets and cut into 4 portions. Sit on squares of greaseproof paper on the pizza baking tray. Pour some boiling water into the wok.

6 Arrange the salmon with a spoonful of brandy and dill mayonnaise and a wedge of lemon. Serve immediately with sliced potatoes and a green leafy salad.

Watchpoint!

Minimizing the salt
Make sure excess salt is wiped or rinsed off after marinating. There'll still be a residue of salt left on the salmon afterwards, so go easy on the seasoning when making the brandy and dill sauce to serve with it.

Variations on a theme

Thai-style white fish

Thai-style fish has the hot and aromatic allure of ginger, chillies and lemon grass, cooled with a soothing creamy sauce. The marinating and steaming method is the same as for the salmon.

Although fragrant rice would be more traditional with a Thai-style dish, crusty white bread is ideal for mopping up the minty soured cream sauce.

serves 4

preparation time
15 minutes, plus 2-3 hours for marinating

cooking time
10 minutes

ingredients
900g (2lb) skinned halibut or prime cod fillet, fine bones removed with tweezers

for the marinade
1 tsp freshly grated ginger
zest and juice of 1 lime
juice of ½ lemon
25g (1oz) caster sugar
25g (1oz) coarse sea salt
1 tbsp finely sliced lemon grass
2 small hot red chillies, deseeded and very finely sliced

for the sauce
150ml (5fl oz) soured cream
150ml (5fl oz) natural yoghurt
juice of 1 lime
2 tsp finely chopped fresh mint
salt and pepper

1 Pack the fish into a shallow dish. Mix the marinade ingredients and rub over the fish. Cover and refrigerate for 2-3 hours, turning fish over halfway through the marinating time.
2 Whisk together the sauce ingredients, going easy on the salt. Pour into a serving bowl, cover and leave in the fridge until ready to serve.
3 Wipe excess salt from the fish and cut it into 4 portions. Sit it, skinned side down, on squares of buttered greaseproof paper. Pour boiling water into the steamer or frying pan to come just below level of steaming rack.
4 Bring to a good simmer and open steam the fish for 8-10 minutes, depending on the thickness of the fillet.
5 Serve with the soured cream, lime and mint sauce and a mixture of stir-fried vegetables – mangetout, green beans and asparagus, seasoned with soy sauce.

why not try...

With open steaming there's no need to cure the fish at all. Keep it simple and just season fillets of any firm fish before cooking. Serve with a creamy sauce and fresh vegetables.

cod with coriander butter
Season 4 cod or salmon fillets and steam as before. Chill and cube 250g (9oz) butter. Gently fry finely chopped shallots and ½ star anise in a knob of butter until just soft, without colouring. Add 85ml (3fl oz) white wine vinegar, then 175ml (6fl oz) white wine, then 150ml (5fl oz) water, reducing each time by three-quarters. Add ¾ bunch of coriander, chopped, and 1 tsp crushed coriander seeds. Bring to a simmer, and gradually whisk in chilled butter. Season. Strain through a sieve and add remaining coriander leaves. Thin the sauce with lemon juice if it's too thick and serve with the fish.

turbot on a bed of leeks, mushrooms and spinach
Open steam 4 x 175g (6oz) turbot fillets over a pan of water mixed with 150ml (5fl oz) dry white wine until tender. Meanwhile, stir-fry ½ tsp grated fresh root ginger and 450g (1lb) each of sliced mushrooms, leeks and spinach in 55g (2oz) unsalted butter. When almost cooked, add 8 blanched asparagus spears, ½ bunch flatleaf parsley, lime juice, seasoning. Serve with the turbot on top.

grilled tuna

Grilling is the simplest way of cooking fish. Steaks and fillets cook in minutes, the high temperature sealing in flavour and moistness

Fresh tuna is a lovely meaty fish. A tuna fillet has a texture similar to beef and is cooked in the same way – it is best cooked medium-rare to medium. The firm, close-grained, dark red flesh grills well, needing only 2-3 minutes each side to keep it pink, moist and tender inside. Don't overcook the tuna – it turns dry very quickly.

When buying, go for an even, deep colour – pale flesh is not fresh. Dark marks indicate bruising – avoid these. Tuna steaks are generally quite thick and still have the skin on while fillets are thinner and skinless.

Spicy Cajun style
Cajun cooking – noted for its sizzling hot flavours – comes from the New Orleans area. In this recipe tuna fillets are grilled with a peppery Cajun-style coating and served with spicy potato wedges. For the best flavour, let the fillet stand in its coating for an hour or two before cooking.

Flavour variation
Very fresh tuna can simply be grilled or pan-fried with a knob of butter. But the flesh can turn out dry – so give it a boost with a tangy lime marinade. Serve with a green salad or tagliatelle.

Gary's special touch

I think the tingly tart flavour of lime has a special affinity with the meatiness of fresh tuna – it's slightly sweeter than lemon juice and offers a hint of the exotic which blends in perfectly with the Cajun spice coating. Since lime works so well with tuna, I've used it again for the sour cream and lime dressing variation.

making the 'blackened' Cajun tuna

You will need

serves 4

preparation time
10 minutes plus up to 2 hours to marinate the tuna; 5-10 minutes for the spicy potato wedges

cooking time
4-8 minutes for the tuna; 30-35 minutes for the spicy potato wedges

pre-heat oven
220°C/425°F/gas 7

ingredients
½ tbsp olive oil
4 x 125-175g (4½-6oz) tuna fillets
2 limes, cut into quarters
large bunch of watercress, rinsed and trimmed

for the Cajun spice mix
2 tsp chilli powder
1 tsp black peppercorns
1 tsp white peppercorns
1 tsp dried oregano
1 tsp dried thyme
1 tsp cumin seeds
1 tsp garlic granules
1 tsp onion granules
1 tsp salt

for the spicy potato wedges
8 medium sized potatoes, peeled and sliced into 4-6 wedges each
2 tbsp vegetable oil
salt
2 tsp paprika

equipment
coffee grinder, mini-processor or pestle and mortar for processing the Cajun spice mix
large roasting tin
ridged grill pan

1 Place all the Cajun spice ingredients in a coffee grinder, mini-processor or pestle and mortar and grind or pound to a fine powder. Spread out on a plate.

This recipe relies for its appeal on a hot, spicy outside crust that protects the succulent meaty texture of the tuna. The fish comes off the grill moist, dark and delicious – the name 'blackened' refers to the colour of the grilled coating – and is perfectly complemented by crispy, spicy potato wedges, watercress and a squeeze of lime which cools down the Cajun heat.

Grilling times
The amount of time you need to grill tuna fillets or steaks depends on their thickness. Average size fillets, 2cm (¾in) thick, take 2-3 minutes each side. The tuna is cooked when the surface feels firm to the touch – if you want it rare it should still be a little pink in the centre. Allow 1-2 minutes more if you want the fish medium to well done, but be aware that overcooked tuna quickly becomes dry. Heat the grill to a very hot temperature before starting to cook the fillets, so that they sear at once, sealing in all the juices.

Making the coating
The ingredients for the spicy Cajun coating need to be ground or processed to a fine powder so that they stick to the fish and form a crust when grilled. Use dried oregano and thyme – fresh leaves won't grind down finely enough. Buy onion and garlic granules, not flavoured salts. Granules are available in most supermarkets.

4 Roast the spicy potato wedges in the pre-heated oven for 30-35 minutes, turning them halfway through, until they are slightly crispy and golden brown on the outside and tender inside.

diamond grill marks

Fillets cooked on a ridged grill pan come out with attractive marks. You can use a hot skewer to achieve the same effect.

2 Coat all 4 tuna fillets on both sides with the spice mix, then leave them in the fridge for 1-2 hours to absorb the spicy flavours. Take them out again 20 minutes before cooking.

3 Meanwhile, make the spicy potatoes. Spread the potato wedges in a large roasting tin in one layer. Add the oil, salt and paprika and toss until the potatoes are well coated.

If you don't have a ridged grill pan, cook the tuna under your cooker grill. Heat a skewer in the gas flame or on an electric hob and mark a diamond pattern on each fillet before cooking. For safety use long skewers and an oven glove.

5 Heat the grill pan until very hot, brush with olive oil and cook the fillets for about 2-3 minutes each side – the exact time depends on the thickness. The fillet is cooked when it feels firm to the touch.

6 Squeeze a little lime juice over each tuna fillet and serve with the spicy potato wedges, watercress and quarters of lime.

Variations on a theme

marinaded tuna with soured cream and lime dressing

The tuna fillets are marinaded in olive oil, lemon zest, pepper and sea salt, then grilled and served with a soured cream and lime dressing. The intense lime flavour cuts through the oiliness of the fish, while the red onion slices add crunch.

Perfect timing
The tuna must have time to absorb the marinade flavours – this helps it stay moist. Coat the fish in the marinade, cover it tightly, then refrigerate for up to 2 hours. Allow the fish to come back to room temperature for about 20 minutes before cooking. For a highly flavoured soured cream and lime dressing, make it about 30 minutes in advance .

ingredients
4 x 125-175g (4½-6oz) tuna fillets
grated zest from 1 lemon, juice from ½ lemon
1 tbsp olive oil
1 tsp coarsely ground white pepper
½ tsp coarse sea salt
1 red onion, thinly sliced

for the dressing
142ml soured cream
juice of 1 lime
salt
1-2 tbsp shredded basil

1 Mix the lemon zest and juice, olive oil, salt and white pepper. Turn the tuna fillets in the mixture until coated. Cover and refrigerate for up to 2 hours (but not less than 30 minutes).
2 To make the dressing, mix the soured cream with the lime juice, salt and basil, then leave to infuse for 30 minutes.
3 Grill the tuna fillets as before (see page 73, step 5).
4 Serve the fillets with some dressing spooned on the side and sprinkled with thinly sliced red onion. Accompany with a green or mixed salad.

why not try...

grilled tuna and cucumber brochettes
Cut tuna into 4cm (1½in) cubes. Peel, halve and deseed a cucumber and slice into 2.5cm (1in) segments. Put fish and cucumber into a dish and add a marinade of olive oil, white wine, herbs and lemon juice. Toss the fish and cucumber in the marinade, then leave to steep for at least 1 hour. Put alternate tuna and cucumber pieces on skewers and place on an oiled pan or grill rack. Cook under pre-heated grill for about 10 minutes, turning occasionally and basting frequently with the marinade. Serve with rice or a mixed salad.

gorgeous garlic
Rub the tuna with a cut clove of garlic, then grill as before and serve with the soured cream, lime and basil dressing. Alternatively, serve with spicy potato wedges made with sweet potatoes tossed in dried oregano instead of ordinary potatoes and paprika.

tuna and salade niçoise
Try grilled chunks of fresh tuna in a salade niçoise. Mix cooked tuna with cherry tomatoes, shredded lettuce, black olives, cooked green beans, boiled new potatoes and quartered hard-boiled eggs, then toss in a vinaigrette of olive oil, Dijon mustard, white wine or tarragon vinegar and seasoning.

steamed mussels

Gentle steaming enhances the distinctive flavour and juicy succulence of fresh mussels

Mussels are favourite dish on the menus at French and Belgian pavement cafés, where all types of seafood are extremely popular and widely available. Often served with thin-cut potato chips (*frites*) and a glass of beer, steamed mussels are a classic part of seafood cuisine. Crusty bread is also an essential part of the meal, as it is used to soak up the rich, fishy juices.

Moules marinière
One of the most famous steamed mussel dishes is moules marinière. The mussels take on the flavours of the wine-enriched stock in which they are steamed, while double cream, added at the end of cooking, gives the finished dish a luxurious smoothness. Served in individual bowls, the mussels are shelled and eaten one by one.

Added crunch
For a more formal presentation, try the variation recipe where the mussels are served in their half-shells with a buttery almond and parsley sauce and topped with breadcrumbs. There are many other flavour ideas for steamed mussels, from using cider in the stock to an easy pasta meal.

Gary's special touch

My own twist on moules marinière comes from star anise, which lends a subtle spiciness to the flavour. A mirepoix of sautéed diced vegetables is also added at the end to make the dish more colourful. For the best results, dice the vegetables to 3mm (⅛in) so that they cook evenly and quickly in the sauce.

making the moules marinière

You will need

serves 2	**for the mussels and sauce**
preparation time 15 minutes, plus 20 minutes cleaning mussels	250ml (9fl oz) white wine
cooking time 15 minutes	400ml (14fl oz) fish stock (see page 9)
	1 star anise
for the vegetables	1kg (2lb 4oz) mussels, cleaned
55g (2oz) butter	and soaked
2 heaped tbsp finely diced shallots or onions	85ml (3fl oz) double cream
1 heaped tbsp finely diced carrot	a squeeze of lemon juice
1 heaped tbsp finely diced celery	salt and pepper
1 garlic clove, crushed	2 tbsp chopped mixed fresh herbs, for
1 heaped tbsp finely diced leek	example parsley, tarragon and chervil

The quantities in this recipe serve two people as a main course. If you want to cook mussels for four people, double the ingredients but cook them in two batches.

Why steaming?
Steaming in a small amount of stock is the most efficient way to open and cook mussels, and retains the delicate flavour of the flesh. You'll need a large pan with a tight-fitting lid as the mussels must be covered at the beginning of cooking to build up the heat inside. The mussels are then turned gently in the hot liquid until the shells open and the flesh is cooked.

Essential preparation
Many people avoid serving mussels because of the preparation needed before cooking. Although mussels require thorough washing and checking, they do not take long to cook. For convenience, mussels are often sold in 1kg (2lb 4oz) bags. Sometimes they are available partially

cleaned so that the preparation time at home is made shorter.

Quick cooking
Mussels have a limited season and are at their best from autumn through to spring. They take only a few minutes to cook, but the stock and wine must be boiling before they can be added to the pan.

In this recipe, the mussels are first covered and cooked in the simmering stock for 30 seconds, then stirred until they open. After steaming, remove the mussels from the pan with a slotted spoon. Do not over-cook the mussels, or they turn rubbery. It is essential to discard any mussels that are unopened.

Gentle sautéeing
The sautéed vegetables enhance the finished dish and lend extra colour to its appearance. Take care to dice them very finely and evenly. Sweat them over a low heat in step 1 so they soften, but do not brown.

1 Melt two-thirds of the butter in a pan. Add the shallots, carrot, celery and garlic. Sweat them for 3 minutes or until softened. Add the leek and cook for 1 minute.

4 Boil the mixture over a high heat until reduced by a third. Reduce the heat. Add the cream, then whisk in the lemon juice and the rest of the butter.

2 For the mussels, heat wine, stock and star anise in a large pan. Add the mussels. Cover and cook for 30 seconds. Stir for 4 minutes, until the mussels open, then remove from pan.

3 To make the sauce, carefully pour the cooking liquid from the large pan into a jug. Then strain this liquid through a sieve on to the vegetables and stir to mix them well.

Watchpoint

Use lightly seasoned stock for making moules marinière as too much salt can mask the delicate flavours of the mussels and fresh herbs.

If you are using fish stock made from stock cubes, dissolve them in twice the amount of water stated on the packet to reduce their saltiness. If you are using chilled stock, dilute it with half its own volume of water before using it.

It is a sensible idea is to taste the sauce at step 5 to check its flavour before adding any salt.

5 Lightly season the sauce with salt and pepper (see Watchpoint, above). Add the chopped mixed herbs and stir together until well mixed.

6 Tip the mussels into a bowl and pour over the sauce. Serve with crusty bread, toasted if you prefer, to soak up the juices.

Variations on a theme

mussels with buttery almonds and parsley

Served in half shells and topped with shallots, almonds, parsley and breadcrumbs, these mussels have a special flavour and texture.

serves 4 as a starter
preparation time
15 minutes
cooking time *15 minutes*

for the shallots
6 shallots, finely chopped
1 large garlic clove
250g (9oz) unsalted butter

for the mussels
½ onion, chopped
1 carrot, chopped
2 sticks celery, chopped
1 small leek, chopped
1 garlic clove, crushed
1 bay leaf
1 sprig thyme
½ bottle dry white wine
600ml (1 pint) diluted fish stock (see page 9)
1kg (2lb 4oz) mussels, cleaned and soaked
55g (2oz) blanched almonds, cut into slivers
2 tbsp chopped parsley
toast, cut into small pieces

1 Sweat the shallots and garlic in 1 tbsp butter until soft. Stir in all but 2 tbsp of the remaining butter.
2 For the mussels, sweat the vegetables, garlic, bay leaf and thyme in 2 tbsp butter until soft. Stir in the wine, then boil until almost dry. Add the stock and bring to the boil. Add the mussels and stir until they open.
3 Strain off the liquid and discard the vegetables. Shell the mussels, discarding any that are unopened. Put into a bowl with a little cooking liquid, cover and set aside. Rinse the shells.
4 Boil the cooking liquid until thickened. Add the mussels, shallots in butter, almonds and parsley.
5 Arrange the shells on plates and put a mussel into each shell. Spoon shallot mixture over the top and sprinkle with the toast pieces.

why not try...

Cooked mussels can be added to a variety of recipes and the cooking liquid is ideal for flavouring sauces and soups.

Normandy style
For a sharper flavour, replace the white wine in these mussel recipes with dry cider. Accompany with apple slices, sautéed in butter.

egg-enriched sauce
After reducing the cooking liquid in the moules marinière recipe or mussels with almonds, leave to cool slightly, then beat in two egg yolks. Transfer to a double boiler and stir or whisk until thickened. Serve the mussels in or out of their shells, with the enriched sauce poured on top.

mussel and leek soup
Use the unreduced cooking liquid to flavour a home-made cream of leek soup. Add the mussels at the end of cooking and serve with garlic croûtons.

mussels with pasta
Flavour a thick white sauce with the reduced cooking liquid. Stir in the cooked mussels and serve with fresh pasta and seasonal vegetables.

eats well with...

To bring out the star anise taste in the moules marinière, serve with a glass of Pernod, or add a drop to the sauce.

fish pie

Homely and welcoming, fish pie combines juicy fish in a smooth white sauce with a creamy mashed potato topping

Fish pie brings together familiar ingredients and favourite flavours in one satisfying dish. Various techniques are used to create the pie, but all are straightforward.

A tasty assembly
First, the spinach leaves are briefly wilted, then spread out in a baking dish. The fish is gently poached in milk, then drained and broken up into chunks. The same milk is then used to make a delicious white sauce, to which the fish and prawns are added (4 hard-boiled eggs can be added as an optional extra). Simple seasonings – parsley, lemon juice, salt and pepper – perfectly complement the mild flavours of the fish and prawns.

Lashings of mash
Boiled potatoes mashed with butter and milk or cream create a smooth, super-rich topping for the pie, with grated cheddar for richness and flavour.

Classic combo
Pink salmon and green leeks under dill-flavoured mashed potato make an attractive alternative recipe. Smoked salmon and grated lemon zest are included to sharpen the flavours.

Gary's special touch

I've replaced plain white fish with smoked haddock for its irresistible smokiness which flavours the milk as it poaches. Try to find uncoloured smoked haddock rather than the bright yellow variety as it has a more subtle flavour. A layer of fresh spinach leaves lifts the colour and flavour of the pie.

making the smoked haddock pie

You will need

serves 4

preparation time
30 minutes

cooking time
30 minutes

pre-heat oven
200°C/400°F/gas 6

ingredients
*600g (1lb 5oz) skinless smoked
haddock fillet*
500g (1lb 2oz) spinach, washed
salt and white pepper
600ml (1 pint) milk
85g (3oz) butter

55g (2oz) plain flour
150g (5½oz) cooked prawns
3 tbsp chopped fresh parsley
juice of ½ lemon

for the topping
*750g (1lb 7oz) potatoes, peeled and
quartered*
85g (3oz) butter
*100ml (3½fl oz) milk or double
cream, or a mixture of the two*
115g (4oz) mature cheddar, grated

equipment
large baking dish

I Put the spinach into a sieve or colander. Pour boiling water over the spinach to wilt it. Squeeze excess water from the spinach, arrange it in the base of a baking dish and season well.

The ingredients for this fish pie are cooked twice – first separately, then baked together in the oven – so it is important not to overcook them in the early stages. Cook the spinach lightly to wilt the leaves – any longer and all the flavour is lost. Similarly, poach the fish only until the flesh turns opaque and flakes easily – it is better to undercook it a little, rather than overcooking it.

Make sure, however, that you cook the sauce well to avoid the taste of raw flour. After thickening, simmer gently for a further 2-3 minutes, stirring continually to remove any lumps.

Simple finish

For a homely finish, the mashed potato is simply spooned over the fish mixture, then lightly manipulated with a fork to create soft peaks that brown in the oven as the pie bakes. To create patterns, score the mashed potato with a fork into wavy lines. To give the pie a smarter finish, spoon the mash into a piping bag and pipe a neat topping over the filling.

Different vegetables

An alternative to spinach in this pie is broccoli – blanch in boiling water and use the same way as the spinach. Also try mashing some carrot with the mashed potato topping.

Tip

If you can't find any skinless smoked haddock fillet in your supermarket, poach the fish with its skin on, then carefully peel the skin off when the fish is cooked and discard it. Don't try pulling the skin off the fish when it is raw as it won't come away easily or evenly.

5 Spoon the fish and prawn mixture in the sauce over the spinach in the dish and level it out, leaving plenty of room for the topping.

2 For the topping, boil the potatoes for 20 minutes until tender. Meanwhile, put the fish and milk into a large shallow pan. Poach gently for 7 minutes, or until the fish is opaque.

3 Lift the fish out of the pan with a fish slice, then strain the milk into a jug and reserve. Break the fish into chunks or flakes, removing any small bones.

4 Melt 55g (2oz) butter in a pan. Mix in the flour, cook for 1-2 minutes and add the milk. Stir until thickened, then simmer for 2 minutes. Add seasoning, parsley, lemon, fish and prawns.

6 Drain the potatoes, then mash with 40g (1½oz) of butter, milk or cream. Stir in the cheese and season. Spoon over the fish and fluff up with a fork.

7 Cut the remaining butter into tiny pieces and scatter over the pie. Bake for 30 minutes, or until golden. Serve with peas, mangetout and buttered brown bread.

Variations on a theme

salmon and leek pie

Sautéed leeks and strips of oak-smoked salmon join salmon fillet in this tasty pie. The mashed potato topping is speckled with chopped fresh dill.

serves 6

preparation time
30 minutes

cooking time *30 minutes*

pre-heat oven
200°C/400°F/gas 6

ingredients
900g (2lb) skinless salmon fillet
600ml (1 pint) milk
115g (4oz) butter
700g (1lb 9oz) leeks, cut in 1cm (½in) slices
55g (2oz) plain flour
55g (2oz) oak-smoked salmon, cut into strips
salt and white pepper
zest and juice of 1 lemon
2 tbsp chopped fresh dill

for the topping
mashed potatoes (see page 81, replacing the cheese with 2 tbsp chopped fresh dill)

1 Make the mashed potatoes (see page 81, steps 2 and 6), with dill instead of cheese.
2 Poach salmon fillet in milk for 7 minutes until it flakes easily.
3 Lift fish out and break into chunks. Strain milk into a jug and reserve.

4 Melt 25g (1oz) of the butter in a pan. Add leeks and fry over a low heat for 5 minutes until softened. Remove from pan and set aside.
5 Melt 55g (2oz) of the butter in the pan. Mix in flour and cook for 1-2 minutes. Add milk and whisk to make a smooth sauce. Stir in leeks.
6 Add poached and smoked salmon, lemon zest and juice and dill to sauce. Season, then transfer to baking dish.
7 Top with mashed potato. Dot with remaining butter and bake for 30 minutes until golden brown.

why not try...

other fish
Use other white fish to make the pies – try cod, haddock, plaice, hake or whiting.

mushrooms or greens
Replace the spinach with half the quantity of sautéed sliced mushrooms or shredded spring greens.

touch of spice
For a warm spicy flavour, season the sauce with ½ tsp grated nutmeg, mustard powder or paprika.

petit pois
Add 55g (2oz) thawed, frozen garden peas or petit pois to the sauce at the last minute.

crisp topping
For an instant topping, roughly crush a large bag of ready-salted potato crisps. Mix with 55g (2oz) finely grated cheese and spread over the pie.

sharpen up
Add 2 tbsp capers or rinsed, diced gherkins to the sauce.

short-cut mash
Cover either of the pies with instant mashed potato made from a packet mix. Prepare the mix according to the instructions on the packet, but replace a third of the recommended water with double cream. Add grated cheese, if using, and spoon or pipe over the fish mixture.

roast beef

Tender roast beef is given a tasty twist with a fiery peppercorn crust

Roast beef with Yorkshire pudding and horseradish sauce is about as traditional as you can get – but there are simple ways of livening up this old favourite. Peppered roast beef is a spicy version that sets the tastebuds alight – yet still goes well with the traditional trimmings.

Which joint?
The best joints for roasting are sirloin, topside or rolled rib – they all have a good flavour and are reasonably priced. All you need to do is roast the beef until it is cooked the way you like it – rare, medium or well done.

When buying beef, remember that meat from a young animal has bright red flesh and white fat marbled through the flesh. The fat on meat from older animals is a creamy colour and the flesh may be a little tougher.

A change of coat
A prime beef joint only needs salt and pepper to bring out its flavour – but you can transform it with a host of other flavourings.

For the variation recipe, the beef is marinated in red wine, olive oil, herbs and mustard, then given a mustard seed coating. The marinade is used to baste the beef during cooking.

You can also coat the beef with breadcrumbs, garlic, onion, nuts, spices and dried fruit.

Gary's special touch

You may think that the pepper coating masks the flavour of the beef, and this can happen with peppered steaks because all the meat is coated. But with a large joint, only the top is covered, so the beef has the prominent flavour – each slice is meltingly tender inside, with a thin peppery layer just around the edge.

roasting the peppered beef

You will need

serves 8

preparation time *20 minutes*

chilling time *1 hour*

pre-heat oven *200°C/400°F/gas 6*

cooking time *1-1 hour 20 minutes, depending on the cut of beef and how well done you like it*

ingredients
1.8kg (4lb) beef – sirloin, rolled rib or topside
2-3 tbsp crushed or coarsely ground black peppercorns
salt
vegetable oil

Yorkshire pudding batter (see Making the pudding batter, below)

for the horseradish sauce
150ml (5fl oz) double cream
1-2 tbsp freshly grated horseradish or bottled horseradish relish
2 tsp white wine vinegar
½ tsp prepared English mustard
salt and white pepper
caster sugar to taste

equipment
roasting tin
2 x 4-cup Yorkshire pudding tins or a muffin tray

I Firmly press the pepper into the fat on the top of the beef with your fingers. Season the joint all over with salt. Chill in the fridge for 1 hour.

The beef is sealed before roasting to lock in the juices, to keep the meat tasty and moist. Seal the joint by cooking it over a high heat until it is lightly browned all over.

Time it to your own taste
The length of roasting time depends on three things: the type of beef cut, the temperature of the oven and your own preference as to how well done you like it.

As a rough guide, if the joint is sealed first, then roasted at 200°C/400°F/gas 6, give rare beef 15 minutes per 450g (1lb), medium 20 minutes and well done 25 minutes.

Rest and relaxation
Resting any joint after roasting is one of the main keys to tender meat. Leave the beef to stand for at least 15 minutes to let the muscle fibres relax and tenderize.

Resting also makes carving easier because the meat firms up. It retains heat for a surprisingly long time when it's covered with foil and left in a warm place on a warmed serving platter.

Making the pudding batter
Make enough Yorkshire puddings for eight people to have two each. Sift 450g (1lb) of plain flour and two pinches of salt into a large bowl. Beat 6 eggs lightly, then add to the flour. Whisk together with a balloon whisk or electric whisk to form a paste. Gradually whisk in 600ml-800ml (1-1¼ pints) milk to form a smooth batter which thinly coats the back of a wooden spoon. Put the batter in a jug.

Bake the puddings in two batches – put the first batch in the oven about 35 minutes before the beef is ready, and the second batch while the beef is resting. Warm the first batch 5 minutes just before serving.

Recipe tip

Beetroot crisps
Prepare the beetroot crisps while the beef is resting.

ingredients
4 raw beetroot
vegetable oil for deep frying
plain flour for dusting
salt

I Peel the beetroot and slice thinly with a mandolin, food processor or sharp knife. Dry with kitchen paper. **2** Heat the oil in a deep-fat fryer or chip pan to 180°C/350°F/gas 4. Lightly coat the beetroot in flour. Deep-fry in batches for 15 seconds each, or until crisp. Remove the slices with a slotted spoon. Drain on kitchen paper. Season with salt.

2 Pre-heat the oven. Heat some oil in a roasting tin on the hob. Fry the beef until lightly browned. Roast for 1 hour to 1 hour 20 minutes, depending on how rare you like your beef.

3 About 35 minutes before the beef is ready, grease the Yorkshire pudding trays with oil and heat in the top of the oven. Pour in the batter and bake the first batch for 20 minutes.

Cook's notes

A meat thermometer is useful for showing you how cooked the beef is in the centre. Push it into the thickest part of the joint: rare beef registers 60°C/140°F, medium beef reads 70°C/150°F and well done reads 80°C/170°F.

If you don't have a meat thermometer, press the flesh firmly so some of the juices come out. If the juices are red, the beef is rare, if they are pink, it is medium, and if they are clear, the meat is well done.

Remember that the hot beef keeps cooking as it is resting, so take it out of the oven a little less done than you like.

4 Mix the horseradish sauce ingredients in a bowl. Test the beef (see Cook's notes) and transfer to a warm platter. Cover and leave for 15 minutes. Bake a second batch of puddings.

5 Uncover the beef and surround with Yorkshire puddings and beetroot crisps (see Recipe tip). Carve the beef into slices. Serve with the horseradish sauce, roast potatoes and vegetables.

Variations on a theme

marinaded mustardy roast beef

This is an ideal recipe for a less expensive joint – the marinade keeps it moist during roasting.

serves 8

preparation time
10 minutes

marinating time *8 hours*

cooking time *1 hour to 1 hour 20 minutes*

pre-heat oven
220°C/425°F/gas 7

ingredients
1.8kg (4lb) beef sirloin, topside or rolled rib
150ml (5fl oz) double or whipping cream

for the marinade
300ml (10fl oz) red wine
5 tbsp olive oil
1 tbsp dried herbes de Provence
2 tsp Dijon mustard
1 tbsp coarsely ground black pepper

for the crust
2 tbsp mustard seeds
2 tbsp plain flour
salt and black pepper

1 Mix the marinade ingredients. Add the beef and turn to coat. Cover and chill for 8 hours, turning occasionally.
2 Pre-heat the oven. For the crust, crush the mustard seeds. Mix with the flour and seasoning.
3 Remove the beef from the marinade and pat dry. Roll it in the crust mixture. Put in a roasting tin and add marinade.
4 Roast for 1 hour to 1 hour 20 minutes, depending on how well done you like the beef. Baste with the marinade to keep the beef moist.
5 Put the beef on to a warmed platter and cover with foil. Leave to rest for 15 minutes.
6 Meanwhile, skim the fat from the roasting juices. Deglaze in the tin over a low heat, then boil and reduce by half. Add the cream. Simmer for 4 minutes, season and serve with the beef.

why not try...

garlic and herb crust
Season 55g (2oz) fresh white breadcrumbs with salt, pepper, crushed garlic and herbs. Moisten the mixture with olive oil. Seal the beef as before and roll the joint firmly through the breadcrumb mixture before roasting.

almond and apricot crust
For a north African flavour, mix 55g (2oz) fine fresh white breadcrumbs with 2 tbsp each very finely chopped almonds and dried apricots. Season with salt, pepper and paprika, then moisten with olive oil. Apply to the beef as above.

eats well with...

Serve hot with boiled, roast or sautéed potatoes and seasonal vegetables. Serve left-over roast beef with cold braised red cabbage or beetroot salad, or make it into sandwiches with the horseradish sauce.

any left...

For a cottage pie, mince any left-over cold beef. Fry finely diced onions and carrots until softened. Stir in the beef and any left-over gravy or horseradish sauce. Transfer to an ovenproof dish and top with mashed potato. Bake in a medium oven until the potato topping is golden.

braised meat

After slow braising in the oven, even the toughest meat is meltingly tender. Some of the meat juices are then reduced to a wonderfully rich glaze

Braising is a combination of steaming and simmering in the oven. It is ideal for cooking tougher cuts of meat and larger cuts of poultry – the lengthy cooking time breaks down any sinews. Braising the meat on a bed of vegetables with enough liquid to half-cover it also keeps it very moist.

Shiny pieces of beef

The braising method transforms an inexpensive cut of meat into a luxurious experience. Rolled and skewered chuck steaks are used here, but blade or brisket of beef works just as well. The cooking liquid is reduced to make a thick gravy, some of which is used to create a shiny glaze. Braised beef is very good served with parsnip mash and Savoy cabbage.

Steeping in flavour

Cooked slowly on a bed of vegetables, half covered with stock and wine, the meat takes up the flavours surrounding it. You can alter the dish by varying these – cooking the beef with garlic, olives and tomatoes gives a Mediterranean flavour. Or you can change the meat itself. Why not try gently braising a double turkey breast in white wine?

Gary's special touch

Meat can be braised in stock alone, but here I add chopped vegetables, tomatoes and a whole bottle of good red wine.

Once cooked, I remove the beef from the pot and strain the meat juices. I reduce some to a shiny glaze for the beef. Then I add concentrated veal jus – you can use canned consommé – to the rest of the meat juices to create a rich gravy.

making the glazed beef

You will need

serves 6

preparation time 1 hour

cooking time 3½ hours

pre-heat oven
170°C/325°F/ gas 3

ingredients

6 x 225g (8oz) chuck steaks, rolled
(see Cook's notes, below)

7 large onions - 6 halved, skins left
on, 1 roughly chopped

1 large carrot, roughly chopped

½ leek, roughly chopped

2 celery sticks, roughly chopped

85g (3oz) butter

300g (10½oz) tomatoes, roughly
chopped

salt and pepper

for the sauce

75cl bottle of red wine

600-900ml (1-1½ pints) beef stock
(see page 8) or water

300ml (10fl oz) good-quality canned
consommé or reduced veal jus

equipment

large, flame-proof casserole

frying-pan

large roasting tin

1 Lightly fry the chopped onion, carrot, leek and celery in 25g (1oz) butter in the casserole for 5-6 minutes until they start to soften and turn pale golden.

In this recipe the beef is first sealed by quickly frying it until it is lightly and evenly browned. It's then slowly braised in the oven in a rich mixture of stock and red wine on a bed of roughly chopped and sautéed vegetables.

To ensure that the finished dish has an attractive appearance, the chuck steaks are rolled into neat cigar shapes – see Cook's notes. When the meat is tender, it's taken out of the casserole and kept warm while the dish is being finished.

Making the sauce

Reducing a little of the cooking liquor by fast boiling results in a spectacularly shiny, sticky glaze for the beef. Adding reduced veal jus or high-quality canned consommé to the remaining cooking liquid creates an ultra-rich and thick sauce with a really concentrated flavour.

Cook's notes

Buy chuck steaks that are about 1cm (½in) thick. There are three good ways to prepare them for cooking – the first is used in the cooking steps.

a Trim off any excess fat. Then roll the chuck into neat cigar shapes and secure with wooden cocktail sticks at each end.
b Roll chuck into cigar shapes as before, and tie neatly with string.
c With steak flat on a board, run long wooden skewers through it from corner to corner diagonally. This will keep the meat flat.

Remove cocktail sticks, skewers or string before serving – the cooked meat holds its shape without support.

5 Meanwhile, melt the rest of the butter in a roasting tin and sit the onion halves on top. Cover with foil and put into the oven below the beef, removing the foil after 30 minutes.

2 Stir the tomatoes into the vegetable mixture and cook for a further 5-6 minutes. Pour in the wine and boil until reduced to a quarter of the original volume.

3 Heat the frying pan and add 25g (1oz) butter. Season the beef steaks and, once the butter has melted, add to the pan and seal quickly over a high heat.

4 Place the chuck in the casserole with enough stock to half cover it. Bring to a simmer, cover and cook in the oven for 2½-3 hours, turning the meat every 30 minutes.

6 After 2 hours check that the meat is becoming tender. Return to the oven for another hour then remove the meat, cover and keep warm.

7 Strain the meat juices and boil to reduce to 450ml (15fl oz). For the glaze, transfer 150ml (5fl oz) to a small pan and boil until syrupy. To make the gravy, add the consommé or veal jus to the rest of the meat juices. Bring to the boil. Skim off any fat. Slip the skins off the onions and sit the beef on top. Drizzle the glaze over the meat and serve the gravy separately.

Variations on a theme

turkey crown braised in white wine

This special double breast or 'crown' is an ideal candidate for braising as the meat stays truly moist and tender. Turkey crowns are not always available at supermarkets, but a good butcher will prepare one for you.

Ask the butcher to leave the breastbone in, but take the wishbone out to make carving easier. Leave the skin on.

serves 6
preparation time
25 minutes
cooking time *1 hour*

pre-heat oven
200°C/400°F/gas 6

ingredients
1.5kg (3lb 5oz) turkey crown
25g (1oz) butter
2 tbsp olive oil
salt and pepper
6 thick rashers of bacon, cut into strips
600ml (1 pint) white wine
450g (1lb) carrots, sliced
450g (1lb) onions, sliced
1 bouquet garni sachet
2-3 tbsp brandy (optional)
300ml (10fl oz) chicken stock (see page 8)
150ml (5fl oz) double cream
2-3 tbsp chopped fresh parsley

equipment
large casserole dish

1 Heat the butter and oil in a frying-pan and season and brown the turkey. Set in the casserole. Sauté the bacon until golden then add to the turkey.
2 Deglaze the pan with the wine. Place the vegetables around the turkey, add the bouquet garni and brandy. Pour in the stock and bring to a simmer.
3 Braise with the lid off to get a golden skin. After 30 minutes, baste and then cook for another 30 minutes, basting every 10 minutes, or until cooked. Test for doneness by piercing with a skewer – the juices should run clear and the flesh be white when it's cooked.
4 Remove turkey and keep warm. Discard the bouquet garni. Lift out the vegetables and bacon and set aside. Boil the stock to reduce it by a third. Then add the cream and bring it almost back to the boil.
5 Thinly slice the turkey and serve with the creamy sauce and vegetables.

why not try...

Mediterranean beef
Sauté 2 diced onions with 3 crushed garlic cloves in 2 tbsp olive oil until soft. Add 400g (14oz) fresh chopped tomatoes and cook for 5 minutes. Pour in 75cl red wine and reduce by three quarters. In a frying-pan seal 6 x 225g (8oz) chuck steaks, rolled as before.

Set the vegetables in a casserole with the chuck on top. Season and add enough stock to half cover the meat. Simmer and place in the oven for 2½-3 hours or until tender, turning the meat every 30 minutes. Once cooked, add 18 pitted black olives and warm through before serving.

eats well with...

turnip and onions
Simmer 350g (12oz) turnips in three parts milk to one part water for 5-10 minutes. Add 1 crushed garlic clove and a pinch of salt. When tender, pureé the turnips with 5 tbsp milk. Remove the skin and centre of the roast onions and spoon in the pureé.

any left?

beef rissoles
Mince the beef and mix with mashed potato. Add a beaten egg and shape into cakes. Roll in flour or bread-crumbs and fry in a little oil.

steamed meat puddings

Treat an inexpensive cut of meat to long, slow cooking in light pastry and it will become fragrant and tender

The traditional recipes for steamed meat puddings use suet pastry which encases a filling of beef, stock and herbs. The pastry seals in the filling and allows the flavours to mingle and intensify, while absorbing the meat's fragrant liquor to become soft and tasty.

Slow steaming in a pastry jacket makes meat meltingly tender. This method is often used for lean, less expensive cuts of beef such as chuck or blade. Prime cuts, such as sirloin, disintegrate during lengthy cooking.

Cornish tribute
This steamed version of the traditional Cornish pasty is delicious. Lean tasty beef cooks in its own juices with potato, onion, swede and a little stock. Serve it with some fiery mustard and a jug of rich gravy on the side.

Traditional favourite
A good old-fashioned, slow-cooked steak and kidney pudding is hard to beat. This recipe uses stout and plenty of mushrooms to fill out its flavours and the filling is cooked first to reduce steaming time. Fresh thyme is mixed into the suet pastry to create a deliciously flavoured crust.

Gary's special touch

Suet pastry is the perfect companion to rich, slow-cooked meat and it's particularly good when perked up with an extra flavouring. I put mustard powder into the pastry for the Cornish pasty pudding and thyme in the steak and kidney version. Mix any flavourings into the dry ingredients before binding the pastry with water.

making the Cornish pasty pudding

You will need

serves 6

preparation time *40 minutes*

cooking time *2 hours*

for the suet pastry
350g (12oz) plain flour
25g (1oz) baking powder
pinch of salt
225g (8oz) dried suet
1 tbsp English mustard powder
300ml (10fl oz) cold water

for the filling
225g (8oz) potato, peeled and sliced

225g (8oz) swede, peeled and sliced
450g (1lb) beef chuck or blade, sliced into very thin strips
1 large onion, sliced
salt and pepper
25g (1oz) butter
150-250ml (5-9fl oz) beef stock (see page 8)
a few drops of Worcestershire sauce

equipment
1.2 litre (2 pint) pudding basin, buttered; saucepan large enough to contain basin

1 Sieve the flour, baking powder and salt together, then add the suet and mustard powder. Add the water and mix to a soft dough. Cover and rest for 5 minutes.

Suet is pure beef fat which, when mixed with flour, makes an incredibly light, flavoursome pastry. It's sold dried and shredded so it's easy to incorporate into a flour mixture. There's no rubbing in and it's not important to keep the mix cool, as with other pastries. Indeed, suet pastry is more forgiving than pastry made with butter and much easier to roll and handle.

Baking powder is added to the flour to lighten the pastry. It starts to work as a raising agent as soon as it's mixed with the water so use the pastry almost at once, leaving it to rest for just 5 minutes before rolling it out.

Meat matters
For this pudding, use chuck or blade of beef from the shoulder of the animal. These are excellent when cooked slowly to allow their flavours and tenderness to develop. Both meats are naturally lean but should be marbled with some fine veins of fat and have a thin fatty crust which will help to keep

them moist. If chuck or blade are unavailable, you can use other lean cuts of stewing beef, such as shin or flank.

Gold top
For a rich golden crust, try steaming your pudding in the oven. Cover the pudding with foil, fasten it with string, then sit it in a roasting tin. Pour in hot water to come half-way up the basin. Steam at 170°C/325°F/gas 3 for about 2 hours, topping up with hot water if necessary.

Recipe tip

Tasty gravy
Make a gravy for this pudding with 2-3 litres (3-5 pints) fresh beef stock. Boil, skimming often, until the stock thickens. If the flavour is good but it's too thin, thicken with cornflour. For making beef stock, see page 8.

5 Once the basin is filled, mix a few drops of Worcestershire sauce into the beef stock and pour over the ingredients in the suet pastry.

2 Roll out three-quarters of the dough, making the pastry at least 1cm (½in) thick, and line the basin. Roll the remaining dough into a circle to cover the pudding.

3 In separate bowls, season the sliced vegetables, onion and meat with plenty of salt and pepper. Then melt the butter and trickle it over the vegetables.

4 In the pastry-lined basin, alternate layers of meat with individual layers of swede, potato and onion. Overlap the vegetables to create neat, distinct layers.

6 Brush water around the edge of the pudding. Cover with the pastry lid. Pinch to seal, then cover with buttered, pleated foil. Fasten with string.

7 Steam the pudding for 2 hours. Once cooked, remove from the saucepan and leave to rest for 10 minutes before turning out.

Variations on a theme

traditional steak and kidney pudding

This pudding has a tender filling of beef, kidney and mushrooms in a rich stout gravy. Serve with carrots and shredded cabbage.

serves 6

preparation time
1¾ hours

cooking time *1½-2 hours*

for the filling
350g (12oz) braising steak, trimmed and cut into 2.5cm (1in) dice
115g (4oz) ox or lambs' kidneys, trimmed and cut into 2.5cm (1in) dice
55g (2oz) unsalted butter
3 celery sticks, diced
3 carrots, diced
2 onions, diced
115g (4oz) mushrooms, quartered
1 garlic clove, crushed
½ tsp fresh chopped thyme
150ml (5fl oz) Guinness
750ml (1¼ pints) beef stock (see page 8)
salt and white pepper

for the pastry
350g (12oz) plain flour
25g (1oz) baking powder
pinch of salt
225g (8oz) dried suet
1-2 tsp dried thyme
300ml (10fl oz) water

equipment
1.2 litre (2 pint) pudding basin, buttered; large saucepan to contain basin

1 Fry the steak and kidney in half the butter, colouring them well.
2 In another pan, sweat the vegetables, garlic and thyme in the remaining butter for a few minutes. Add the Guinness and boil until almost dry.
3 Add the meat and enough stock to cover it. Bring to a simmer, cover and cook for about 1 hour until the meat is tender. Season and cool.
4 For the pastry, sieve the flour, baking powder and a pinch of salt into a bowl. Add the thyme and suet, then mix in the water to form a soft dough. Rest the pastry for 5 minutes.
5 Roll out the pastry and use ¾ of it to line the basin. With a slotted spoon, transfer the meat mix to the basin – you only need a little liquid.
6 Roll out the remaining pastry. Dampen the edges and place on the pudding, pressing the pastry edges together. Cover with buttered, pleated foil, and tie with string. Put the pudding in the large pan, half-filled with water. Cover and steam for 1½-2 hours, topping up the pan with hot water as necessary.
7 Boil any liquid left over from stewing the meat; strain and use as gravy.

why not try...

crust ideas
Flavour suet pastry with herbs and spices to enhance the meat filling. For a wonderful herby flavour, try finely chopped rosemary or sage. Alternatively, add plenty of freshly ground black pepper for a delicious bite.

meat mixes
Experiment with the filling for a steamed pudding: try spicing up the beef with ground mace and cayenne pepper or enriching the filling with 2 tbsp tomato purée. Mushroom ketchup enhances the flavour of mushrooms and red wine is a good alternative to stout.

seafood treat
Many years ago, oysters were cheap and plentiful and often used in steak and kidney pudding to add flavour. If you want to push the boat out, they make a delicious addition to the meat filling.

eats well with...

A glorious steamed meat pudding needs only simple vegetable accompaniments that throw its rich flavours into relief. Steamed carrots, cabbage or parsnips work well. If you feel the need for potatoes, serve them mashed into a melting purée with butter and cream. A dollop of mustard or horseradish sauce is the perfect finishing touch.

steak and chips

Steak is always a great favourite and this peppered rib steak, served with game chips, is no exception

For special occasions, a plate of steak and chips is a popular choice. The tender juicy meat combined with the crisp chips is a happy marriage of textures and flavours.

This recipe calls for rib steak, a cut of meat on the bone that's taken from the forerib – it looks like a large beef chop. You cook just the one rib steak and then carve it at the table. Since a good cut like rib steak is fairly expensive, this is a recipe just for two.

A wafer-thin chip
This rib steak is served with game chips – wafer-thin slices of potato that have been deep-fried until crisp and golden. The steak is coated with crushed peppercorns to give it added flavour and texture. A bunch of watercress or a simple leafy salad is all you need as accompaniment.

Spicy steak
The variation is a spicier twist on the peppered steaks – curry spices are crushed and used to coat the meat. This dish is served with an unusual alternative to traditional chips – sweet potato chips. These are roasted in the oven – much in the same way as peppers are roasted – and they are soft rather than crisp.

Gary's special touch

To make very thin game chips, I use a mandolin. This tool is excellent for slicing all sorts of vegetables. A good-quality mandolin has several detachable blades for cutting a variety of shapes and thicknesses – such as thin French fries or julienne vegetables. But be very careful, the blades are particularly sharp.

making steak and game chips

You will need

serves 2

preparation time
20 minutes, plus soaking

cooking time
25 minutes, plus resting

pre-heat oven 220°C/425°F/gas 7

ingredients
750-900g (1½-2lb) rib steak, on the bone, trimmed of fat
2 tbsp black peppercorns
2 tbsp olive oil

knob of butter

for the game chips
225g (8oz) large potatoes
oil for deep-frying
coarse sea salt, to serve

equipment
large, heavy-based frying-pan,
large saucepan or deep-fat fryer,
roasting tin

1 Wash and peel the potatoes and then slice them very thinly, using a mandolin. Leave the potatoes in a bowl of cold water for 30 minutes, to remove excess starch.

Start this meal by getting the potatoes ready. If you want even game chips, you can trim the potatoes into tidy cylinders before slicing. A mandolin will give you the ultra-thin slices of potato that are ideal for game chips, but if you don't have a mandolin, use a very sharp knife and slice the potatoes as thin as you possibly can. Cut the potatoes widthways and don't forget to be careful when using the mandolin – the extra sharp blade can easily slice off a finger tip or two! After slicing, leave the potatoes to soak in cold water for 30 minutes to remove as much of the starch as possible.

Evenly ground

While the potatoes are soaking, you'll have plenty of time to crush the peppercorns and prepare the steak. You can use an electric spice mill but a pestle and mortar gives you a more even result – in an electric mill, some of the pepper will be ground fine and some coarse, and the finer grindings can burn during cooking.

When the potatoes have soaked, you need to dry them thoroughly with a clean tea-towel. This is important – if the potatoes are too wet the hot oil could spatter when you are frying.

You can be draining and drying the potatoes and heating the oil for deep-frying during the last stage of frying the steak. You have enough time to deep-fry the potatoes while the meat is in the oven and when it's resting.

How do you like it?

A rib steak is usually preferred medium or medium-rare. For this thick cut you'll need to fry it first – 6 minutes on each side – and then transfer it to a hot oven for a further 10-12 minutes. This may seem like a long time but as this steak is on the bone it takes quite a while to cook. Once the steak is done, leave it to rest in a warm place for 6-7 minutes before carving. This will give the meat time to relax, making it more tender.

To serve the steak, bring it to the table and then cut the meat away from the bone. Cut the meat in half and serve immediately. The game chips need a sprinkling of coarse sea salt to serve.

5 Drain the potatoes and dry well in a clean tea-towel. Heat the oil in a large pan – when a cube of bread sizzles in the oil, it's hot enough.

2 Meanwhile, crush the peppercorns in a pestle and mortar or a spice mill. Using your fingertips, press the crushed peppercorns firmly into each side of the meat.

3 Heat the oil in a frying-pan over moderate heat. Add the peppered steak and leave it to fry for 6 minutes – don't push it around the pan – before turning it over.

4 Add the butter. Continue to fry for a further 6 minutes. Put the meat in a roasting tin and pour over the pan juices. Transfer to the oven for 10-12 minutes. Set aside to rest.

6 Deep fry the chips in batches until golden brown. Transfer to an ovenproof dish lined with kitchen paper and keep warm.

7 Using a sharp knife, cut the meat from the bone. Then cut it in two and transfer to individual serving plates; drizzle on some of the pan juices. Serve the hot game chips sprinkled with sea salt.

Variations on a theme

spicy steaks and sweet potato chips

serves 2

preparation time
20 minutes

cooking time
25 minutes, plus resting

pre-heat oven
220°C/425°F/gas 7

ingredients
750-900g (1½-2lb) rib
steak, on the bone,
trimmed of fat
2 tsp coriander seeds
1 tsp nigella seeds
1 tsp cumin seeds
6 cardamom pods
2 tbsp sunflower oil
25-55g (1-2oz) ghee or
butter
½ onion, finely chopped

150ml (5fl oz) ready-
made vegetable stock
2-3 tbsp full-fat natural
yoghurt

for sweet potato chips
1 large or 2 small sweet
potatoes, peeled
2-3 tbsp sunflower oil
1 tsp ground coriander
½ tsp ground cinnamon

equipment
baking tray; large, heavy-
based frying-pan;
roasting tin

1 Cut the sweet potato
into thick chips and put
in a large bowl with the
oil and ground spices.
Using your hands, mix to
thoroughly coat the
chips. Spread them on a
baking tray and roast for
25-30 minutes until soft
and slightly browned.
2 Meanwhile, crush the
whole spices in a pestle
and mortar or spice mill.
Press the crushed spices
firmly into each side of
the meat.
3 Heat the oil in a
frying-pan over
moderate heat and fry
the steak for 6 minutes,
each side, basting with
the pan juices.
4 Place the steak in a
roasting tin and pour on
the pan juices. Put in the
oven for 10-12 minutes
until cooked through;
rest for 6-7 minutes.
5 Meanwhile, add a
knob of ghee to the
roasting tin and cook the
onion until soft. Stir in
the stock, a little at a
time. Let each addition
bubble until it reduces
slightly. When there's
about 100ml (3½fl oz) of
liquid in the pan, reduce
the heat to low and stir
in the yoghurt – don't let
the sauce boil or the
yoghurt might curdle.
6 Cut the steak off the
bone and carve into
2 slices. Serve on
individual serving plates
with the sauce and the
sweet potato chips.

why not try...

sauce for the meat
It's easy to make a tasty sauce
to go with the peppered steak
by deglazing the roasting tin.
When the steak has finished
cooking, take it out to rest and
place the tin over moderate
heat. Pour in a glass of red
wine and let this bubble for a
few minutes until only a few
spoonfuls of liquid are left.
Add 1-2 tbsp brandy and let
that bubble for a couple of
minutes to reduce slightly.
Pour in 150ml (5fl oz) good-
quality beef stock (see page 8)
or consommé and simmer
until reduced by a third. Serve
poured over the steak.

peppered pork
Both the peppercorn and
spicy coating work well with
pork chops. Just rub them into
the pork as you do with the
steak. Fry the chops in butter
over medium heat for
10-15 minutes, turning once,
until the juices run clear.

eats well with...

For a cooked vegetable
accompaniment to the
peppered steak, why not
serve some yellow courgettes,
cooked in butter and lemon
juice, or some wilted spinach?

The spicy steak eats well with
some traditional curry
vegetable side dishes, such as
bindi bhaji or sag aloo.

breaded veal

Inspired by the classic wiener schnitzel, this breaded veal recipe marries the tenderness of the meat with a crisp breadcrumb coating

Coating food in breadcrumbs before it's fried is an ideal way to keep it succulent at the same time as giving it a crispy golden shell. It's an excellent method for veal which is a very lean meat – the protective coating of breadcrumbs and the quick cooking time mean the meat stays moist and tender. Escalopes – thin slices taken from the leg – are often cooked in this way, but you can also bread other smaller veal cuts, such as cutlets or chops, for pan-frying.

Finer flavours
Marinating the veal before you bread and cook it is an excellent way of adding extra flavour. The escalopes are marinated in lemon and tarragon – flavours which complement the delicate veal. Extra taste is added by covering the escalopes in grated parmesan cheese, prior to coating them in breadcrumbs.

A coated chop
The variation recipe is for breaded veal chops. These are marinated with juniper berries and bay leaves to give the meat a robust flavour before the chops are coated in breadcrumbs and then shallow-fried.

Gary's special touch

Before coating food with breadcrumbs, it is usual to dust the food with flour first. However, I like to coat my veal escalopes with some finely grated parmesan or pecorino cheese, rather than using just flour. The cheese helps the breadcrumbs stick to the meat – and adds a wonderful taste too.

making breaded veal escalopes

You will need

serves 4	
preparation time *30 minutes,* *plus marinating and chilling*	*zest of ½ lemon*
	30g (1oz) fresh chopped tarragon
cooking time *10 minutes*	*salt and pepper*
	55g (2oz) finely grated parmesan
ingredients	*2 eggs*
4 veal escalopes, each weighing about 100g (3½oz)	*150g (5½oz) fresh white breadcrumbs*
4 tbsp olive oil	*large knob of butter*
juice of 1 lemon	*2-4 tbsp olive oil*

I Lay the veal escalopes
between 2 sheets of plastic
wrap and beat lightly with a
rolling pin or the flat side of a
cleaver until evenly flattened.

For this dish, the veal escalopes are flattened until they are about 3mm (⅛in) thick. The coated meat is fried for only a few minutes – any longer would cause the breadcrumbs to burn – the meat needs to be thin to ensure it is properly cooked through. Don't flatten the meat too hard – you aren't trying to tenderize the meat, since it's soft enough already.

By marinating the veal before coating with breadcrumbs, you can add even more flavour to the finished dish. Remember to pat the meat dry with kitchen paper when you take it out of the marinade, otherwise the coating will not stick properly. Don't worry about wiping away all traces of lemon zest and tarragon – any bits that remain only add to the flavour.

Cheesy coating

Instead of coating the escalopes in flour before dipping in the egg, this recipe uses grated parmesan. The cheese sticks the egg to the meat just as well as flour – and gives even more flavour. It also melts during frying and so further binds the breadcrumb coating to the veal.

The escalopes are dipped in beaten egg before being covered with breadcrumbs. But before you do this, you need to beat a little water in with the eggs – this helps keep the coating supple.

Once the veal is covered in breadcrumbs, a criss-cross pattern is lightly scored through the coating – don't cut the meat. The breadcrumb coating shrinks during frying and these indentations help prevent the coating breaking up as it shrinks. Chilling the escalopes for about 30 minutes also helps the coating to stick.

Shallow-frying escalopes

The escalopes are shallow fried in melted butter and olive oil. They are quite large so you'll probably need to fry them in batches – keep the cooked ones warm in a low oven. You might need to add a little more oil with each batch to make sure there's enough fat in the pan.

Serve the escalopes at once accompanied by simple potato and green salads. And don't forget some lemon wedges so you can squeeze the fresh juice over the meat.

5 Spread the breadcrumbs on
a plate. Dip the escalopes,
one at a time, into the egg and
then in the breadcrumbs. Turn
until evenly coated.

2 Mix together the olive oil, lemon juice, zest and tarragon and use to coat the escalopes. Set aside, in a non-metallic dish, for about 1 hour.

3 Put the grated parmesan on a plate and season. Pat the escalopes dry and press both sides lightly into the cheese, to coat evenly.

4 Put the eggs into a bowl and pour in 1 tbsp cold water. Beat lightly to mix the whites with the yolks. Pour into a shallow dish.

6 Make criss-cross lines through the breadcrumb coating by pressing down lightly with the back of a large knife. Chill for about 30 minutes.

7 Melt the butter with 2 tbsp oil over moderate heat. Fry the escalopes one by one for 2-3 minutes on each side, until golden brown, adding more oil between batches if necessary.

Variations on a theme

breaded veal chops

serves 4

preparation time
30 minutes, plus marinating and chilling

cooking time
10 minutes

ingredients
4 veal chops, no more than 1cm (½in) thick
1 tbsp juniper berries, lightly crushed
juice of 1 lemon
4 tbsp olive oil
4 bay leaves, cut in half lengthways
flour for dusting
2 eggs
150g (5½oz) fresh white breadcrumbs
55g (2oz) butter
1 tbsp vegetable oil

1 Using kitchen scissors, snip around the edges of the chops at intervals – this will help prevent the meat curling up during cooking.
2 Mix together the juniper berries, lemon juice and olive oil and use to coat the chops thoroughly; lay them in a non-metallic dish. Place half a bay leaf under each chop and then put the remaining halves on top of the chops. Leave the meat to marinate for at least 1 hour.
3 After marinating, remove the bay leaves and pat the chops dry with kitchen paper.

Lightly dust with the flour.
4 Lightly beat the eggs with a spoonful of cold water. Dip the floured chops in the beaten egg and then straight in the breadcrumbs. Chill for about 30 minutes.
5 Heat the oil and butter in a large frying-pan over moderate heat and fry the chops, in batches if necessary, for 5 minutes on each side until golden and cooked through. Serve immediately with some simple boiled vegetables and garnished with some strips of lemon zest and slices of lemon.

why not try...

herby breadcrumbs
If you use a food processor to make your breadcrumbs, you can use it to add extra flavour at the same time. Simply toss a handful of fresh herbs in with the bread and process until the breadcrumbs are fine. The herbs will be finely chopped at the same time as being thoroughly mixed in with the breadcrumbs.

different breadcrumbs
Plain white bread does make perfect breadcrumbs for these recipes but you might like to try using different breads as an alternative. Why not try some flavoured breads, such as tomato or walnut? Or try breads from around the world, such as ciabatta, focaccia or chollah.

other meats
You can coat other meats in breadcrumbs for frying. Chicken or turkey breasts, flattened into thin escalopes, work particularly well. And you could also try this method on pork and lamb chops or lamb medallions.

stroganoff

Tender strips of meat, simmered in a soured cream sauce, are the essence of a stroganoff

Beef stroganoff is a classic dish that has been around since the 18th century. The name is rumoured to come from the Russian Stroganoff family who were wealthy financiers and merchants. A French cook employed by the family is said to have invented the dish and given it the name of his master.

Easy – but impressive
The dish is amazingly quick and easy to make. The beef is quickly seared over as high a heat as possible to seal in its juicy tenderness, then briefly flambéed with brandy which gives extra flavour without the strong taste of alcohol.

Sliced onions and mushrooms are sautéed separately, then mixed with the beef before it's simmered very gently in soured cream. Lemon juice adds a final touch of piquancy and parsley a splash of colour. Beef stroganoff is often served with boiled rice but lightly buttered tagliatelle works well too.

Pork with mustard
Classic stroganoff is made with beef but it tastes equally good with other meats. Pork with mustard and tasty horse mushrooms gives it a delicious, pale new twist. Serve this with boiled new potatoes.

Gary's special touch

You can use button mushrooms for either of these stroganoff recipes – but with the fantastic choice available, I like to try other varieties. For the beef stroganoff I've opted for mild, nutty chestnut mushrooms which have a 'meaty' texture. For the pork stroganoff I've chosen horse mushrooms.

making beef stroganoff

You will need

serves 4

preparation time *15 minutes*

cooking time *30 minutes*

ingredients

500g (1lb 2oz) fillet of beef, sliced in strips about 6cm (2½in) long and 5mm (¼in) wide

salt and pepper

3 tbsp oil

3 tbsp brandy (optional)

55g (2oz) butter

1 large onion, peeled, quartered and

thinly sliced in wedges

225g (8oz) chestnut mushrooms, thinly sliced

1 tsp paprika

284ml (10fl oz) carton soured cream

juice of 1 lemon

1-2 tbsp fresh chopped parsley

equipment

large, heavy-bottomed frying-pan

It's important to cut the meat into similar size pieces so that they cook evenly. The meat must also be seared quickly so that it doesn't become tough. Make sure the oil in the pan is as hot as possible – almost at smoking point. As soon as the beef hits the hot oil, move the meat around the pan as briskly as you would a stir-fry.

At this stage, the meat only needs sealing and browning on the outside, while remaining rare and tender inside. You may have to sauté the beef in batches if your pan is not large enough. An overcrowded pan just steams rather than browns the meat. The onions and mushrooms are then cooked separately in the same pan.

On your marks...

As stroganoff is a speedy dish to cook, ensure you have all the ingredients prepared before you begin. Have a saucepan of boiling salted water waiting for the pasta as soon as you start the final stage of the stroganoff.

Inside info

Flamboyant flambé

The word *flambé* is a cooking term which describes the process of pouring a spirit over food, lighting it and leaving it to flame. The purpose is to burn off the alcohol while enhancing and concentrating the flavour of the food.

When flambéing food, make sure the spirit is warm before you ignite it. For a stroganoff, pour in the brandy and allow it to heat through before lighting. Take care when lighting the brandy in the pan. Use a long taper rather than a match as the flames can ignite very quickly and may catch you unawares. Let the flames subside before continuing with the next step of the recipe.

Season the meat with plenty of salt and pepper. Heat oil in a frying-pan until very hot. Add beef to the pan and sauté briskly over a high heat until lightly browned.

5 Pour the soured cream into the pan and heat through gently. Return the beef, onions and mushrooms to the pan and bring to a simmer.

2 Sprinkle the beef with brandy, heat gently and set alight with a taper. When the flames have died down, transfer the beef to a bowl with a slotted spoon and keep warm.

3 Melt half the butter in the pan, add the onion and fry gently for about 5 minutes until softened but not browned. Transfer the cooked onions to a plate and keep warm.

4 Melt the remaining butter in the pan, add the mushrooms and paprika, and sauté for about 5 minutes until tender. Add the mushrooms to the onions and keep warm.

6 Simmer the stroganoff very gently over a low heat for 10-15 minutes until it is thick and very creamy. Add the lemon juice and cook for 1-2 minutes.

7 Taste the sauce and adjust the seasoning. Then transfer the stroganoff from the frying-pan to a warmed serving dish. Sprinkle with chopped parsley and serve piping hot with a bowl of tagliatelle.

Variations on a theme

pork stroganoff with grainy mustard

This dish uses horse mushrooms – large white mushrooms with long stems and a stronger flavour than button mushrooms. They are best eaten young as they toughen with age. The seasoning of grainy mustard and fresh thyme adds plenty of extra flavour.

serves 4

preparation time
15 minutes

cooking time
30 minutes

ingredients
500g (1lb 2oz) pork tenderloin, sliced into
strips 6cm (2½in) long and 5mm (¼in) wide
salt and pepper
3 tbsp oil
55g (2oz) butter
225g (8oz) shallots, finely chopped
225g (8oz) horse mushrooms, trimmed and sliced if large, otherwise trimmed but left whole
284ml (10fl oz) carton soured cream
1 tbsp wholegrain mustard
small glass dry white wine
1 sprig fresh thyme
1-2 tbsp fresh thyme leaves, to garnish

equipment
large heavy-bottomed frying-pan

1 Season the pork well with salt and pepper. Heat oil in frying-pan until very hot. Add pork strips to pan and sauté briskly over a high heat until lightly browned. Transfer the meat to a bowl with a slotted spoon and set aside.
2 Melt half the butter in the pan, add the shallots and fry slowly until they are softened but not browned. Transfer to a plate and keep warm.
3 Melt the remaining butter in the pan, add the mushrooms and fry until tender – about 5 minutes. Add to the shallots and keep warm.
4 Pour the soured cream into the pan with the mustard, the white wine and the sprig of thyme. Stir, then bring to the boil. Cook until the sauce thickens to a coating consistency.
5 Return the pork, shallots and mushrooms to the pan and bring to a simmer. Simmer gently over a low heat for 10-15 minutes until the stroganoff is thick and creamy. Then remove and discard the thyme.
6 Taste the sauce and adjust seasoning. Transfer to a warmed serving dish. Garnish with fresh thyme and serve with floury boiled potatoes.

why not try...

chicken, prawn and dill
Cut 350g (12oz) chicken breasts into strips. Season well with salt and pepper. Heat 3 tbsp oil in a frying-pan, add chicken and sauté briskly over a high heat. Add 350g (12oz) tiger prawns and cook for a further 1-2 minutes. Transfer to a bowl and set aside. Melt 25g (1oz) butter in the pan, add the onions and fry slowly until softened but not browned. Transfer to a plate and keep warm. Melt another 25g (1oz) butter in the pan, add the mushrooms and fry until tender. Add to the onions. Pour the soured cream into the pan with 1 small glass white wine. Stir and bring to the boil. Cook until the sauce thickens to a coating consistency. Return the chicken, prawns, onions and mushrooms to the pan and bring to a simmer. Cook gently over a low heat for 10-15 minutes until the stroganoff is thick and creamy. Season well. Stir in 1-2 tbsp chopped fresh dill. Serve with fresh cooked tagliatelle.

eats well with...

As an alternative to buttered tagliatelle or potatoes, try plain boiled rice or smooth creamy polenta.

roast leg of lamb

A perfectly cooked traditional roast leg of lamb is a great favourite. Adding a shiny sticky coat looks wonderful and enhances the taste, too

L amb is a tender meat, and while nearly all cuts are good for roasting, the leg joint is especially good. The delicate sweetness of lamb means that it can be roasted with nothing more than a dusting of salt and pepper, but it works beautifully with lots of other tastes.

Mastering the method
The recipes here show how to achieve a perfectly cooked and presented roast, with or without a sticky glaze. The secret lies in searing the joint to give a golden finish on the outside and to seal in the juices that keep the meat moist and tender. There's also a chart to help with roasting times so that the meat is cooked exactly as you like it.

Delicious variations
Once you have mastered the basics, tackle the variations. Give the outside of the joint a crisp crumb coating or flavour from inside with a parsley and garlic stuffing. Roast the lamb in the French way, spiked with rosemary and garlic, or stuff it with nuts, apricots and spices for a Moroccan feel.

Gary's special touch

You'll find that this sticky glaze lifts the lamb into a class of its own. Simply baste the joint as it roasts with a marinade of honey, teriyaki and soy, then reduce the pan juices until they're like black treacle. Brush this marinade thickly over the joint, to give it a lustrous glaze that adds extra flavour to every slice.

cooking the sticky roast lamb

You will need

pre-heat oven 200°C/400°F/gas 6	1-2 glasses white wine for basting
ingredients leg of lamb, pelvic bone removed (ask the butcher to remove the pelvic bone to make carving easier or to leave space for stuffing) garlic clove, halved 2-3 tbsp groundnut oil 2-3 onions, halved horizontally	**for the marinade** 2 tbsp clear honey 2 tbsp teriyaki marinade 2 tbsp light soy sauce **for the gravy** 1-2 glasses of white wine 600ml (1 pint) good-quality meat stock (see page 8)

For a moist and tender roast, the outside is first sealed at a high heat, and the rest of the cooking completed at a lower temperature.

To seal a joint, sear the meat on all sides in a large frying-pan before putting it into the oven. If the joint is very large, pre-heat the oven to maximum and cook the meat for 10-12 minutes. Reduce to 200°C/400°F/gas 6 and complete cooking.

Timings
Use the cooking times on the chart below. If in doubt about judging how cooked the joint is, buy a meat thermometer. Seal the joint, then insert the thermometer into the thickest part, avoiding the bone. Towards the end of the cooking time, check the temperature; as a guide, 70-75°C gives medium rare

meat, 80°C well done – medium is midway between the two.

Making gravy and serving
When the meat is done, cover it with foil on a carving dish and let it rest for 15 minutes to tenderize. Remove the onions – they've done their job of giving colour and flavour to the gravy.

Tip off any excess fat, then deglaze the tin with a glass of wine, stirring constantly – deglazing dissolves any tasty meat juices and sediment left in the tin. To finish the gravy, add the stock and wine.

The finished joint looks so good you'll want to carve it at table – it's easy using the method opposite. Serve with vegetables – green beans stir-fried are particularly good – and pour the gravy into a jug.

1 Rub the lamb with the cut garlic clove. Mix the marinade ingredients together. Heat the oil in a large frying-pan until hot, but not smoking. Put in the lamb, meaty side down.

4 For the gravy, tip excess fat from the tin, set over a low heat and deglaze with wine. Slowly add the stock, bring to the boil, then simmer for 5 minutes.

Average roasting times ●

medium rare	medium	well done
15 minutes per 450g (1lb)	20 minutes per 450g (1lb)	25-30 minutes per 450g (1lb)

● **Note**
These timings are based on the joint being sealed first and then finished at 200°C/400°F/gas 6

Easy carving

Put the lamb on a carving dish to prevent it slipping and to catch all those lovely juices.

2 Once one side is browned, keep turning the leg until it is brown all over. Set the halved onions in the roasting tin, sit the browned lamb on top and put it into the oven for 20 minutes.

3 Add a glass of wine and the marinade and baste. Baste again every 20 minutes, adding more wine if necessary. When the joint is cooked, remove it from the tin and rest it under foil.

I Put the joint meaty side up and cut out a V-shaped wedge from the bony end. Working towards the thick end, cut slices away from the wedge.

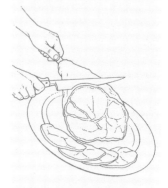

5 Strain the gravy and reserve two thirds in a jug and keep warm. Reduce the remaining gravy in a small pan until it is the consistency of black treacle.

6 After leaving the roasted leg to rest for 15 minutes, brush or spoon the dark reduced gravy all over the joint to give it a rich sticky coating. Now it's ready to carve.

2 When all the slices have been cut from the meaty side, turn the joint over. Start slicing from the thick end and carve the meat from the bone. This side is always more done, so mix this type of meat with slices from the meaty side when serving.

Variations on a theme

parsley stuffed lamb

Instead of basting a tasty glaze over the outside of the joint, an aromatic stuffing flavours the lamb from within as it cooks. The basis of this stuffing is a *persillade* (a blend of parsley and garlic) to which other ingredients are added.

For an intense garlicky flavour, use just the parsley, garlic and sea salt – or keep back a spoonful of this mixture to add to the gravy.

ingredients

leg of lamb, pelvic bone removed
5 garlic cloves, peeled
½-1 tsp coarse sea salt
1 bunch flatleaf parsley
4 tbsp fresh breadcrumbs
55g (2oz) mushrooms, finely chopped
115g (4oz) ham or bacon, finely shredded
zest of 1 lemon
pepper

1 To make the persillade, crush the garlic with the sea salt. Chop the parsley finely and then stir it into the garlic.
2 Add the breadcrumbs, mushrooms, ham or bacon, and lemon zest. Mix well to bind the mixture together and season with pepper – the sea salt and bacon make it salty enough already.

3 Pack the stuffing into the pelvic cavity, pressing it in as tightly as possible. Shape any left-over stuffing into balls, sit them in a buttered dish and bake them for the last half hour in the oven with the joint.
4 Cook the joint in the same way as the sticky roast lamb, without using the marinade.

why not try...

crunchy crumbed lamb
Ten minutes before the joint is done, remove from the oven, brush the skin with mustard, and press on a mixture of fresh breadcrumbs, lemon zest and chopped fresh herbs. Bake for 10 more minutes until golden.

garlic spiked lamb
The classic French flavouring for lamb is rosemary and garlic. Slice 2 garlic cloves and roughly chop 2-3 sprigs of rosemary. With a sharp knife make small slits in the lamb and press in the garlic. Scatter rosemary over joint and roast as usual.

twice peppered lamb
Mix 1 tbsp each of crushed green and pink bottled peppercorns. Make slits over the lamb skin, and stuff with pepper. Roast as usual. While the joint rests, add finely chopped onion and extra peppercorns to the pan juices, 2 tbsp of warmed brandy and then flambé (set alight in the pan). Add a glass of white wine and 300ml (10fl oz) stock to make gravy. Just before serving, beat in some cream and a knob of chilled butter.

eastern promise lamb
Make a stuffing of chopped apricots, almonds, pistachios, seasoned with salt and pepper and ½ tsp each of ground coriander, ginger and cinnamon. Flavour the gravy with a glass of Marsala.

stuffed crown roasts

When you want to impress, a stuffed crown roast is ideal as the centrepiece of a festive occasion

A crown roast is made from racks of lamb or pork. A rack is one side of the animal's ribcage. Rack meat, full-flavoured and lean, comes in quantities of 6-9 chops per rack. When two racks are sewn together they look like a crown. You can pack stuffing into the centre of the crown, or bake it separately.

The main recipe here is for a stuffed crown roast of pork, served with baby carrots and caramelized apple wedges. Since a crown of pork can consist of up to 18 chops, invite lots of hungry guests. The variation is a crown roast of lamb, which is much smaller than a rack of pork. Here we use 2 small racks of 4 lamb cutlets each for a small crown.

Order from the butcher
Order ready-trimmed racks from the butcher. Then all you have to do is slit the membranes between the ribs and bend the racks around to form a crown shape, and sew the ends together with a trussing needle and string.

Luscious lamb
The sweetness of the apricot and apple stuffing cuts through the slightly fatty lamb and mingles beautifully with the savoury meat.

Gary's special touch

Crown roast is usually made with lamb, but here I've chosen pork. The stuffing is great with the rich roast pork flavour and gives moisture as well as taste. The roast's own juices make a savoury sauce. My trick is in the roasting – I give the meat a couple of hours in the oven before packing the centre with stuffing.

making stuffed crown roast of pork

You will need

serves 10-14	**for the stuffing**
preparation time *30 minutes*	*2½ heaped tbsp white breadcrumbs*
cooking time *3½-4 hours, plus*	*1 onion, peeled and finely chopped*
10-15 minutes resting after roasting	*1 tbsp finely chopped fresh sage*
pre-heat oven *200°C/400°F/gas 6*	*450g (1lb) pork sausagemeat*
	1 egg, beaten
ingredients	*salt and pepper*
2 prepared racks of pork	
salt and pepper	**equipment**
oil for brushing	*trussing needle and string*

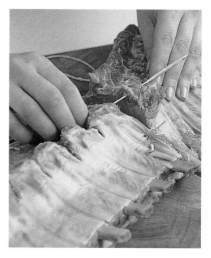

When you buy your pork, ask the butcher for two racks of 7 to 9 ribs from the same animal, so that they are of matching size. You can ask your butcher to make the whole crown for you, but if you are preparing the crown yourself, sew the two racks together with a trussing needle and string, with the bony ends pointing upwards and ribs curving outwards in a crown shape. (You can buy a trussing needle from good kitchen equipment shops.)

Adding the stuffing

While the crown is roasting you can make the stuffing. Then remove the crown from the oven about half-way through roasting so that you can insert the stuffing into the centre. The fat from the sausagemeat keeps it moist and the stuffing will make a richly browned, crusty accompaniment to the roast. Protect the tips of the bones with foil caps to prevent them from charring. But remember to remove these before serving. There should be enough meat juices left from the joint for you to make a savoury gravy.

Roasting the crown

The roasting time for the pork depends on its weight. In general, allow about 25 minutes per 450g (1lb) for the initial roasting of the pork crown, without the stuffing. Pork should always be cooked through thoroughly (it's never served rare like beef). The pork crown used here weighed 2.3kg (5lb) before the stuffing was added, and it was roasted for 2 hours without the stuffing, then taken out, stuffed, and returned to the oven at a lower temperature for another 1½ to 1¾ hours.

If you have bought a pork crown which is smaller or larger than the one shown here, you will need to adjust the initial roasting times accordingly. Allow another 1½-1¾ hours roasting after the stuffing has been added if the stuffing contains meat – such as sausagemeat or belly pork. The lamb crown roast in the variation recipe doesn't need pre-roasting because the racks are much smaller, and because there aren't any meat ingredients in the stuffing – instead, this recipe experiments with fruit stuffing.

1 Place racks side by side, with the ribs uppermost. Sew end ribs together half-way down. Cut and knot string, then stitch again near base. Loop string around two end ribs and tie.

5 Remove roast from oven, turn it so ribs face up and sit it back in tin. Pack stuffing inside. Cover tips of ribs with foil, then brush ribs with oil.

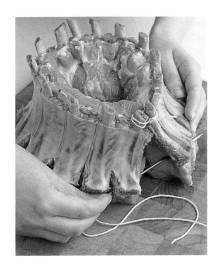

2 Bend racks into a circle, ribs outwards. If ends don't meet, trim more fat or meat away. To secure crown, tie tops of end ribs together and make a single stitch at base of the ribs.

3 Place crown, rib ends down, in a roasting tin, then season with salt and pepper. Roast in pre-heated oven for about 2 hours, basting with pan juices from time to time.

4 Prepare stuffing. Mix breadcrumbs with onion and sage, pour over a little boiling water and stir. Add the beaten egg and sausagemeat, season, then mix in thoroughly.

6 Reduce oven heat to 180°C/350°F/gas 4 and roast stuffed crown for another 1½-1¾ hours. Baste with the pan juices from time to time. Cover the top of the stuffing with foil if it starts to singe.

7 Remove the roast from the oven, cover with foil and leave to rest for 10-15 minutes. Remove the foil and lift the roast on to a warmed serving plate. Make gravy with the pan juices. Carve the crown at the table, cutting between the ribs to separate each of the chops. Serve with baby carrots and some caramelized apple wedges.

Variations on a theme

crown roast of lamb with apricot and apple stuffing

serves 4

preparation time
30 minutes

cooking time *1-1½ hours*

pre-heat oven
200°C/400°F/gas 6

ingredients
2 prepared small racks of lamb (best end of neck)
oil for brushing over lamb

for the stuffing
25g (1oz) butter
1 small onion, chopped
2 celery sticks, diced
1 dessert apple, peeled, cored and diced
40g (1½oz) dried, no-soak apricots, finely chopped
70g (2½oz) fresh white breadcrumbs

1 tbsp finely chopped fresh parsley
finely grated rind and juice of ½ lemon
1 egg, beaten
salt and pepper
1 tbsp plain flour
300ml (10fl oz) chicken stock (see page 8)

equipment *as before*

1 Make crown – bend lamb racks into a circle, fat side in. Sew as before.
2 Make stuffing. Melt butter in pan, add onion, celery and apple and brown lightly. Take off heat and stir in apricots, breadcrumbs, parsley, lemon rind and juice.

Leave mix to cool, then add egg and seasoning.
3 Pile stuffing into crown. Place in roasting tin and brush meat with oil. Cover rib tips with foil.
4 Roast joint in oven for 1-1½ hours, basting from time to time. Remove from oven and rest for 10 minutes. Remove foil and transfer meat to a serving dish. Keep warm.
5 Drain fat from roasting tin. Add flour to pan juices and stir. Cook for 1 minute, stirring, then add stock and cook for 2-3 minutes. Season gravy and serve hot with the joint. Carve chops and serve with stuffing.

why not try...

minty stuffing
Here's a fresh-tasting alternative stuffing for crown roast of lamb. In a large bowl mix together 55g (2oz) fresh breadcrumbs, 1 chopped onion, 1 tbsp chopped fresh parsley, 1 tbsp chopped fresh mint, 1 tsp grated nutmeg, 1 tsp crushed rosemary, the grated rind of half a lemon and salt and pepper to taste. Bind all the ingredients together with 1 beaten egg, then use to stuff the crown.

pork alternative
You can replace the sausagemeat in the pork crown roast stuffing with the same weight of chopped or minced belly pork.

eats well with...

Traditional roast or boiled potatoes are excellent accompaniments for crown roasts, as are carrots and broccoli, Brussels sprouts and cauliflower. Both pork and lamb are delicious with fruit accompaniments.

To make caramelized apples to serve with the pork crown roast, peel and cut 6 small dessert apples into eighths. Heat 55g (2oz) butter in a frying-pan, add the apples and turn to coat in butter. Then sprinkle with 1 tsp sugar and sauté for 3-4 minutes until the apples start to crisp. Don't let the apples cook too long or they will turn mushy.

shepherd's pie

That great British
institution, shepherd's
pie, is a satisfying dish and
a firm family favourite

Ashepherd's pie is traditionally
made with a minced lamb filling –
a cottage pie uses beef. Originally a
method of using up leftovers, a
shepherd's pie was filled with minced
leftover roast lamb and vegetables,
mixed with leftover gravy. Any boiled
potatoes that hadn't been eaten were
mashed to top the pie. However, the
best shepherd's pie is one cooked
from scratch.

A meaty pie
This recipe uses raw minced lamb
which is quickly browned to seal in
the juices. More flavour is added by
sautéing chopped carrot, celery and
onion before mixing with the meat.
Simmering the filling gently in red
wine, tomato sauce and stock gives it
a rich and tasty sauce. Finally, the
mashed potato topping is finished
with a layer of grated mature cheddar
cheese that melts to give the pie
a delicious golden crust.

Going green
The variation recipe is for a vegetarian shepherd's pie. It's full of
lentils and split peas which give
the pie an almost meaty texture.
It's also bursting with an array of
fresh vegetables and spiced up
with paprika. And even if you are
a meat-eater, you probably won't
miss the lamb!

Gary's special touch

I use raw rather
than cooked lamb
to make this
shepherd's pie. As
the meat is
simmered with the
other ingredients,
it infuses the sauce
with its flavour.

I also prefer to use
coarsely minced
lamb so that the
meat doesn't break
down completely
during cooking –
which is what a
more finely minced
meat would do.

making shepherd's pie

You will need

serves 4-6

preparation time
25 minutes

cooking time
2 hours

ingredients
675g (1½lb) coarsely minced lamb
salt and pepper
25g (1oz) lamb or beef dripping or
2 tbsp vegetable oil
55g (2oz) butter
3 onions, finely chopped
3 carrots, diced
4 celery sticks, diced
½ tsp cinnamon

½ tsp chopped fresh thyme
½ tsp chopped rosemary
2 tsp Worcestershire sauce
2 tbsp tomato purée
2 tbsp tomato ketchup
2-3 glasses of red wine
25g (1oz) plain flour
200ml (7fl oz) chicken stock (see
page 8)
900g (2lb) mashed potato, made
with minimal butter and milk
55-85g (2-3oz) mature cheddar
cheese, grated

equipment
flameproof dish

Use lean, coarsely minced lamb for this recipe. It's a good idea to buy a cut of meat, such as shoulder of lamb, and either mince it yourself or ask the butcher to do it.

Sealing the lamb
The first stage of making the filling for this pie is to seal the meat. Do this in a frying-pan over a fairly high heat – you want to seal and colour the meat as quickly as possible so that it retains its flavour. You'll probably need to fry the meat in batches. The lamb is then put in a colander, so that excess oil drains away. This prevents the finished dish from becoming too greasy.

Rich filling
The red wine in this filling adds to the flavour which is further boosted by adding the wine in small amounts. By doing this, and allowing each addition of wine to reduce, the flavour of the

cooked meat isn't boiled away in too much wine. To ensure that the filling is very rich, it has to simmer away for 1-1½ hours. This may seem like a very long time but it greatly improves the taste, as the flavours really get a chance to mature. During this time you have to watch the sauce to make sure that it doesn't become too thick. If it looks like this is happening, add a little water. But don't let the sauce become too thin either, or the mashed potato will sink into it.

Tip
You could prepare this in advance. Just make the filling and mashed potato and leave to cool. When ready, assemble the pie and then bake in an oven pre-heated to 200°C/400°F/gas 6 for 35-40 minutes.

1 Season the lamb. Heat the dripping or oil in a large frying-pan over high heat and fry the lamb in batches to seal it. Remove from the pan and drain in a colander.

5 Add the stock and bring to a simmer. Leave to cook for 1-1½ hours. If the sauce becomes too thick during this time, add a little water to it.

2 Melt half the butter in a saucepan and add the vegetables. Stir in the cinnamon and herbs; season to taste. Cook for 5-6 minutes until the vegetables begin to soften.

3 Add the fried lamb to the vegetables and cook for a few minutes over medium heat. Then add the Worcestershire sauce, tomato purée and ketchup and mix well.

4 Stir in the wine, half a glass at a time, letting each addition reduce by three-quarters. Sprinkle in the flour and cook for 2-3 minutes until slightly thickened.

6 Meanwhile, make the mashed potato and keep it warm. Put the hot filling in an ovenproof dish. Spoon the mashed potato on top.

7 Using a palette knife, smooth the topping and make an even scalloped pattern. Melt the remaining butter and brush on the top. Sprinkle with the cheese. Cook under a hot grill until golden.

Variations on a theme

lentil shepherd's pie

A vegetarian alternative to the traditional shepherd's pie.

serves 4

preparation time
30 minutes

cooking time *1¾ hours*

pre-heat oven
190°C/375°F/gas 5

ingredients
175g (6oz) green lentils
115g (4oz) yellow split peas
600ml (1 pint) ready-made vegetable stock, hot
900g (2lb) mashed potato, made with very little butter and cream or milk
55g (2oz) butter
2 celery stalks, chopped
1 red onion, chopped
1 carrot, chopped
1 red pepper, chopped
450g (1lb) spinach, cooked and chopped
1 garlic clove, chopped
1 tsp fresh oregano
½ tsp grated nutmeg
¼ tsp paprika
salt and pepper
225g (8oz) tomatoes, peeled and sliced
25g (1oz) parmesan

equipment
ovenproof dish, piping bag and nozzle

1 Wash the lentils and peas and put them in a saucepan with the stock. Cover and simmer for 45-60 minutes, until they have absorbed all the stock.

2 Meanwhile, make the mashed potato using less butter, cream or milk than you would usually.

3 Melt half the butter in a frying-pan and add the celery, onion, carrot and pepper. Cook over low heat for 8-10 minutes until tender.

4 Add the cooked vegetables and spinach to the lentils and split peas. Then stir in the garlic, oregano, nutmeg and paprika; season to taste.

5 Spoon the filling into the ovenproof dish and arrange the slices of tomato on top.

6 Spoon the mashed potato into a piping bag and use to pipe a decorative lattice pattern on top of the filling. If you don't have a piping bag, spoon the potato on the top.

7 Melt the remaining butter and brush over the top of the mashed potato. Grate the parmesan cheese and sprinkle over the potato. Bake in the pre-heated oven for 20 minutes until golden on top.

why not try...

potato slices
Instead of using mashed potato as the topping for your pie, you could top it with slices of cooked potato instead. Peel 4-5 potatoes and boil for about 15 minutes until cooked through. Cut into slices about 5mm (¼in) thick. Arrange the potato slices over the filling so that they overlap slightly. Then dot with butter, sprinkle with grated cheddar cheese and finish under the grill.

any left?

If you have any of the lamb shepherd's pie left over you can make it into shepherd's pie fritters. Cut away any of the cheese topping and discard. Then mix the mince and the mash together before storing in the fridge. To make the fritters, dust your hands with flour and roll the mixture into small balls about 2.5cm (1in) in diameter. Dust the balls in seasoned flour. Then dip into some beaten egg and roll in white breadcrumbs. Dip into the egg and crumbs again, and then refrigerate for at least an hour. Pour some vegetable oil into a large saucepan and heat until a breadcrumb sizzles in the oil. Deep-fry the balls until golden; drain on kitchen paper and serve.

honey-roast pork belly

For a simple, relaxed Sunday lunch, a slow roast is ideal, and this delicious honey-coated pork belly recipe is the perfect option

Slow roasting is a great way to cook a joint – it ensures the meat stays succulent and tender. Pork belly is quite a fatty cut of pork and during the slow cooking much of this fat melts, helping to keep the meat moist. The addition of some honey during the roasting gives the pork belly a glistening, golden glaze. The pork is roasted on a bed of onions and the juices seep from the meat during cooking to give the onions a rich meaty flavour and wonderfully gooey texture. The cooking juices and onions are then served with the pork.

Something soft on the side
This pork dish is excellent combined with soft and creamy mashed potato or a vegetable purée. For side dishes, choose simple but flavoursome vegetables, such as carrots or leeks.

Slow and spicy
The variation recipe is for a spicy slow roast that has been marinated overnight for even more flavour. The Chinese-inspired ingredients give the roasted pork a real Oriental flavour. It's ideal served with rice or noodles and stir-fried vegetables.

Gary's special touch

I think a simple side dish is always best with this kind of sweet and succulent, highly flavoured roast. Try this recipe of pea and potato mash. Just cook and then purée 225-450g (8oz-1lb) frozen peas and mix this and a knob of butter into 450g (1lb) hot mashed potatoes – it tastes sensational!

slow honey-roasting pork belly

You will need

serves 4	**ingredients**
preparation time	1-1.1kg (2¼-2½lb) piece of pork
15 minutes	belly, boned but with rind left on
cooking time	5 large onions, halved and sliced
3 hours, plus resting time	vegetable oil
pre-heat oven	1 tsp white peppercorns, crushed
160°C/325°F/gas 3	coarse sea salt
	2-3 tbsp honey
	salt and pepper

Before the pork belly is roasted, the rind is scored all over using the tip of a very sharp knife. Keep the cuts at least 1cm (½in) apart. Rubbing the pepper and salt into the rind helps flavour the meat and make the rind more crisp.

The pork is cooked on top of a bed of sliced onions. As the meat roasts, the fat and juices drip down into the onions, keeping them moist. This also helps stop the onions burning during the long cooking time. Instead, they become soft and full of flavour.

Basting for the best

After the meat has roasted for an hour, it's a good idea to start basting it with the fat and juices that have come out of the pork. This helps the joint to stay moist and succulent. To do this, just take the roasting tin out of the oven and tip it slightly to one side. Spoon out some of the juices and pour over the meat; return the pork to the oven. Keep doing this at intervals of 15-20 minutes.

Once the meat has been roasting for 2½ hours, you pour the honey over the rind. As it cooks, the honey begins to caramelize and form a rich and golden glaze over the meat.

When the meat is cooked through, it needs to be taken out of the oven and left to rest for 10-15 minutes. While it is resting, put the roasting tin on the hob and deglaze with a little water. This lifts any interesting juicy and sticky bits from the tin and makes a moist liquor.

The pork belly is cut into four portions and each piece is presented on a bed of the cooked onions. Pour any cooking liquor over the meat and serve with pea and potato mash.

Inside info

Pork belly

This cut, taken from the underside of the pig, is also known as streaky or flank. It is a thin piece of pork, made up of layers of meat and fat, in roughly equal proportions.

Pork belly can be slow-roasted in one flat piece, as here, or it can be stuffed and rolled for roasting. It is also popular in casseroles, such as cassoulet, where it adds a richness and flavour.

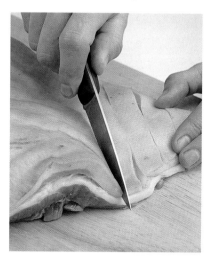

1 Using kitchen paper, wipe the pork belly rind to ensure it is dry. Take a very sharp knife and, with the tip, score through the rind, making cuts 1cm (½in) apart.

5 Take the pork out of the oven and test for doneness with the point of a knife or skewer – the juices should run clear. Remove pork from the tin and rest for 10-15 minutes.

2 Put the onions in a roasting tin and put the belly, rind-side up, on top. Trickle with a little oil and press on the white peppercorns and a little sea salt. Roast for 1 hour.

3 Remove from the oven and baste the meat with any fat and juices. Add 1-2 tbsp water to stop the onions from drying out. Cook for 1½ hours more, basting every 15-20 minutes.

4 Take the meat out of the oven and increase the heat to 200°C/400°F/gas 6. Pour the honey over the belly and roast for 30-40 minutes, basting a few more times.

6 Meanwhile, put the roasting tin over moderate heat and pour 2-3 tbsp water into the onions. Stir well to incorporate any juices and crusty bits left in the tin; set aside.

7 To serve, cut the pork belly into four portions. Spoon the onions on to plates and top with the pork. Drizzle with any remaining cooking liquor and serve with pea and potato mash.

Variations on a theme

spicy slow-roast pork

An Oriental-inspired marinade and a gingery honey glaze give a spicy twist to this slow roast.

serves 4

preparation time
20 minutes, plus overnight marinating

cooking time
3 hours, plus resting

pre-heat oven
160°C/325°F/gas 3

ingredients
1-1.1kg (2¼-2½lb) piece of pork belly, boned but with rind left on
vegetable oil
1 tsp Chinese five-spice powder
coarse sea salt
350g jar crystallized ginger in syrup
2 tbsp honey

for the marinade
85ml (3fl oz) light soy sauce
2 tbsp dry sherry
3 garlic cloves, crushed
2 star anise
6cm (2½in) piece root ginger, peeled and grated
2 tbsp honey

1 Wipe the pork belly rind with kitchen paper and, using the tip of a sharp knife, score the rind, making cuts 1cm (½in) apart. Mix together the marinade ingredients and set aside 3 tbsp of the mixture.

2 Cover the pork belly with the marinade and, using your hands, rub it into the flesh and rind. Set aside to marinate for 24 hours, or overnight.

3 Place the pork on a rack in a roasting tin and trickle on a little vegetable oil. Rub the five-spice powder and some sea salt into the rind. Put in the oven and roast for 2½ hours.

4 Mix the honey with 1 tbsp syrup from the jar of crystallized ginger and pour over the pork belly. Turn the oven up to 200°C/400°F/gas 6 and roast for a further 20-30 minutes, basting a couple more times.

5 When the pork is tender and cooked through completely, set aside to rest for 10-15 minutes. Put the roasting tin on the hob and stir in the reserved marinade and 100ml (3½fl oz) water to deglaze the tin. Leave the sauce to simmer for a few minutes to thicken.

6 To serve, cut the pork belly into slices. Finely chop 2-3 pieces of crystallized ginger and sprinkle over the pork. Pour on the sauce. Serve on a bed of cooked rice.

why not try...

hotter coating
For a crispy coating with a slightly hotter flavour, try mixing 1 tsp English mustard powder in with the honey. You could also try using coarsely ground black pepper instead of the white pepper to rub into the rind. Alternatively, use some chilli oil to rub into the rind.

eats well with...

Since this is a slow-roast dish, it's a good idea to slow-cook a potato dish in the oven at the same time – such as dauphinois or boulangère potatoes. The soft, melting texture of the potatoes goes well with the tender meat.

Purées and mashes of vegetables other than potato make delicious accompaniments – why not try a celeriac or parsnip purée or mashed sweet potatoes?

any left?

This slow honey roast is delicious eaten cold. And if you've any of the onions and the pea and potato mash left, mix them together and fry for a wonderful version of bubble and squeak.

roast stuffed tenderloin

Tender by name and tender by nature, pork fillet is even more succulent when stuffed

Pork tenderloin, also called pork fillet, is an exceptionally lean, boneless cut of meat. It's found under the pig's lower backbone, where there is little muscle movement, which is why it is so tender. It requires very little preparation and cooks quite quickly, even when stuffed. To accompany it, all it needs is some simply cooked vegetables and an excellent wine.

Dining with ease

Stuffed tenderloin is a great dish to serve at a dinner party. It's easy to carve and produces neat, uniform slices of meat, with a morsel of stuffing at the centre, that look very impressive. And of course, the stuffing also flavours the delicate meat as it roasts, producing a dish your guests will truly enjoy.

Your choice

The main recipe is for a pork tenderloin stuffed with a delicious mixture of spinach, ham and herbs. Pork is often combined with fruit in dishes and the variation recipe follows this tradition by using dried apricots in a stuffing that's also full of spicy flavours from the East. Other classic fruity choices for pork tenderloin stuffings are apples, raisins and prunes.

Gary's special touch

I find that lean tenderloin is its own worst enemy – its lack of natural fat can make the meat rather dry. I like to stuff the joint with a moist and tasty stuffing and then cover it with rashers of streaky bacon. The bacon helps baste the meat and keep it moist – as well as giving the pork an even more sensational flavour!

ham and spinach stuffed tenderloin

You will need

serves 4

preparation time *25 minutes*

cooking time *45-50 minutes*

pre-heat oven *180ºC/350ºF/gas 4*

ingredients

large pork tenderloin

2 rashers streaky bacon

2 roughly chopped red onions

2 rosemary sprigs

3 tbsp olive oil

for the stuffing

25g (1oz) butter

2 shallots, finely chopped

½ tbsp finely chopped sage leaves

115g (4oz) baby spinach leaves, shredded

25g (1oz) sliced ham

55g (2oz) fresh breadcrumbs

1 beaten egg

¼ tsp grated nutmeg

for the gravy

2 glasses of white wine

150ml (5fl oz) chicken stock (see page 8)

equipment

kitchen string; roasting tin

Choose a fairly large tenderloin, weighing about 450g (1lb). This should produce ample slices for four people. As tenderloin is such a lean meat, you might want to serve it with a moist and creamy side dish such as mashed potatoes or pommes dauphinois. And choose some tender and tasty vegetables as an accompaniment, such as some deliciously sweet baby carrots and leeks.

Making the gravy

A good gravy is just what this dish needs and this recipe includes a richly flavoured sauce. The red onions and sprigs of rosemary on which the tenderloin are roasted add intense flavours to the cooking juices and the roasting tin is deglazed with a fair amount of white wine. If you want a gravy that's even more indulgent, then deglaze the pan with port. If the gravy gets too thick, just add a little water while it's still in the roasting tin.

Serving up

Make sure that the dinner plates have been warmed through before you serve the meat, so that the slices of meat do not cool down too quickly between the kitchen and the dinner table. Place a couple of slices on each plate, pour some of the hot gravy around them and serve.

Cook's notes

In this recipe, the tenderloin is roasted on a bed of onions and rosemary that add to the flavour of the gravy but which could also be served as a tasty accompaniment. You might like to try roasting the pork on a layer of apples and leeks, cut into rough chunks. Or why not try a bed of red and yellow peppers with sprigs of thyme?

I Slice open the tenderloin lengthways, two-thirds of the way through. Open out the split tenderloin and pound it gently with a rolling pin, to flatten and widen it slightly.

5 Roast for 35-40 minutes, basting it a few times during cooking. Once cooked, remove the tenderloin, cover with foil and rest for about 5 minutes.

2 For the stuffing, melt the butter and fry the shallots and sage for about 10 minutes. Add the spinach and cook until it wilts. Then mix in the rest of the stuffing ingredients.

3 Spread the stuffing along the centre of the tenderloin, patting it down firmly. Roll up the tenderloin and tie it with kitchen string, at roughly 4cm (1½in) intervals.

4 Lay the meat in a roasting tin, cover with the slices of bacon and surround with the onions and sprigs of rosemary. Drizzle the olive oil over the meat and onions.

6 Meanwhile, discard the onions and rosemary, and deglaze the pan with wine. Add the stock and boil rapidly until reduced by half; strain.

7 Cut the string off the tenderloin, then slice it slightly on the diagonal. Serve immediately with the hot gravy.

Variations on a theme

tenderloin with apricots and almonds

Full of spicy flavours and succulent apricots, this version of stuffed tenderloin is served with a tasty Marsala gravy.

serves 4

preparation time
20 minutes

cooking time
40-45 minutes

pre-heat oven
180°C/350°F/gas 4

ingredients
large pork tenderloin (about 450g/1lb)
3 tbsp olive oil
2 onions, roughly chopped
2 rashers streaky bacon

for the stuffing
25g (1oz) butter
1 onion, finely chopped
¼ tsp ground coriander
¼ tsp ground cinnamon
½ tbsp parsley, chopped
1 tbsp ready-to-eat dried apricots, chopped
1 tbsp almonds, chopped
55g (2oz) cooked bulgar wheat
1 beaten egg

to serve
2 glasses of Marsala, for the gravy
ready-made tabbouleh

equipment
kitchen string; roasting tin

1 Slice the tenderloin lengthways, two-thirds of the way through. Open it out and flatten slightly with a rolling pin.
2 To make the stuffing, melt the butter in a saucepan, add the onions and spices and fry for about 10 minutes.
3 Remove from the heat and mix in the other stuffing ingredients. Spread the stuffing along the tenderloin, roll it up and tie with string at 4cm (1½in) intervals.
4 Heat the oil in a roasting tin on the hob and brown the meat. Add the onions, toss in oil and sit the tenderloin on top; cover with the streaky bacon.
5 Roast the tenderloin for 35-40 minutes, basting it a few times with the cooking juices. Remove from the oven, cover with foil and rest for about 5 minutes.
6 To make the gravy, discard the onions and place the roasting tin over a low heat. Deglaze the pan with the Marsala. Cook until reduced by about a third, then strain into a jug and keep warm.
7 Carve the tenderloin into slices about 2cm (¾in) wide. Then serve with the gravy on a bed of tabbouleh.

why not try...

rocket and sun-dried tomato stuffing

Melt a knob of butter in a small pan and cook 1 chopped onion until soft. Then add 115g (4oz) finely shredded rocket leaves and 25g (1oz) of sun-dried tomatoes. Fry for a few minutes until the rocket has wilted. Remove from the heat and pour off any excess liquid. Then add 55g (2oz) fresh breadcrumbs and one beaten egg. Mix thoroughly and season to taste.

cranberries and orange zest stuffing

Make the stuffing as above but substitute 55g (2oz) cooked cranberries and the zest of 1 orange for the rocket and sun-dried tomatoes.

fresh herb stuffing

You could just simply stuff the tenderloin with some fresh herbs. Make two cuts along the joint and fill with chopped fresh herbs – why not try sage, fennel or tarragon? The tenderloin looks wonderful when it's sliced through.

eats well with...

The apricot and almond stuffed tenderloin is perfect served on a bed of fluffy white rice or steaming couscous that will soak up the rich gravy. A simple green salad, with a few toasted pine nuts tossed in, is an ideal accompaniment.

hot hams

Boiled in cider, baked with a sweet mustard and brandy glaze, then served with a creamy sauce, hot ham is a treat

These days, the names ham and gammon are nearly always used interchangeably – both refer to the cured (salted) meat from the leg of a pig, which is sometimes also smoked.

The joint you need here is usually sold as gammon and becomes known as ham after it is cooked. You can use unsmoked or smoked gammon, depending on your taste.

Soaking before cooking?

Check the labelling on a pre-packed gammon joint, or consult your butcher, to find out whether the joint you're buying needs soaking. In the past, gammon joints required lengthy soaking to dilute the saltiness of the curing process. Nowadays, however, cures are much milder and most gammon joints need no soaking at all. You simply boil them in water, stock, cider or wine.

In this recipe, the boiling stage cooks the ham. Subsequent baking crisps up the thin crust with a sweet shiny mustard glaze.

Crunchy nut crust

An equally tasty alternative approach is to give the gammon a sweet crunchy crust with an irresistible mixture of almond, honey, mustard and sesame seeds.

Gary's special touch

If you like the taste of apples, you'll see that the main ham recipe certainly uses a lot of them. The poaching liquid is cider, flavoured with fresh apples, and I serve the ham with baked dessert apples. Then, just for good measure, I splash some Calvados (brandy distilled from cider) into the lovely sweet, succulent glaze.

making ham with a mustard glaze

You will need

serves 12 or more
preparation time 15 minutes
cooking time 2 hours
pre-heat oven 180°C/350°F/gas 4

ingredients
2.25kg (5lb) mild-cure corner
gammon joint, smoked or unsmoked
cider – enough to cover joint and for
baking the apples
1 large carrot, peeled and cut into
3 or 4 pieces
1 stick celery, cut into 3 or 4 pieces
1 onion, peeled and cut into quarters
1 cooking apple, quartered
1 bay leaf
10 black peppercorns

12 small dessert apples, cored
55g (2oz) butter
demerara sugar for sprinkling

for the glaze and sauce
15-20 cloves
300ml (10fl oz) Calvados
2 tbsp grainy mustard
1 tbsp English mustard powder
85g (3oz) demerara sugar
2 tbsp double cream

equipment
large saucepan with lid, big enough to
take the gammon joint; roasting tin;
shallow ovenproof dish, lightly
buttered, for apples

I Put joint in a large pan. Cover with water and bring to the boil. Then pour the water away and cover joint with cider. Add carrot, celery, onion, cooking apple, bay leaf and peppercorns.

Buy a mild-cure joint, if possible, because it won't need soaking before you cook it. However, it's still a good idea to start cooking the ham in water, bring that to the boil, then throw it away to avoid over-saltiness and eliminate any scum. Replace the water with the cider and flavourings.

Added apple
There's no doubt that ham and pork have a natural affinity with apples. The sharp fruitiness of apples complements the rich meat and cuts through its fattiness. The ham is also glazed with a mixture of cider, apple brandy, sugar and mustard which creates a flavourful, crisp crust that brings out the best in the sweet, tender meat.

Less than a pinch
You definitely don't need to add any salt to this recipe – the ham should

provide more than enough on its own. When you come to score the fat just before glazing, don't cut right through to the meat or it becomes dry and stringy. You can serve the ham hot or cold.

Cook's notes

A corner gammon joint is excellent for baking. This is a triangular cut from the top of the pig's leg; you should be able to order a corner piece weighing anything from 1.3-2.25kg (3-5lb). These sometimes come pre-cooked, in which case you can go straight on to the glazing and roasting stages without having to boil the ham first.

5 Mix Calvados, mustards and sugar and spread over joint. Pour reduced joint cooking liquid into tin. Bake joint for 30 minutes until brown, basting often.

2 Bring to the boil, reduce heat, cover and simmer for 1½-2 hours (20 minutes per 450g/1lb). Then lift joint out, drain and put on a rack in a roasting tin. Leave until cool enough to handle.

3 Meanwhile, top each apple with a knob of butter and a little sugar. Pour 3-4 tbsp cider into the dish and bake for 30 minutes. Reduce 600ml (1 pint) of the joint cooking liquid by half.

4 Turn oven down to 160°C/325°F/gas 3. Remove skin from the joint in the tin and trim fat to a 5mm (¼in) thick layer. Score fat in a diamond pattern and stud with cloves.

6 Remove ham from tin, then simmer juices in tin for 1-2 minutes, stirring. Add cream, and more cider if needed, season to taste and pour into a sauceboat.

7 Carve the hot ham into slices and serve with the creamy sauce, the baked apples and some mashed potatoes and green beans.

Variations on a theme

gammon with crunchy nut crust

This ham joint has a gorgeous crunchy, nutty crust. To make sure it stays crisp, don't baste too often while the ham is baking in the oven. If you like, you can buy a ready-cooked gammon joint and proceed straight to the oven-baking after coating the top with the crust mixture. You can serve this ham hot or cold.

serves 8

preparation time
15 minutes

cooking time
2 hours 15 minutes

pre-heat oven
200°C/400°F/gas 6

ingredients
1.8kg (4lb) gammon joint, smoked or unsmoked
white wine to cover joint
1 large carrot, peeled and cut into 3 or 4 pieces
1 parsnip, peeled and cut into 3 or 4 pieces
1 onion, peeled and cut into quarters
1 leek, cut into 4 pieces
1 bay leaf
10 black peppercorns

for the glaze
15 cloves
4 tbsp runny honey
1 tbsp Dijon mustard
2 tbsp sesame seeds
1 tbsp white mustard seeds
25g (1oz) flaked almonds or crushed hazelnuts

55g (2oz) fresh white breadcrumbs

equipment
saucepan big enough to take gammon joint; roasting tin

1 Put joint in large pan. Cover with water and bring to boil. Remove from heat, drain off water, then re-cover with white wine and add the vegetables, bay leaf and peppercorns.
2 Bring to the boil and simmer the joint for 1½-2 hours (20 minutes per 450g/1lb). Then lift ham out, drain and put in a roasting tin. Leave until cool enough to handle.
3 Remove skin and trim fat to a 5mm (¼in) thick layer. Score fat in a diamond pattern and stud with cloves.
4 Mix the honey and Dijon mustard and brush half the mixture over the fat on the joint. Then mix the sesame and mustard seeds, nuts and breadcrumbs into the remaining glaze and press on to the joint over the glaze.
5 Add 3-4 tbsp of the ham liquor to the tin, then bake for 15 minutes in the pre-heated oven, basting occasionally, until the crust is crispy and golden. Serve in slices.

why not try...

glazing over
For the simplest glaze, just sprinkle brown sugar on top of the boiled ham after skinning. For a richer glaze, pour several tablespoons of Madeira on top of the sugar before roasting for 30 minutes, basting frequently. For a sweet and sour option, mix mustard with runny honey (or melted redcurrant jelly, marmalade or apricot jam) and a spirit, wine or a liqueur. (If you're using marmalade, then try a dash of Cointreau with it, for example.)

crunchy crusts
If you like a crusty topping, then mix brown sugar, breadcrumbs and crushed nuts – almonds, hazelnuts, pistachios, walnuts or pecans.

liquid flavours
White or red wine, cider, sherry and even Coca Cola (never Diet Coke) all impart extra flavour to the gammon joint. They also form the basis of a sauce to go with the ham.

sauce it up
Three sauces are particularly good with hot or cold ham: apple sauce, parsley sauce and onion sauce.

any left?

Glazed hams are great served hot but just as good cold with apple sauce or chutney, or in sandwiches with mustard.

sausage casseroles

These hearty sausage casseroles make delicious, flavoursome meals in themselves

Sausages are ideal for casseroles and stews; they are quickly browned before slow cooking to release lots of flavour into the accompanying sauce. Choose good-quality pork sausages to ensure a good flavour. Alternatively, choose venison or game sausages for a more refined edge to a casserole or a spicy sausage, such as chorizo, for a more exotic flavour.

Browning for colour

For most casseroles, sausages are browned first to add colour to the dish. Leave them whole and brown well on the outside but don't worry about cooking them through at this point. If you are using ready-to-eat sausages, such as chorizo or kabanos, cut them into chunks first and fry them briefly before adding them to the dish.

All-in-one

Sausages and pulses provide a delicious combination; for the main recipe casserole, plump pork sausages are cooked with butter beans, bacon, red wine, herbs and passata — it's guaranteed to become a firm family favourite. In the variation recipe, venison or beef sausages are delicately braised with red wine and button onions.

Gary's special touch

I like to buy good-quality pork and herb sausages from my local butcher, or if I have the time, I make my own – I particularly like using thyme and sage. Good pork sausages from your supermarket are perfectly fine, but they can lack the flavour of home-made or freshly made sausages from the butcher.

making sausage and bean casserole

You will need

serves 4	1 large onion, halved and sliced
preparation time 30 minutes, plus overnight soaking for beans	3 garlic cloves, finely chopped
	1 tbsp finely chopped fresh rosemary
cooking time 1 hour 50 minutes	500g jar passata
pre-heat oven	300ml (10fl oz) red wine
180°C/350°F/gas 4	300ml (10fl oz) chicken stock (see page 8)
	2 bay leaves
ingredients	salt and pepper
450g (1lb) pork and herb sausages	2 tbsp chopped fresh parsley
225g (8oz) dried butter (lima) beans	Savoy cabbage, to serve
3 sprigs of fresh thyme	
2 tbsp olive oil	**equipment**
125g (4½oz) lean bacon, chopped	large flameproof, ovenproof casserole
1 leek, thinly sliced	

Generally speaking, a stew is made up of ingredients that are cooked together, without prior browning, on top of the stove. In a casserole, the ingredients are usually browned, often with flour, on top of the stove, then finished in the oven. However, the boundaries between stews and casseroles have become somewhat blurred over time.

Soaking times

This casserole needs some forward planning as the dried butter beans need to be soaked for at least eight hours or overnight. The longer dried beans are stored, the longer they will take to cook until tender, so don't keep them for too long and buy from a shop with a high turnover. If you forget to soak the beans you can use a quick method – bring the beans to the boil in plenty of water and boil for 2 minutes, then remove from the heat, cover and stand for about an hour, then continue as for the recipe.

Putting it together

The sausages are browned in the casserole dish until golden brown. You can use a large frying-pan if this is easier, and transfer them to the casserole later.

The sausages are taken out of the pan while you soften the other ingredients. Bacon, leek, onion, garlic and rosemary are cooked in the casserole before adding the liquid and beans to the dish. The casserole is cooked for 40 minutes before returning the sausages to the dish, to ensure that the butter beans are tender.

Tip

You can use canned beans if you don't want to use dried. Drain and rinse the beans and add to the casserole. Add the sausages at the same time and then cook for just 40 minutes.

Put the butter beans in a large bowl, cover with plenty of water and leave to soak overnight. The next day, drain the beans, discarding the soaking water.

5 Stir in the passata, wine, stock, bay leaves and drained beans. Bring to the boil, cover, then transfer to the oven and cook for 40 minutes.

2 Put the soaked beans in a pan with the thyme and cover with water. Boil for 10 minutes, reduce heat, and simmer for 10 minutes. Drain, discarding thyme, and reserve.

3 Meanwhile, heat the oil in the casserole dish and add the sausages. Fry gently, turning them over with tongs, until golden brown all over. Remove and set aside.

4 Add the chopped bacon to the pan with the leek, onion, garlic and rosemary and cook gently for 5 minutes, stirring occasionally, until softened but not coloured.

6 Take the casserole out of the oven, add the sausages return to the oven to cook for another 40 minutes until sausages and beans are tender.

7 Season to taste with salt and pepper. Stir in the fresh parsley and serve with some shredded and cooked Savoy cabbage.

Variations on a theme

venison sausage and red wine stew

Venison sausages are braised in red wine with button onions and flavoured with redcurrant jelly for this smart dinner party stew. If you can't find venison sausages use beef sausages instead.

serves 4

preparation time
20 minutes

cooking time *30 minutes*

ingredients
450g (1lb) good-quality venison or beef sausages
2 tbsp olive oil
225g (8oz) rindless
streaky bacon, chopped
225g (8oz) button onions, peeled and halved
350g (12oz) mixed root vegetables (carrots, parsnips, swede, turnip), cut into matchsticks
2 celery sticks, diced
1 tbsp plain flour
300ml (10fl oz) red wine
salt and pepper
1 garlic clove, peeled and crushed
2 bay leaves
2 tbsp redcurrant jelly
sprigs of thyme, to garnish

equipment
large flameproof casserole dish

1 Heat oil in the casserole dish and add the sausages. Fry until browned all over. Remove from the dish with a slotted spoon and set aside.

2 Drain off all but 2 tbsp of the fat from the sausages, and add the bacon, onions, mixed root vegetables and celery. Fry quickly, stirring occasionally, until well browned all over.

3 Sprinkle the flour into the pan and stir well so that it's thoroughly mixed in. Cook for 1-2 minutes. Add the wine to the casserole and stir well to blend.

4 Return the sausages to the pan, season to taste with salt and pepper, then add the garlic and bay leaves. Bring the stew gently to the boil and cook for about 5 minutes.

5 Cover the casserole dish tightly and simmer for a further 20 minutes. Add the redcurrant jelly to the stew about 10 minutes before the end of the cooking time; stir well until the jelly is completely dissolved.

6 Season to taste with salt and pepper and sprinkle with the sprigs of thyme. Serve on a deep bed of creamy mashed potato.

why not try...

chilli sausage casserole

Brown 450g (1lb) beef sausages in a little oil in a casserole dish; set aside. Fry 1 sliced onion and 1 crushed garlic clove gently in the dish until softened. Add 1 tsp chilli powder and cook for 1 minute. Return the sausages to the dish with a 400g (14oz) can kidney beans, drained and rinsed, and a 400g (14oz) can chopped tomatoes. Take 2-3 tbsp out of 350ml (12fl oz) cold beef stock and mix with 1 tbsp cornflour to form a paste. Add the paste and remaining stock to the dish, with a few drops of Tabasco and 2 tbsp tomato purée. Bring to the boil, cover and cook for 1 hour in an oven, pre-heated to 170°C/325°F/gas 3.

cider sausage casserole

Brown 450g (1lb) herby pork sausages in melted butter in a casserole dish; set aside. Cook 1 sliced onion and 2 sliced dessert apples in the casserole for 5 minutes until soft. Add a pinch of cinnamon and nutmeg and stir in 1 tbsp flour; cook for 1 minute. Return the sausages to the dish and pour in 425ml (15fl oz) dry cider. Bring to the boil and put in an oven pre-heated to 180°C/350°F/gas 4 for 40-50 minutes.

roast turkey

Serve a succulent golden turkey with a moist, fruity stuffing as the ultimate Christmas treat

A good-quality turkey, properly roasted, is succulent, appetising and makes a great centrepiece to the Christmas spread. Turkey has a reputation for being a dry meat but this should not happen if you choose a plump young bird – especially a free-range or organic one. The right roasting techniques will also help to seal in moisture and produce a mouth-watering result.

Big bird

Buy a fresh turkey if you can, choosing a bird which is smooth to the touch with a layer of fat on its back. Reserve the giblets to make a rich stock (see Using giblets, page 138). After the bird is roasted, make gravy with the pan juices and flavour it with port.

Veggie feast

For a vegetarian Christmas dish, the aim is to create something that goes just as well with the roast vegetables, stuffings and sauces as the turkey does. Mushroom and apricot parcels are ideal. Their firm, moist texture and 'meaty' flavour works well with roast potatoes, Brussels sprouts and other winter vegetables. The gravy can be served on the table with the rest of the trimmings.

Gary's special touch

A tasty stuffing not only adds new flavours to roast turkey, it also helps to keep the bird moist while roasting. This delicious stuffing contains apricots and fresh sage to give a hint of herby sweetness to the sausagemeat, breadcrumbs and onions. It can be made in advance and refrigerated until needed.

roasting the turkey

You will need

pre-heat oven *220°C/425°F/gas 7*
preparation time *20 minutes*
cooking time *3½-5 hours*

ingredients
1 turkey
55-85g (2-3oz) butter, softened
salt and pepper
6-10 slices streaky bacon

for the stuffing
(enough for a 4.5-6.3kg/10-14lb bird)
450g (1lb) pork sausagemeat
115g (4oz) fresh white breadcrumbs

115g (4oz) dried apricots, chopped
1 medium onion, finely chopped
2 tbsp fresh chopped sage
1 egg, beaten
salt and pepper

for the gravy
2-3 tbsp plain flour
850ml (1½ pints) chicken stock (see page 8) or turkey giblet stock (see page 138)
150ml (5fl oz) port

1 Thoroughly mix all the stuffing ingredients in a large bowl – you may find it easiest to do this with your hands. Season the mixture, cover and set aside.

As a rough guide, 4 people require a 3.6-4.5kg (8-10lb) turkey, 6-10 people a 4.5-6.3kg (10-14lb) turkey and 12 people a 6.3-8kg (14-18lb) turkey. This allows for generous portions with plenty left over.

If the turkey is frozen, defrost it in a plastic bag in a cool place (not the fridge), removing the giblets as soon as possible. Refrigerate the defrosted turkey for up to 24 hours. Return it to room temperature before cooking.

Roasting

Begin cooking the turkey in a hot oven to heat it through, then turn the heat down so it continues to cook more gently. Baste every 45 minutes.

To test that the turkey is cooked, pierce one thigh with a skewer and press out the juices. They should run clear. Put the bird on a platter and rest it for 30 minutes before carving. This allows the meat to reabsorb its juices, making it more succulent.

Recipe tip

Ham-wrapped trimmings
Cut 300g (10½oz) prosciutto into 5cm (2in) strips. Cut 6-8 chipolatas into 5cm (2in) lengths. Wrap 450g (1lb) cooked chestnuts and each piece of sausage in ham. Roast in oven with turkey for 15-20 minutes until ham is crisp and sausages are cooked.

5 Reduce temperature and continue roasting. Remove bacon when well done. Baste regularly. Remove foil 45 minutes before end of roasting.

Turkey roasting times *(weigh the bird after stuffing)*

weight	cooking time
3.6-4.5kg (8-10lb)	*30 minutes 220°C/425°F/gas 7; 3-3½ hrs 180°C/350°F/gas 4*
4.5-6.3kg (10-14lb)	*30 minutes 220°C/425°F/gas 7; 3½-4 hrs 180°C/350°F/gas 4*
6.3-8kg (14-18lb)	*30 minutes 220°C/425°F/gas 7; 4-4½ hrs 160°C/325°F/gas 3*

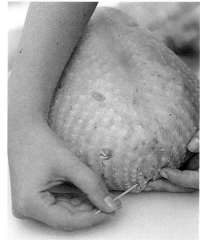

2 Loosen the skin around the neck end of the turkey. Delve inside to locate the wishbone and cut it out with a small sharp knife. (This makes carving easier.)

3 Pack stuffing into neck end of bird only, pushing it up under the skin. Fold the skin over the end and secure with cocktail sticks. Weigh turkey and calculate roasting time.

4 Put turkey in roasting tin, breast side up. Tie legs with string. Smear with butter, season and lay slices of bacon on the breast. Cover with foil. Roast for 30 minutes.

6 Rest cooked turkey for 30 minutes. Spoon off most of fat from tin. Add enough flour to absorb juices and create loose paste. Stir until smooth.

7 Place on hob, add stock and whisk until thickened. Add port and season. Cook, stirring, for 3-5 minutes until smooth and thick.

Variations on a theme

mushroom and apricot tarts

These succulent tarts mirror the apricot and sage flavouring used in the turkey stuffing. Simply pop them into the oven after you've taken the turkey out. Serve with a jug of onion gravy.

serves 4

pre-heat oven
190°C/375°F/gas 5

preparation time
20 minutes

cooking time 20 minutes

ingredients
1 medium onion
2 garlic cloves
3 tbsp olive oil
350g (12oz) mushrooms
2-3 tbsp red wine
500g (1lb 2oz) packet

puff pastry
85g (3oz) dried apricots, chopped
2 tsp fresh chopped sage
55g (2oz) fresh white breadcrumbs
55g (2oz) mature cheddar, grated (optional)
salt and pepper
1 egg, beaten

for the onion gravy
4 onions, finely chopped
knob of butter
1 tsp demerara sugar
300-450ml (10-15fl oz) carton vegetable stock
cornflour (optional)

equipment
1 baking sheet, buttered

1 Blitz onion and garlic in food processor until finely chopped. Heat oil in a large frying-pan and fry onion and garlic gently until golden.
2 Blitz mushrooms in a processor until finely chopped. Add to onions and cook, stirring, until soft – keeping heat high.
3 Add wine and cook briefly until liquid evaporates. Remove from heat to cool a little.
4 Meanwhile, roll out pastry to about 35cm (14in) square. Cut into 4 squares and trim edges.
5 Stir apricots, sage, breadcrumbs and cheese (if using) into mushroom mix and season. Pour in half egg and mix to bind.
6 Distribute mixture between pastry squares, forming square portions lying at an angle to pastry edges. Pull up corners of pastry to middle, sealing edges with egg. Peel the corners of pastry right back to expose filling. Brush pastry with egg and bake for 20 minutes until golden brown.

making onion gravy

1 In a large saucepan, cook onions in butter until golden. Add sugar, cooking for 1-2 minutes.
2 Add stock and cook, stirring, for 6-8 minutes. Thicken with 1 tbsp cornflour mixed with water if necessary.

why not try...

using giblets
To create a rich stock, put the washed turkey giblets in a pan with 1 onion, halved, and 850ml (1½ pints) water. Bring to a simmer, skim off any scum then add a few parsley stalks, 2 chopped celery stalks, 2 chopped carrots, 1 bay leaf and salt and pepper. Half-cover the pan and simmer for 1½-2 hours. Strain. Use the stock straight away or allow to cool and store in the fridge for 1-2 days. Reboil before use.

oyster stuffing
For a luxurious stuffing, try smoked oysters. Melt 115g (4oz) butter and cook 1 finely chopped onion until golden. Add 2 tbsp fresh white breadcrumbs and stir until butter is absorbed. Put in a bowl with 2 more tbsp breadcrumbs, 3 finely chopped sticks celery, 2 chopped garlic cloves and 1 tbsp fresh chopped herbs. Drain 2 cans smoked oysters, chop and add. Season and bind with cream.

nutty parcels
Adapt the mushroom tarts by replacing the apricots with 55g (2oz) coarsely chopped pine nuts and 3-4 finely chopped sun-dried tomatoes. Use parmesan instead of cheddar and 2 tsp dried basil instead of sage. Wrap in filo pastry instead of puff and brush with melted butter before baking.

roast duck

A crispy, succulent roast duck is an excellent choice for a dinner party

The beauty of roast duck is that it can be left to its own devices in the oven for 2-3 hours after an initial sealing at high heat. All you need to do is remove the fat from the pan once or twice during roasting.

You can buy fresh or frozen duck, with or without giblets, and in a range of sizes to suit the number of people you have to feed. Since duck is so fatty, it loses a lot of weight during roasting, so allow at least 450g (1lb) of meat per person. A 1.3-1.8kg (3-4lb) duck is plenty for 2-3 people. Allow a 2.7kg (6lb) duck for 4, and two 1.8kg (4lb) birds for 6. Try to buy a duck with giblets, which can be used to make a really sumptuous gravy.

Crisp and tasty

For crispy skin over the breast meat, cook the duck until the drumsticks and wings are frazzled. This doesn't matter since these parts don't have much meat. The breasts and thighs provide the bulk of the meat. Long slow cooking releases most of the fat and gives the crispy finish.

Duck and apple

In the main recipe the duck is served with a classic orange sauce. The variation is roast duck with sage, onion and apple stuffing balls, served with apple sauce on the side.

Gary's special touch

You can continue the duck flavour by using the leftover fat from the duck to make delicious roast potatoes. Just place the boiled potatoes in a roasting tin and pour the fat over them. When they are cooked, transfer them to a serving dish and sprinkle with salt and pepper and you will have a tasty side dish.

roast duck with orange sauce

You will need

serves 4

preparation time *15 minutes*
cooking time *3 hours 20 minutes*
pre-heat oven *220°C/425°F/gas 7*

ingredients
1 x 2.25-2.7kg (5-6lb) oven-ready duck, with giblets if available
salt and pepper
1 small orange, quartered
1 small onion, quartered
1 bunch watercress, washed

for the orange sauce
2 small Seville oranges, or sweet oranges plus the juice of 1 lemon
1 tbsp plain flour
600ml (1 pint) duck giblets stock (see page 142) or chicken stock (see page 8)
3 heaped tsp brown sugar
4-5 tbsp port
salt and pepper

equipment
roasting tin with a trivet or rack

1 Dry duck inside and out, place on rack in roasting tin, then prick skin all over with fork or skewer. Season with salt and pepper, then place orange and onion quarters inside.

For a crispy finish a duck needs to be dry before it goes into the oven. Dry inside and out with kitchen paper or a tea-towel. If possible, also leave in a cool dry place for several hours to air-dry. The initial oven temperature for roasting duck is hot (220°C/425°F/ gas 7) which ensures crispness. After 20 minutes turn down the heat. If you prefer the meat to be slightly pink at the end of roasting, then simply cut down a little on the roasting time.

Because duck is so fatty, it's not a good idea to stuff the cavity – the stuffing absorbs far too much fat and becomes almost inedible. But a quartered orange or lemon, or an apple and a quartered onion placed in the cavity does wonders for the flavour.

Dealing with duck fat
Duck is self-basting, producing more than enough fat for lubrication. Prick the skin all over with a fork so fat can escape, and season well inside and out with salt and pepper. Place the duck on a trivet in the roasting tin on a high oven shelf. Don't cover with foil. Spoon out or pour off the fat from the roasting tin once or twice during roasting time. Don't discard the fat – use it for roasting potatoes. When the cooking time is up, remove the duck from the tin, then tip it to drain fat and juices from the cavity.

Orange sauce
Oranges go well with duck – their sweetness and citrus sharpness cut through the fatty meat. Bitter Seville oranges are best – but if these are out of season, use sweeter oranges and add lemon juice for sharpness.

Use a large fat separator to remove as much fat as possible from the pan juices, then make the sauce with the remaining juices.

Tip
If you're in a great hurry, use marmalade instead of orange juice and zest to make the sauce. Just stir 2-3 tbsp marmalade into the gravy after you have thickened the duck juices with flour.

5 Pour juices back into tin, discarding fat. Sprinkle flour in, stir to a paste and cook over a low heat for 2-3 minutes to brown slightly.

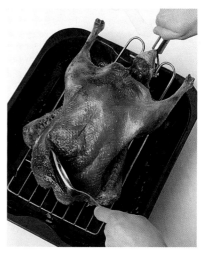

2 Roast duck on a high oven shelf. After 20 minutes turn heat down to 180°C/350°F/gas 4 and roast for 3 hours. Spoon out fat from roasting tin once or twice during this time.

3 Meanwhile, peel rinds from oranges, then cut them into thin shreds. Put in a pan, cover with boiling water and blanch for 5 minutes. Drain. Squeeze juice from oranges and reserve.

4 Remove duck from oven, tip up in tin to drain juices from body cavity, then take duck off the rack and leave to relax for 5-10 minutes. Remove fat from juices using a fat separator.

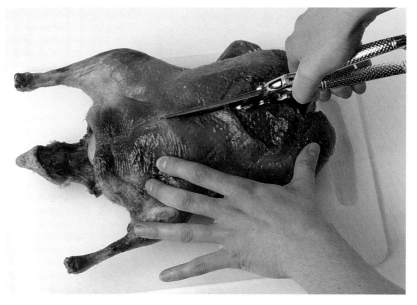

6 Add the stock gradually, stirring to make a smooth sauce, then add the sugar. Cook for 1-2 minutes, then add orange juice and rind. Season.

7 Divide duck into four by cutting along the breast and through the backbone, then across each half. Arrange on watercress. Stir port into orange sauce and serve immediately with the duck.

Variations on a theme

roast duck with sage, apple & onion balls

Roast duck served with apple sauce and sage, onion and apple balls.

serves 2
preparation time
15 minutes
cooking time *2 hours*
pre-heat oven
200°C/400°F/gas 6

ingredients
1 x 1.3-1.8kg (3-4lb) oven-ready duck
½ lemon, quartered
1 small onion, quartered
1 tsp plain flour
300ml (10fl oz) chicken stock (see page 8) or duck giblet stock (see above right)

for the stuffing
15g (½oz) butter
1 onion, finely chopped
1 small eating apple, peeled, cored and grated
115g (4oz) fresh white breadcrumbs
1 tbsp fresh chopped sage
1 small egg, beaten
salt and pepper

for the apple sauce
450g (1lb) cooking apples, peeled, cored and chopped
grated zest of ½ lemon
2 tbsp sugar
1 tbsp butter

equipment *as before*

1 Prepare duck as before. Season cavity and place onion and lemon inside. Prick skin and sprinkle with salt.
2 Put duck upside down on a rack in a roasting tin and roast for 30 minutes. Spoon off fat, turn duck over (breast-side up) and roast for 1-1½ hours. Test by piercing thigh with skewer. If juices run pink, continue cooking.
3 Meanwhile, make stuffing. Melt butter in pan and cook onion until soft. Cool. Stir in apple, egg breadcrumbs, sage, and seasoning. Shape into small balls and cook in roasting tin with duck for last 30 minutes of roasting time.
4 Make apple sauce. Put apples in heavy-bottomed pan with lemon zest, 3 tbsp water and sugar. Cover and cook slowly until apples are soft. Remove from heat and beat in butter. Add extra sugar to taste. Cool.
5 Remove duck from oven. Tip juices from cavity into bowl and reserve.
6 Make gravy. Pour off all but 1 tbsp fat from tin, stir over a low heat and scrape off sediment. Stir in flour, add reserved juices and stock and whisk until smooth. Season.
7 Carve duck. Serve with gravy and apple sauce in boats.

why not try...

making giblet stock
If your duck comes with giblets, you can make a delicious stock – the basis for gravy or sauce. To make stock, rinse giblets in cold water, then put into pan with 850ml (1½ pints) cold water, bring to boil and skim off scum. Add bouquet garni, 1 small onion, peeled and halved, 6 black peppercorns, 4 allspice berries and 1 small carrot, peeled and sliced. Bring back to boil, partially cover and simmer for 1 hour. Strain, discarding flavourings. Reserve for use in sauce or gravy.

cheerful cherries
Make a quick morello cherry sauce with 175g (6oz) morello cherry jam and 150ml (5fl oz) red wine. Put jam and wine in a saucepan and simmer for about 10 minutes. You can make this well in advance, then re-heat before serving.

orange and redcurrant
Mix 4 tbsp redcurrant jelly with grated zest of 1 orange. Stir in 1 tbsp fresh chopped mint for a stronger flavour. Or make with crab apple and rowan berry jelly – the rowan berries give a sharp tangy edge to the jelly that is superb with the duck. Blackcurrant, blackberry, cranberry and raspberry jellies are all suitable for this sauce.

⊦ roast chicken

Golden pot-roast chicken takes on the tastes of spring when served with a creamy sauce flavoured with fresh mint

Chicken that's been pot-roasted in a rich stock has all the taste of a roast, plus a moist tenderness that comes from soaking up the cooking juices. The golden colour comes from a quick browning in the frying-pan, but the main cooking is done with the bird surrounded by vegetables and stock. Regular basting ensures that all the flavours permeate the chicken.

It's so easy
There's very little preparation to do apart from chopping the vegetables to go into the stock. To finish the dish, simply let the cooking liquor bubble away for 10 minutes or so to produce a good rich sauce.

Simple to adapt
Try the same method for a bistro-style dish, using a classic French flavour combination of red wine and shallots – it makes a good warming meal for the winter season. For a spring option, try a lemon and sage version, or add extra veg-etables to make a more hearty meal in a pot. Make a strong cassoulet-style pot-roast by cooking a whole chicken with smoked ring sausage and butter beans and tomato.

Gary's special touch

I love doing the unexpected with a dish. Here I've used fresh mint as a spring-like flavouring for chicken, instead of the usual lamb. I add the mint twice – first to the stock during cooking, then to the finished sauce. Tossed in at the end, the mint stays green and gives off a lovely minty aroma as the pot-roast is served.

pot-roasting the minty chicken

You will need

serves 4-6

preparation time
20 minutes

cooking time
approximately 1½ hours

pre-heat oven
200°C/400°F/gas 6

ingredients
1.3-1.8kg (3-4lb) chicken
salt and pepper
2 tbsp olive oil
knob of butter
1 onion, roughly chopped
2 celery sticks, chopped
1 whole garlic clove
4-5 fresh mint leaves
850ml (1½ pints) chicken stock (see page 8) or water

for the sauce
225g (8oz) frozen peas
225g (8oz) button or chestnut mushrooms
150ml (5fl oz) double cream
55g (2oz) cold butter, cubed, plus an extra knob of butter
6 fresh mint leaves, finely shredded, plus extra mint to garnish
salt and pepper

equipment
covered casserole dish or earthenware braising pot

Traditional pot-roasting is a long, slow process where tougher cuts of meat are left to tenderize for hours in a sealed pot in a warm oven.

A faster method
The chicken recipes here are a faster adaptation of the traditional method, but the chicken still tastes wonderful. The vegetables and chicken are sautéed first to add colour and to seal in flavour. Then they're placed in a pot, covered with a close-fitting lid and cooked at a medium temperature for the same time that it takes for a conventional roast.

The ingredient that transforms the cooking is liquid – the recipes here use chicken stock – which adds flavour and ensures that there is no risk of burning. Vegetable stock or water, further flavoured with wine, herbs or spices, is also suitable for quick pot-roasting.

I Season the chicken with salt and pepper. Heat the oil and butter in a frying-pan and brown the chicken on all sides until very golden. Put the chicken into the casserole dish.

4 For the sauce, cook the peas in boiling salted water until tender. Quarter the mushroom caps, season and shallow-fry in the knob of butter until golden and tender.

5 Strain the chicken cooking liquor into a pan and boil rapidly to reduce it by half; this will take about 10 minutes. Add the cream and simmer for 3-4 minutes.

Easy carving

Allow the chicken to 'rest' covered in foil. It makes it much easier to cut into clean pieces.

2 In the same frying-pan sauté the onion, celery, the stalks cut from the mushrooms being used in the sauce, the whole garlic clove and the mint leaves for 4-5 minutes. Add to the chicken.

3 Warm the stock and pour over the chicken and vegetables in the pot. Cover. Cook in the oven for 1 hour, basting occasionally. When done, remove the bird and let it rest, loosely covered in foil.

1 First remove the legs. Steadying the chicken with a fork, cut between the thigh and breast with a sharp knife. Push the thigh outwards to find and cut through the hip joint. Split the leg in two by cutting the joint between thigh and drumstick.

6 Carve the chicken following the carving instructions (see right). Add mushrooms and peas to the sauce and warm through. Stir in the cubed butter and season with salt and pepper. Then add the shredded mint and serve immediately, garnishing each portion with extra mint.

2 To remove a breast, with the neck end nearest you, cut along one side of the breastbone, easing the meat away from it. Pull the wing off and continue cutting down against the bone to the wing joint, until the breast comes free. Cut the breast diagonally in half.

Repeat for the other side to end up with 4 halves of breast, 2 drumsticks, 2 thighs and 2 wings.

Variations on a theme

pot-roast chicken in red wine

Adding wine, bacon and whole shallots to the cooking stock gives a rich coq-au-vin flavour to the bird.

Once again the stock is reduced to form a good sauce, then cold butter is beaten in to make it glossy. Garnish the chicken with a lavish sprinkling of parsley and croutons for extra colour and crunch.

preparation time
20 minutes
cooking time
approximately 1½ hours
pre-heat oven
200°C/400°/gas 6

ingredients
1.3-1.8kg (3-4lb) chicken
knob of butter
2 tbsp olive oil
115-175g (4-6oz) shallots
115-175g (4-6oz) button onions
4 rashers streaky bacon, cut into thick strips
chopped parsley to garnish
crispy croutons to garnish (see Tip, right)

for the sauce
300ml (10fl oz) chicken stock (see page 8)
4 glasses good red wine
25-55g (1-2oz) cold butter
salt and pepper

1 Heat butter and oil in a large frying-pan, add the shallots, button onions and bacon, and sauté until they begin to take some colour. Put into the cooking pot.
2 Seal bird as before, and put into the pot.
3 Pour the stock and wine over the chicken, cover and cook in the oven as before.
4 Once cooked, remove the chicken from the pot and leave to rest, covered. Take out the vegetables and keep warm.
5 To make the sauce, strain the cooking juices into a pan, and boil rapidly to reduce them by half. Beat in the cold butter and stir until melted. Season to taste.
6 Serve chicken with the sauce and a garnish of chopped parsley and crispy croutons.

Tip

For perfect croutons, remove the crusts from some thickly sliced white bread and cut into cubes. Sauté in oil and butter in a frying-pan until evenly browned. Drain on kitchen paper. Reheat in oven, wrapped in foil.

why not try...

lemon sage chicken
Season and seal chicken as before. Put a halved lemon and 2 sprigs of sage into its cavity. Sprinkle with lemon zest and pot-roast for 1 hour in 600ml (1 pint) of stock. Remove and rest chicken. To make a sauce, reduce cooking liquor by half, add 1 large tbsp double cream, salt and pepper, extra lemon juice and chopped fresh sage. Serve with buttery noodles sprinkled with a little fresh sage.

all-in-one pot roast
Add large chunks of vegetables such as swedes, potatoes, carrots, onions and leeks to the pot with the sealed, seasoned chicken and cook in chicken stock. Then reduce the sauce or treat the dish as a soup-style stew.

quick smoky chicken
Pot-roast the chicken with a whole smoked ring sausage in the original stock and vegetable mixture. After 30 minutes, add a can of drained butter beans. Remove the chicken when ready and cut the sausage into pieces. Reduce the cooking liquid, stir in 4 tbsp chopped tomatoes or passata and season with salt and pepper.

blanquettes

In this classic French dish, tender chicken is gently poached and served in a creamy sauce with button mushrooms and onions

A blanquette is a stew or ragout of pale meat – poultry, veal or lamb – cooked in white stock or water with a variety of aromatic flavourings. The name probably derives from the French word *blanc* – meaning white.

Classic cuisine

The sauce for the blanquette is created by thickening the clear poaching stock with a basic roux, then enriching it with cream and egg yolks.

Throughout the cooking process you must be careful not to allow the chicken or the sauce to brown. The blanquette is meant to be very pale in colour and delicate in taste. Flavour comes from using the poaching liquid in the sauce – and from the onions, mushrooms and white wine. A garnish of chopped fresh parsley lifts the overall colour of the dish.

Make the most of turkey

Turkey can also be made into a blanquette. In the variation recipe, the poaching liquid is enriched with sherry, while the sauce is flavoured with chopped fresh sage for a vibrant herby flavour. Baby carrots and parsnips add a mild sweetness and enhance the colour and texture of the overall dish.

Gary's special touch

To highlight the pale, delicate nature of these blanquettes, I've chosen to make crispy golden croûtons with the chicken recipe, and a triangle of polenta with the turkey. Croûtons give a nice change of texture against the soft chicken, while the polenta helps soak up all the delicious turkey juices.

making the blanquette of chicken

You will need

serves 4	150ml (5fl oz) dry white wine
preparation time 15 minutes	salt and white pepper
cooking time 30-35 minutes	2 sprigs fresh thyme
	2 tbsp butter
	2 tbsp plain flour
ingredients	225g (8oz) button mushrooms
700g (1½lb) skinless, boneless chicken	150ml (5fl oz) double cream
breasts, sliced into 3-4 pieces each	2 egg yolks
225g (8oz) button onions or shallots	a few drops of lemon juice
600ml (1 pint) chicken stock (see	croûtons (see Recipe tip, below)
page 8)	

Blanquette of chicken is a popular dish that is quick enough for a midweek meal, but also special enough to serve to guests for lunch or dinner at the weekend.

The emphasis is firmly on the pure chicken flavour and the super-creamy sauce – which is based on the stock in which the chicken is poached. The onions and button mushrooms in the sauce blend well with the chicken pieces and complement the classic simplicity of the dish.

If possible, use organic or free-range chicken – it has a much deeper flavour than battery-reared chicken.

The right stock

The stock must be clear and skimmed of excess fat; otherwise it may make the sauce greasy. Skim off any fat from the surface with a metal spoon before using – or use a fat separator.

If you don't have time to make your own stock, use fresh chilled stock and dilute with half the volume of water. Take care with seasoning if you use a bought stock as these are sometimes very salty and can over-whelm the flavour of the chicken.

Take it easy

There is no need to buy a whole chicken for this blanquette recipe. Ready-prepared skinless, boneless chicken breasts are ideal and only need to be sliced before cooking. Serve with saffron rice timbales and garnish with crispy croûtons for a good crunchy contrast.

Recipe tip

Making croûtons

ingredients
2-3 slices of day-old white bread
oil for frying
knob of butter (optional)

Remove and discard the crusts from the bread, then cut the bread into 1-2cm (½in) cubes. Heat a dash of oil in a frying-pan with the knob of butter (if using) until it foams. Add the bread cubes and toss over a high heat for about 2 minutes until crisp and golden. Drain on kitchen paper, then serve.

1 Put the chicken pieces into the pan with onions, stock, wine, seasoning and thyme. Bring to the boil slowly, then simmer for 10-15 minutes.

4 Return the chicken and onions to the pan. Add the mushrooms and simmer gently for 3 minutes, or until the mushrooms are cooked.

2 Remove chicken and onions. Boil the liquid for 5 minutes, to reduce slightly. Strain into a jug, cool slightly, then skim off excess fat. Wash the pan.

3 Melt butter in pan over low heat. Stir in flour and cook for 1 minute without browning. Stir in poaching liquid. Cook for 5 minutes to a smooth sauce.

Cook's notes

For a sunny-coloured saffron rice to accompany the chicken, put a good pinch of saffron strands into a jug, pour 150ml (5fl oz) of boiling water on top and leave to infuse for at least 20 minutes until the water has turned yellow. Strain the liquid and discard the saffron strands.

Pour the strained liquid into the pan of water in which you're going to boil the rice. As it cooks, the rice takes on a lovely yellow colour. Firmly pack single portions of the cooked rice into buttered moulds or ramekins, then turn out on to individual plates to serve.

5 Combine cream and egg yolks in a bowl. Stir in a little sauce, add mixture to pan and simmer for 2 minutes, until thickened. Add lemon juice.

6 Taste the sauce, then season as needed. Serve at once, garnished with chopped fresh parsley and golden croûtons. Accompany with rice (see Cook's notes, above) or new potatoes.

Variations on a theme

blanquette of turkey with sage, baby carrots and parsnips

Sage and sherry make a tasty sauce for turkey.

serves 6

preparation time
15 minutes

cooking time *35 minutes*

ingredients
700g (1½lb) turkey breast steaks
600ml (1 pint) chicken or turkey stock (see page 8)
150ml (5fl oz) white wine
salt and black pepper
225g (8oz) baby carrots
225g (8oz) baby parsnips
2 tbsp pale sherry
2 tbsp butter
2 tbsp plain flour
150ml (5fl oz) double cream
2 egg yolks
1 tbsp chopped fresh sage
triangles of polenta, cut from a ready-made block

1 Cut the turkey steaks crosswise into 3-4 thick pieces. Bring stock, wine and seasoning to boil in a pan. Add turkey, carrots and parsnips. Simmer for 10-15 minutes, or until turkey is just cooked.
2 Remove turkey from pan and reserve. Simmer vegetables in stock for a further 2 minutes until just tender. Remove vegetables and set aside.
3 Add sherry to pan and boil for 5 minutes to reduce a little. Strain liquid into a jug, cool slightly and skim off excess fat. Wash pan.
4 Melt butter in pan over a low heat, stir in flour and cook without browning for 1 minute. Stir in cooking liquid, and cook for 5 minutes to form a smooth sauce.
5 Return turkey and vegetables to pan. Heat through for 3 minutes. Mix cream, egg yolks and chopped sage in a bowl. Stir in a little sauce, then pour into pan. Stir over a low heat for 2 minutes, without boiling, until thickened.
6 Adjust seasoning, then garnish with sage leaves and grilled polenta.

why not try...

extra meaty
Stir in 55g (2oz) chopped crispy bacon, Parma or prosciutto ham to either recipe before you add the eggs and cream.

other roots
If you can't get baby vegetables for the variation recipe, use standard carrots and parsnips and cut into 5mm (¼in) slices. For a pretty presentation on a special occasion, stamp the slices into shapes with *petit fours* cutters. You can also use other root vegetables, such as turnip, swede or sweet potato.

touch of spice
For a delicate spicy flavour, add ½ tsp grated nutmeg or mace to the chicken blanquette – it goes well with the other flavours.

festive cheer
In the turkey blanquette, replace either the carrots or parsnips with whole peeled, cooked canned chestnuts.

blanquette pie
Make either of the recipes and transfer to a baking dish. Cover with mashed potato or a layer of puff pastry. Bake at 200°C/400°F/gas 6 for 30 minutes, or until golden.

chicken kiev

Cut into a crisply coated chicken kiev to reveal a divine melted herby butter filling

An unfortunate victim of its own popularity, this great classic deserves reappraisal. As with any recipe, the finished dish is only as good as its ingredients, and chicken kiev is no exception. Make this with good-quality chicken and the freshest of herbs and you'll have a dish worthy of any dinner party.

Prepare in advance

Chicken kiev is a recipe that involves advance preparation. There are several stages of chilling necessary to ensure the filling is completely firm before deep-frying. If you try to reduce the chilling time or shallow-fry the kievs instead of deep-frying, you'll end up with a soggy mess. However, the advance preparation can be to your advantage. If you make the butter filling and prepare the chicken the night before and coat and chill the kievs in the morning, you'll only have to spend 30 minutes cooking before you serve the meal.

Butter flavours

Traditionally, chicken kiev is filled with a herby butter – the addition of garlic is a more recent innovation. The variation uses porcini mushrooms in the butter filling and polenta and ciabatta breadcrumbs for the coating.

Gary's special touch

I prefer to buy the chicken for this dish from the butcher – tell him what you're planning to make and he'll be able to get you exactly the right cut. It's best to use breasts with the wing bones still attached (also known as chicken supremes) as the bone makes a very useful handle – both for cooking and eating.

making chicken kiev

You will need

serves 4

preparation time *40 minutes, plus at least 3 hours chilling*

cooking time *25 minutes*

ingredients

4 chicken breasts with wing bones still attached

flour, for dusting

2 large eggs, beaten

300g (10½oz) fresh white breadcrumbs, seasoned with salt and pepper

vegetable oil, for deep-frying

for the butter filling

115g (4oz) softened butter

2 tbsp chopped fresh parsley

1 tbsp chopped fresh tarragon

1 tbsp chopped fresh chives

juice and grated zest of 1 fresh lemon

salt and pepper

equipment

deep-fat fryer or large saucepan for deep-frying

The secret of success for chicken kiev is to make sure that the butter filling is well chilled before you add it to the chicken and that the coated kiev is also well chilled before deep-frying. To make the butter filling you simply work the ingredients together and then form the mixture into rough sausage shapes. These are then chilled for at least an hour.

Flattening the chicken

To prepare the chicken breasts, you need to remove the fillets – small flaps of meat under each breast. These are then beaten between two sheets of greaseproof paper until roughly doubled in size. Don't be too vigorous, or you might make holes in the chicken. The large pieces of breast meat are also flattened.

It's important to wipe the chicken dry before wrapping it around the butter filling. If the chicken is wet, the butter won't adhere to the meat properly. Place the butter on the underside of the larger pieces of chicken breast – where the fillets were cut away – and then cover the butter with the flattened fillets. The meat is then wrapped around the butter so that it's completely enclosed.

Coating tips

Put the flour, egg and breadcrumbs in three shallow dishes – it makes coating the kievs a lot easier. Holding each chicken parcel by the bone, roll it first in the flour, then in the egg and then in the breadcrumbs until evenly coated. Lay each one on a baking tray so that they don't touch and chill for a minimum of 30 minutes. Repeat the coating process and then chill the kievs for a further 30 minutes.

To deep-fry the chicken you'll need enough oil to completely cover the breasts. Make sure that the breasts don't touch each other during deep-frying or they'll fuse together. You'll probably find that you have to fry them in at least two batches.

Blend the butter filling ingredients together. Chill until slightly firm and then, with cold hands, form into 4 sausage shapes. Chill again for at least 1 hour until solid.

5 Cover the butter with the flattened fillet. Press the two pieces of chicken together so that the butter is sealed within the meat.

2 Cut away the fillet – the small flap of meat that you'll find under the breast. Lay this between 2 sheets of greaseproof paper and flatten with a rolling pin.

3 Take the remaining larger piece of breast and lay this between 2 sheets of greaseproof too. Using a rolling pin, flatten the meat. Wipe all the chicken pieces dry.

4 Lay the larger piece of breast on a chopping board so that side which the fillet was cut away from is facing upwards. Place a piece of the chilled butter on top.

6 Dust with flour and dip in egg and breadcrumbs; chill for 30 minutes. Coat again with flour, egg and breadcrumbs; chill for 30 minutes more.

7 Heat the oil to about 160°C (300°F) and deep-fry the coated chicken for 10-12 minutes, until crisp and golden, working in batches if necessary. Drain on kitchen paper.

Variations on a theme

porcini and polenta kiev

An Italian-style twist on this great classic, served with griddled polenta.

serves 4
preparation time
*40 minutes, plus
30 minutes soaking, and
at least 3 hours chilling*
cooking time
25 minutes

ingredients
*4 chicken breasts with
wing bones still attached
flour, for dusting
1 large egg, beaten
75g (2¾oz) polenta
75g (2¾oz) fresh ciabatta
breadcrumbs
vegetable oil, for deep-
frying*

for the butter filling
*25g (1oz) dried porcini
mushrooms
115g (4oz) softened
butter
3 tbsp chopped fresh
chervil
1 tsp grated lemon zest
2 tsp lemon juice
salt and pepper*

equipment
*deep-fat fryer or large
saucepan for deep-frying*

1 Cover the porcini with water and leave to soak for 30 minutes.
2 Drain the porcini, reserving 2 tsp of the soaking liquid. Finely chop the porcini and put

in a bowl with the other filling ingredients and the reserved soaking liquid. Beat until well mixed and chill until slightly firm. Form into 4 sausage shapes. Chill for at least 1 hour until solid.
3 Cut away the fillets from under the breasts. Flatten between 2 sheets of greaseproof paper with a rolling pin. Flatten the larger pieces of breast too. Wipe all the chicken dry.
4 Lay the larger pieces so that the side where the fillets were is facing upwards. Place the butter on top and cover with the fillets. Press the pieces of chicken together to seal in the butter filling completely.
5 Mix together the polenta and ciabatta breadcrumbs. Dust the chicken parcels with flour and dip in the egg and then in the polenta and bread mixture. Chill for 30 minutes. Coat the chicken with flour, egg and the polenta mix again; chill for a further 30 minutes.
6 Heat the oil to about 160°C (300°F) and deep-fry the coated chicken kievs for 10-12 minutes, until crisp and golden, working in batches if necessary.

why not try...

a garlic filling
Mixing some garlic into the filling for chicken kiev has become something of a trend and it does give the melted butter a wonderful intense flavour. All you need to do is finely chop 2 garlic cloves and mix these in with the other ingredients for the butter filling.

different herbs
Although parsley, tarragon and chives are a traditional combination of herbs for chicken kiev, you could experiment with any number of different mixes. Why not try chervil, sage, dill, fennel or rosemary?

eats well with...

The rich buttery filling of these recipes needs the simplest of side dishes as accompaniment. Plain boiled new potatoes and some green vegetables – broccoli, mangetout or spinach, for instance – are ideal to serve with the traditional chicken kiev. You can use the potatoes and vegetables to mop up the melted herby butter as it oozes out of the crispy kiev.

single-crust meat pies

Break through the crisp single-crust pastry lid and you'll find a tender filling – creamy chicken and leek or robust steak and onion – all a meat pie should be

Meat pies are always popular and it's not hard to see why. Tender meat in a rich sauce with lots of lovely flavourings, and a featherlight single-crust pastry shell make a satisfying combination of tastes and textures.

Quick and tasty

This combination of succulent chicken and green leeks looks very appetizing and the sauce is creamy and light. Use chicken breasts or a mix of breast and leg meat – make sure you don't overcook the chicken as it will turn stringy. The single-crust puff pastry topping avoids the need for blind baking, and you can make the filling a day or two in advance and keep it in the fridge until needed – saving time.

Steak filling

Another classic pie is steak and onion. This takes slightly longer than the chicken and leek pie as the steak is braised slowly with onions and red wine for a rich, full-bodied flavour. Shortcrust pastry complements this filling very well. You can also vary the pastry – try rich shortcrust pepper pastry, nutty pastry or wholemeal pastry (see page 9-10, for details).

Gary's special touch

I prefer to cook fillings in advance, rather than cooking pies or puddings from raw. Cooking the fillings completely before covering with the pastry shell means I have time to get the consistency and amount of the sauce just right before baking. Ensure the filling is cooled completely before covering with the pastry.

making the chicken and leek pie

You will need

serves 4

preparation time
45-50 minutes, plus 1 hour to rest the pastry

cooking time
50-60 minutes for the filling plus 50 minutes to 1 hour to bake the pie

pre-heat oven
200°C/400°F/gas 6

ingredients
350g (12oz) quick puff pastry (see page 10)
15g (½oz) butter
6 boneless chicken breasts, skinned

and cut into 2.5cm (1in) dice
2 medium onions, diced
1 garlic clove, crushed
600ml (1 pint) chicken stock (see page 8)
salt and pepper
2 medium leeks, trimmed and cut into 2.5cm (1in) pieces
300ml (10fl oz) double cream
a squeeze of lemon juice
1 egg, lightly beaten

equipment
2 litre (3½ pint) pie dish with a rim for anchoring the pastry

1 Make the quick puff pastry (see page 10), rolling, folding and refrigerating the pastry three times.

Here the chicken, leek and cream filling is cooked completely before it is put into the pie dish and covered with pastry. This allows you to check – and adjust – the amount of sauce needed. Make sure you allow the filling to cool completely before covering with the pastry, otherwise it will turn soggy. You can make your own pastry (see page 10). However, if you are in a hurry, you can use bought puff or shortcrust pastry.

If there is any sauce left after you have filled the pie dish, save it for serving with the pie – just warm it through gently before serving.

Short cut
Make use of leftover pieces of roast chicken or turkey for an even quicker pie. Leftover poultry, which is already cooked, just needs heating through thoroughly after being added to the pan – in this case make plenty of sauce to give a moist filling.

5 Lift the chicken and onions from the stock with a slotted spoon, put into a bowl and reserve. Strain the stock through a sieve, transfer into a clean saucepan then boil until reduced by two-thirds.

6 Put the cream in a pan, simmer and reduce for 10 minutes to a thick coating sauce. Adjust seasoning and add a squeeze of lemon juice.

2 Meanwhile, melt the butter in a saucepan, add the chicken and cook for 2-3 minutes until the chicken is white – don't let it brown.

3 Add the onions and cook for 3-4 minutes. Add the garlic, stock and seasoning, bring to simmering point and cook for 15-20 minutes until the chicken is tender.

4 Meanwhile, plunge the leeks into salted boiling water and cook for 2-3 minutes until just tender. Drain thoroughly and leave to cool.

7 Mix the chicken and the leeks and add to the sauce. Pour into the pie dish, reserving any left-over sauce to serve with the pie. Leave to cool.

8 Roll out the pastry and use to cover the pie. Score a pattern on top, make a hole in the centre, glaze with beaten egg and bake in the oven for 40 minutes until golden. Serve with vegetables.

Variations on a theme

individual steak, onion and red wine pies

Robust steak and full-bodied red wine have a special affinity and are ideal together under crisp shortcrust pastry. Individual pies make serving easy.

serves 4

preparation time
35 minutes

cooking time *1½ hours braising, 40 minutes baking*

pre-heat oven
170°C/325°F/gas 3 for filling; 200°C/400°F/gas 6 for baking

ingredients
900g (2lb) beef stewing steak, cubed

1-2 tbsp seasoned flour
1 tbsp olive oil
15g (½oz) butter
4 large onions, sliced
10 crushed juniper berries
1-2 sprigs thyme
1 bay leaf
salt and pepper
1 bottle red wine
150ml (5fl oz) beef stock (see page 8)
350g (12oz) shortcrust pastry (see page 9-10)
1 egg, beaten

equipment
4 individual pie dishes

1 Toss steak in flour. Melt half the butter with half the oil in a pan and brown the steak. Remove steak and keep warm.
2 Melt rest of butter and oil in the pan, and fry onions until soft.
3 Add berries, herbs, seasoning and red wine. Reduce liquid by half.
4 Add steak and stock, cover and braise in oven for 1½ hours until tender. Leave to cool.
5 Make the shortcrust pastry, then rest it in the fridge for 20-30 minutes.
6 Put meat and sauce in pie dishes (remove bay leaf and thyme). Divide pastry into 4, roll out, use to top each dish and brush with egg. Bake for 30-40 minutes until crisp. Serve with vegetables.

why not try...

There are many delicious fillings that you can use in your pie – and try experimenting with the type of pastry too.

steak and mushroom pie
Use the same weight of braising steak (or venison), 2 chopped onions, and 250g (9oz) button mushrooms. Cook the mushrooms with the onions and continue as for the steak, onion and red wine pies. Season with ½ tsp mace rather than juniper berries.

lamb and mushroom pie
Use diced lamb, sliced onions and sliced or whole button mushrooms, and flavour with 1 tbsp redcurrant jelly. For the pastry, mix 1-2 tbsp chopped mint into the flour for a subtle flavour that complements the lamb perfectly.

chicken and vegetable pie
Use half the quantity of chicken breast in the main recipe and boil baby carrots, baby sweetcorn and mangetout with the leeks. Another idea is to add sliced mushrooms, cooking them after the onions, to give the pie extra flavour. Or include crisply fried bacon or pancetta – this gives a delicious savoury-sweet taste. You can also substitute any game birds, such as pigeon or pheasant, for the chicken.

risotto

Constantly stirring a special Italian rice over a low heat produces a creamy risotto. A medley of wild mushrooms adds a rich, earthy flavour

Making a basic risotto involves frying onions in butter, stirring in risotto rice and gradually adding stock little by little until the rice is tender and creamy. Meat, fish or vegetables add flavour and body to the risotto. Extra butter is stirred in at the end of cooking for more creaminess.

Go wild with mushrooms

Unlike numerous other vegetables, mushrooms do not disintegrate during the time it takes to cook a risotto. As the rice cooks, the rich mushroom juices permeate the whole dish.

Wild mushrooms are ideal for this dish as they have a wonderful flavour. Fresh wild mushrooms, such as morels, porcini (ceps) and chanterelles, are only available in the autumn, but you can use half the quantity of dried instead and save the soaking liquid to add to the stock.

Other grains

For the variation recipe, pearl barley replaces the rice. The dish is finished with a mustard dressing and a bright green parsley coulis, both of which you can make in advance.

Gary's special touch

To do justice to the wonderfully creamy texture of the risotto, I've used a mixture of oyster, wild and button mushrooms to give this vegetarian dish a rich, luxurious flavour too. I've also used freshly ground white pepper – it has a milder flavour than black and blends very well with the pale risotto.

making wild mushroom risotto

I Melt the butter in a large saucepan or frying-pan and add the onions and garlic. Sweat for 3 minutes, until soft. Heat the stock in a pan and keep covered over a low heat.

Classic Italian risottos are made with special Italian risotto rice, such as arborio, canaroli and vialone. The grains have a thick outer layer of starch which dissolves when stirred during cooking to produce the famous creamy texture of a risotto. At the same time, the rice retains a delicate 'bite' at the centre of each grain.

Typically, risotto rice absorbs more liquid than any other type of rice, allowing the grains to soak up plenty of flavour from the stock.

The best butter

In a risotto, the butter is not just used for frying – it acts as a flavouring in its own right. Stirred in after cooking also adds a final touch of creaminess.

Unsalted butter guarantees the best flavour – you can season with extra salt to taste as needed. Salted butter often has an inferior flavour as some manufacturers use salt to disguise the taste of low grade fat.

State of the stock

Home-made stock gives this dish the best flavour. If you use stock cubes,

be careful with the salt as they are already very highly seasoned. Make sure you keep the stock hot while you cook the risotto as cold stock will cool the rice and slow down the cooking of the grains.

Keep stirring

When making risottos, it is important to add the stock gradually and to stir the rice mixture almost continuously until each addition is fully absorbed. This softens the rice grains and keeps the mixture creamy. Use a large wooden spoon to stir the risotto and keep the heat low under the pan so it does not catch.

4 Continue adding the stock, a ladle at a time, stirring constantly, until each amount is absorbed and the rice is tender. This should take 20 minutes.

2 Stir in the sliced mushrooms to the onion mix and cook gently for a further 3 minutes. Add the rice and stir over a low heat until the grains are slightly softened and coated in butter.

3 Add a ladle of the hot stock to the pan. Stir the mixture constantly over a low heat until all the stock is absorbed. Take care not to let the mixture stick to the bottom of the pan.

Watchpoint!

Avoiding burnt pans

To prevent the rice sticking to the bottom of the pan and burning, keep the risotto topped up with hot stock and try not to leave it unattended. If you do leave the pan even for a few minutes, add more stock than usual and turn down the heat to very low.

If, for any reason, the rice does catch, transfer the risotto to a clean pan to finish cooking, leaving the burnt bits behind. Do not stir the burnt bits into the risotto as they will spoil its delicate flavour and texture.

5 Finely grate three-quarters of the parmesan cheese. Use a potato peeler or cheese slicer to shave the remaining cheese into flakes.

6 Season the risotto with salt and pepper. Stir in the grated cheese and the extra butter. Serve at once, garnished with the parmesan cheese shavings.

Variations on a theme

barley risotto with mustard dressing and parsley coulis

This dish is finished in the oven as the barley does not need constant stirring to produce a creamy result. Serve with turkey or chicken saltimbocca, as an unusual side dish.

serves 4-6
pre-heat oven
200°C/400°F/gas 6
preparation time
15 minutes
cooking time *1 hour*

ingredients
2 tbsp olive oil
2 onions, finely chopped
225g (8oz) pearl barley
2 tbsp Dijon mustard
1.2 litres (2 pints) ready-made vegetable stock
55g (2oz) unsalted butter
salt and pepper

for the parsley coulis
1 bunch flatleaf parsley
2 tbsp ice cold water
4 tbsp olive oil

for the dressing
1 tsp mustard
2 tsp white wine vinegar
2 tbsp walnut oil
2 tbsp groundnut oil

1 For the coulis, blanch most of the parsley in boiling water for a few seconds. Refresh in cold water. Drain, then liquidize with the water. Slowly blend in the oil. Season, then sieve. Chill.
2 Heat the oil in an heatproof casserole dish. Sweat the onions until soft. Stir in the barley and mustard and cook for 2 minutes. Stir in 850ml (1½ pints) stock. Bring to a simmer, then cover with greaseproof paper and a tight lid.
3 Bake for 45 minutes, stirring in the remaining stock after 25 minutes.
4 Whisk together the dressing ingredients and season well.
5 Stir the butter and dressing into the risotto. Season again, then serve topped with the coulis and remaining parsley.

why not try...

Risotto is such a versatile dish, you can add a great variety of ingredients to it, either at the start of cooking or near the end to warm through.

breakfast favourites
Stir crispy pieces of bacon or black pudding into the finished barley risotto.

tomato and paprika
For a pinky-red risotto, stir 3 tbsp tomato purée into the stock before heating. Stir in 3 tsp paprika when adding the rice to the pan and add 450g (1lb) chopped, skinned fresh or tinned tomatoes.

taste of the sea
Add 225g (8oz) cooked peeled prawns or white crab meat near the end of cooking.

wholegrain mustard
Use wholegrain mustard in the barley risotto and the dressing.

cut the fat
Halve the quantity of butter for a less rich finish.

blue cheese
Replace the parmesan with blue cheese, such as stilton.

eats well with...

Serve risotto on its own with a tomato and onion side salad, or as an accompaniment to poultry, for example, roast chicken.

rice galettes

Based on a flavourful and sustaining risotto mix, fried savoury cakes are great for winter eating

A galette is simply a flat round cake, which can be sweet or savoury. The term galette comes from *galet*, meaning a flat, smooth pebble which is perfect for skimming across water. The French also use galette to refer to some pancakes, as well as cookies.

Galettes can be made from pastry, potato, rice or other cereals. Savoury galettes are delicious, especially when enhanced with onions, cheese, herbs, fish, eggs, tomatoes and an assortment of vegetables.

Here the recipes are based on rice. Arborio rice is cooked with vegetables or cheese and herbs to make a risotto. This is then cooled until firm, cut into cakes and shallow-fried in oil and butter.

Galettes galore

The main recipe is a chestnut, onion and Brussels sprout risotto cake, which is served with a rich brandy herb butter.

The cheese and herb galette, coloured a soft yellow with saffron, is full of good flavours too – onion, garlic, fresh herbs, and both taleggio and parmesan cheese. It's served cut into generous wedges, accompanied by a green salad. Taleggio is a rich, soft cheese from Italy; if you can't find it in your supermarket, use fontina instead.

Gary's special touch

I find rice galettes are amazingly versatile. You can make them totally vegetarian, like these, or add little pieces of meat or fish. Serve them as a light main course or as a side dish. Liven up the galettes with a rich buttery sauce containing shallots, brandy and parsley. Fried sage leaves are the finishing touch.

Brussels sprout and chestnut galette

You will need

serves 4-6

preparation time 20 minutes, plus cooling and chilling time for risotto

cooking time 50 minutes

ingredients

115g (4oz) unsalted butter

4 onions, finely chopped

225g (8oz) Arborio rice

1.2 litres (2 pints) ready-made vegetable stock, hot

2 tbsp freshly grated parmesan

225g (8oz) Brussels sprouts, finely shredded and cooked in boiling water for 1 minute, then drained

55-85g (2-3oz) cooked vacuum-packed chestnuts, chopped (or canned chestnuts, or dried)

salt and pepper

3 tbsp plain flour

2-3 eggs, beaten

225g (8oz) fresh white breadcrumbs

oil and butter for frying

for the brandy herb butter

1 tbsp chopped shallots

2 tbsp brandy

300ml (10fl oz) ready-made vegetable stock

25-55g (1-2oz) unsalted butter

2 tsp chopped fresh flatleaf parsley

salt and pepper

to garnish

about 20 fresh sage leaves

flour for dusting

a pinch of cayenne pepper

equipment

large frying-pan; 25 x 15cm (10 x 6in) deep tin lined with plastic wrap; 7.5cm (3in) diameter round pastry cutter; shallow sauté pan

1 Make risotto. Melt butter in a sauté pan, add onions and cook until softened. Add rice and cook for 3-5 minutes. Add 1-2 ladles of hot stock and cook until stock is fully absorbed.

Make sure the rice absorbs all the liquid as you make the risotto. Since it needs to set firm enough to cut out round or square cakes, it mustn't be wet and juicy. If it is too wet, the cakes will not stay in shape. Lining the tray with plastic wrap makes turning out the set risotto very easy.

Any chestnuts

If you have got some leftover roast chestnuts, then use those – but if you haven't, then make life easy for yourself and use vacuum-packed, ready-cooked chestnuts. Or, if you can find them, canned chestnuts are good. You can even buy dried chestnuts and reconstitute them.

Time management

You can make the risotto cakes well in advance, breadcrumb them ready for frying, then keep them covered in the fridge until needed. Serve with a big bowl of mixed salad.

Tip

If you are making round cakes, the risotto remaining after the rounds have been cut can be rolled into balls and breadcrumbed for shallow-frying or deep-frying. These are very good if rolled small and served as hot crispy canapés.

5 Heat a little oil and butter in the frying-pan and shallow-fry the cakes on both sides until golden-brown, if necessary in two batches. Keep them warm.

2 Keep adding hot stock, ladle by ladle, until the rice is tender – about 20-25 minutes. Season, then add parmesan. Stir in sprouts and chestnuts, with a drop more stock if needed.

3 Spread hot risotto into plastic wrap-lined tray so it is 2.5cm (1in) thick. Leave to cool, then chill to set firm. Turn out the set risotto and cut into rounds or squares.

4 Lightly flour the cakes, then dip in beaten egg and coat in breadcrumbs. Repeat, giving cakes a second coating of egg and breadcrumbs. Tidy and mark top with a criss-cross pattern.

6 For the butter sauce, heat shallots and brandy in a pan until very hot, then light with a match. Boil until almost dry. Add stock and reduce by two-thirds.

7 Whisk 25g (1oz) butter into sauce. Stir in herbs and seasoning. Heat a little oil in frying-pan, dust sage leaves with flour and cayenne, then quickly fry until crisp. Sit cakes on plates and spoon the sauce around, then garnish with sage leaves.

Variations on a theme

cheese and herb galette

Two cheeses, arborio rice and mixed fresh herbs are a wonderful combination to make into one large risotto cake with a crispy top. Taleggio is smooth and fruity-tasting, with quite a strong flavour, and it melts beautifully. Serve the galette in generous wedges with a salad.

serves 6-8
preparation time
15 minutes, plus cooling
cooking time *1 hour*

ingredients
large pinch of saffron strands
1.2 litres (2 pints) ready-made vegetable stock, hot
55g (2oz) butter
1 onion, finely chopped
3 garlic cloves, crushed
350g (12oz) Arborio rice
125ml (4fl oz) dry white wine
4 tbsp chopped mixed fresh herbs – basil, chives, parsley and tarragon
25g (1oz) freshly grated parmesan
2 large eggs, beaten
225g (8oz) taleggio cheese, derinded and cubed
salt and pepper
oil for shallow-frying

equipment
large frying-pan; 23cm (9in) non-stick, ovenproof frying-pan

1 Infuse saffron strands in hot vegetable stock in a saucepan for 10 minutes.
2 Melt butter in frying-pan, add onion and garlic and fry for 10 minutes until soft and golden. Add rice and stir over heat for 1 minute until all grains are glossy.
3 Add wine and boil rapidly until almost all liquid has evaporated.
4 Heat saffron-infused stock and keep at a low simmer. Add 1 ladle of stock to rice. Simmer gently, stirring constantly, until liquid is absorbed. Continue to add stock and stir rice for 20-25 minutes until all liquid is used up and rice is tender. Season.
5 Remove risotto from heat, then stir in herbs and parmesan. Cover surface with greaseproof paper and leave to cool.
6 Pre-heat oven to 170°C/325°F/gas 3. Stir eggs into risotto, then divide mixture in half. Brush a 23cm (9in) ovenproof pan with a little oil. Spoon half risotto into pan and spread evenly to edges with a palette knife. Sprinkle diced taleggio on top, then spread rest of risotto over cheese. Cook in the oven for 15-20 minutes until piping hot in the centre.
7 Position pan under a hot grill and cook for 5-10 minutes until top is golden. Leave in pan to cool for 10 minutes. Serve warm, cut into wedges, accompanied by a green salad.

why not try...

blue tang
For a stronger flavour, replace the taleggio cheese in the cheese and herb recipe with a blue cheese, such as St Agur or stilton.

potato galette
Bake 6 large floury potatoes until tender. Scoop out the soft potato inside. (You need about 400g/14oz.) Mix it with 4 egg yolks, added one by one, and 1 tsp salt. Mix in 150g (5½oz) softened butter. Shape the potato dough into a ball, then flatten it with the palm of your hand. Repeat twice more. Butter a baking tray and press the dough into it until it is 4cm (1½in) thick. Trace a pattern on the top with a knife, brush with egg and bake in a pre-heated oven at 220°C/435°F/ gas 7, until golden brown.

eats well with...

Any form of green salad goes well with these galettes.

lasagnes

A baked lasagne brought sizzling hot to the table in a big earthenware dish is a truly impressive sight

Lasagne al forno is a classic Italian dish in which large flat sheets of pasta are layered with different combinations of sauce, cheese, meat or vegetables, and baked in the oven. The best-known lasagne is made with Bolognese sauce, based on minced beef and tomatoes, béchamel (or cheese) sauce and lasagne verdi – pasta coloured green with spinach.

Vegetarian version

By using tomato sauce instead of Bolognese, and a tasty mix of roasted mushrooms and peppers, you can make a wonderful vegetarian lasagne. This three-cheese version includes a short cut – instead of béchamel sauce, soft mascarpone cheese is melted with double cream. The cheeses used in the main recipe originate from Italy – mozzarella, mascarpone and parmesan. A sprinkling of parmesan as a final layer gives the lasagne its luscious golden-brown crisp top.

Ratatouille lasagne

The filling for the variation recipe is a quick-roasted version of ratatouille – red pepper, onion, aubergines and courgettes – combined with roast tomato sauce and topped with cheese sauce. You can make the ratatouille and roast tomato sauce in advance.

Gary's special touch

To make sure my three-cheese vegetarian lasagne is packed with luscious flavours I always make it with my special roasted tomato sauce. Use good ripe tomatoes, or Italian plum tomatoes if you can find them in your supermarket, as they have an intense flavour and are ideal for cooking.

making the three-cheese lasagne

You will need

serves 4

preparation time *15 minutes*

cooking time *1 hour*

pre-heat oven *220°C/425°F/gas 7 for roasting tomatoes and vegetables; 190°C/375°F/gas 5 for lasagne*

ingredients

280g (10oz) mascarpone cheese

150-200ml (5-7fl oz) double cream

55g (2oz) freshly grated parmesan, plus 25g (1oz) extra for sprinkling

350g (12oz) green spinach lasagne sheets (lasagne verdi)

2 x 175g (6oz) packets mozzarella cheese, thinly sliced

salt, pepper and nutmeg

for the roast tomato sauce

900g (2lb) ripe plum tomatoes, halved

2 tbsp olive oil

1 tbsp butter

2 garlic cloves, sliced

10 fresh basil leaves

salt and pepper

for the vegetable filling

450g (1lb) chestnut mushrooms, left whole if small, halved if large

1 large green pepper, deseeded and chopped

1 large yellow pepper, deseeded and chopped

1 garlic clove, crushed

olive oil to drizzle over

salt and pepper

equipment

ovenproof dish about 23 x 33cm (9 x 13in) and 5-7.5cm (2-3in) deep

1 Make tomato sauce. Heat oil in flameproof roasting tin. Put in tomatoes, cut side down, in one layer. Roast for 10-15 minutes until golden. (You may need to cook two batches.)

Fresh pasta produces the best result, and is quite easy to find in the supermarket. Dried, pre-boiled lasagne can be too chewy. If you do use the dried type, make sure your sauces are fairly runny to give the pasta plenty of liquid to absorb.

Arrange the sheets so that they fill the dish without overlapping. Trim them to fit with scissors if necessary.

How you layer the ingredients in the dish depends on how much of each sauce you have, and the exact size of your dish. Don't worry if it doesn't work out quite the same as here — the aim is to get layers of different colours — and always finish with the mascarpone and parmesan sauce so that you end up with a well-browned, crisp top.

Cook's notes

Thin – or thick?
In this recipe the lasagne is bathed in a loose cheesy creamy sauce. If you like your lasagne served in neat slices you need to thicken the sauce. Stir 1-2 tbsp potato flour, a little at a time, into the sauce until it thickens, then cook gently for 2 minutes. Potato flour (available from health food stores) thickens sauces without forming lumps and it doesn't give a floury taste. Another alternative is to make the lasagnes in individual portions. Then there's no worry about tidy slices.

5 Grease ovenproof dish and spoon in a layer of tomato sauce. Add a layer of lasagne on top of tomato sauce. Trim lasagne to fit if needed — sheets should not overlap.

2 Turn tomatoes, add butter, garlic and seasoning and cook in oven for 5 minutes, then add basil. Roast for 15-20 minutes. Blitz until smooth. Turn oven down to 190°C/375°F/gas 5.

3 Sprinkle a little olive oil in a roasting tin. Add peppers, mushrooms and garlic. Season, drizzle with olive oil and roast for 15-20 minutes on middle shelf of oven, under the tomatoes.

4 Meanwhile, melt the mascarpone in a pan over a low heat and bring to a gentle simmer. Add parmesan and cream and simmer. Season with salt, pepper and nutmeg.

6 Add some mascarpone sauce, then mushrooms and peppers. Follow with mozzarella slices, layers of tomato, lasagne, mascarpone, mushrooms and peppers, and mozzarella again.

7 Continue with a final layer of tomato and lasagne sheets, then finish with a thick layer of mascarpone sauce. Sprinkle liberally with parmesan and bake in the pre-heated oven for 20 minutes or until golden and bubbling. Serve with green salad and fresh basil.

Variations on a theme

ratatouille and cheese sauce lasagne

Flavourful ratatouille makes a great vegetarian lasagne, both filling and satisfying. The tomato sauce and the ratatouille can be made in advance.

serves 4

preparation time
30 minutes

cooking time
40-50 minutes, plus 1 hour for ratatouille

pre-heat oven
180°C/350°F/gas 4

ingredients
225g (8oz) lasagne sheets
roast tomato sauce (see pages 168 and 169, steps 1 and 2, at ½ quantity)
55g (2oz) freshly grated
parmesan
salt and pepper

for the ratatouille
4 courgettes, sliced
1 small aubergine, diced
1 red pepper, deseeded and diced
1 large onion, sliced
1 tbsp dried oregano
3-4 tbsp olive oil
1 garlic clove, crushed

for the cheese sauce
2 tbsp butter
2 tbsp plain flour
600ml (1 pint) milk
115g (4oz) cheddar cheese, finely grated

equipment
ovenproof dish as before

1 Make tomato sauce as before, halving quantity.
2 Make the ratatouille. Put courgettes, pepper, onion and aubergine in a roasting tin, add oregano, sprinkle with olive oil, garlic and salt and pepper and mix well. Roast at 180°C/350°F/gas 4 for about 1 hour, turning occasionally. Remove from the oven, then pour the tomato sauce on top and stir.
3 Make cheese sauce. Melt butter in a saucepan, add flour and mix to a paste. Cook, stirring, for 1-2 minutes. Add a little milk and stir until mix is smooth. Add rest of milk, a little at a time, stirring well. Season, simmer for 2 minutes, remove from heat and stir in cheese.
4 Grease dish, spoon in cheese sauce to cover base of dish, then line with sheets of lasagne. Cover the lasagne with more cheese sauce, then a layer of ratatouille.
5 Cover ratatouille with lasagne, then cheese sauce, another layer of ratatouille and so on, ending with a thick layer of cheese sauce. Sprinkle evenly with parmesan.
6 Bake for 40-50 minutes until golden brown and bubbling.

why not try...

Whichever sauces you use to make alternative lasagnes, always finish by sprinkling with parmesan cheese to get an appetizing brown top.

mushroom and spinach
Thinly slice 115g (4oz) button mushrooms and fry with a finely chopped onion in a little butter. Layer with lasagne sheets and cooked spinach leaves. Top with béchamel sauce or cheese sauce.

seafood lasagne
Make 600ml (1 pint) of béchamel sauce and stir in 115g (4oz) of cooked, peeled prawns, reserving some of the sauce for the top. Layer with lasagne sheets and finish with béchamel or cheese sauce.

lentil lasagne
Cook 115g (4oz) of Puy lentils until tender. Drain, reserving the cooking liquid. In a saucepan, fry a mixture of diced leeks, carrots and mushrooms with some crushed garlic until softened. Add the lentils, a can of chopped tomatoes and a little lentil stock. Simmer for 15 minutes and season. Layer with lasagne sheets and béchamel sauce.

macaroni cheese

Macaroni cheese is a great favourite – here it appears in a sumptuous pie version and as a traditional supper dish

Hearty and filling, macaroni cheese is perfect comfort food. It's creamy and cheesy and delicious served golden and bubbling straight from the grill. The main recipe here is slightly more sophisticated – perfect for a lunch or supper party. The macaroni, with artichokes and mushrooms, is beautifully served in puff pastry cases.

Lots of sauces

What makes the macaroni cheese pie special is that it is made with three sauces. There's a cheese sauce, a parmesan sauce made with cream, and a hollandaise sauce. If you want to save time, add two egg yolks to the cheese sauce instead of using the hollandaise. Serve the individual pies with a tossed green salad, flavoured with balsamic vinaigrette, sliced red onions, watercress and walnuts or pecans.

Family fare

The variation is a hearty family supper dish of macaroni with mushrooms, leeks and gruyère cheese. The macaroni, mushrooms and leeks are folded into a béchamel sauce – and the gruyère is laid in slices on top and grilled until golden brown.

Gary's special touch

I always think individual portions look smart, and they're easy to serve as well. The contrast in texture between the crisp puff pastry and the creamy soft macaroni is excellent. My little macaroni pies are open at the top, so they bake to a rich, deep golden brown colour. Don't spoil this by letting them burn.

making the macaroni cheese pie

You will need

serves 4

preparation time *20 minutes, plus 20 minutes for pastry to rest in fridge*

cooking time *15-20 minutes for pastry; 20-25 minutes for cheese sauce; 10 minutes for parmesan sauce; 5 minutes for artichokes and mushrooms; 3-4 minutes under grill*

pre-heat oven *200°C/400°F/gas 6*

ingredients

85g (3oz) macaroni, cooked

25g (1oz) butter

450g (1lb) puff pastry (see page 10) or shortcrust (see pages 9-10)

200g (7oz) canned artichoke hearts, drained and sliced

115g (4oz) button mushrooms, sliced

2 heaped tbsp lightly whipped cream

salt and pepper

for the hollandaise sauce

115g (4oz) unsalted butter

1 egg yolk

½ tbsp cold water

squeeze of lemon juice

salt and pepper

for the cheese sauce

1 tbsp butter

1 tbsp plain flour

200ml (7fl oz) milk

½ tsp prepared English mustard

85g (3oz) grated cheddar cheese

for the parmesan sauce

300ml (10fl oz) double cream

85g (3oz) freshly grated parmesan

2 tbsp crème fraîche

squeeze of lemon juice to taste

equipment

4 metal pastry rings, 6cm (2½in) deep, 10cm (4in) diameter, lightly buttered; non-stick baking tray

With this recipe, everything can be prepared ahead and assembled just before serving. Finishing off is just a matter of placing the individual pies under a hot grill for 3-4 minutes to give a deep golden brown colour to the top. The pies are very rich with the three different sauces – so all you need to serve with them is a salad.

Pastry tips

The recipe here uses puff pastry, but you can use basic shortcrust if you prefer. When you are lining the sides of the metal rings, remember to make the sides higher than the side of the rings – and press the pastry edges together very firmly at the base so the bottoms are sealed and don't fall off.

Recipe tip

Making the hollandaise sauce
Melt the butter in a small pan, then leave it to cool. As it cools, the golden butter fat will rise to the top. Put 1 egg yolk in a heatproof bowl with ½ tbsp water, then whisk over a pan of simmering water until pale. Remove from the heat, then slowly whisk in the clarified butter (leaving behind the pale cloudy liquid) until the sauce is smooth and thick. Add a squeeze of lemon juice and salt and pepper to taste.

Sit rings on tray. Roll pastry to 2mm (⅛in) thick, cut out 4 x 10cm (4in) circles and place in base of rings. Cut rest into strips to line sides. Press sides and bottom edge to seal base.

5 Fry mushrooms in 25g (1oz) butter for 5 minutes until soft. Add mushrooms and artichokes to macaroni mix and season. Put into pastry cases.

2 Line rings with greaseproof paper. Fill with baking beans. Rest in fridge for 20 minutes. Bake blind for 10-15 minutes. Remove paper and beans. Bake for another 10 minutes. Unmould.

3 For cheese sauce, melt butter, add flour and cook for 3 minutes. Add milk, then simmer and stir for 10 minutes until thick. Add seasoning, mustard and cheese, and heat until melted.

4 For parmesan sauce, bring cream to simmer in a pan. Lower heat, whisk in parmesan and crème fraîche. Add lemon juice and seasoning. Stir in macaroni and warm through.

6 Warm the cheese sauce, if necessary, and stir in the hollandaise sauce and cream. Spoon into the pies, levelling the tops with the back of a spoon.

7 Cook pies under a pre-heated hot grill until dark golden. Serve with a tossed green salad and vinaigrette (see page 66).

Variations on a theme

macaroni, mushrooms and leeks with gruyère cheese

This makes a tasty, hearty all-in-one family lunch or supper.

serves 4-6
preparation time
15 minutes
cooking time *45 minutes*

ingredients
275g (10oz) macaroni, cooked and drained
25g (1oz) butter
1 tbsp olive oil
225g (8oz) mushrooms
225g (8oz) leeks, sliced
125ml (4fl oz) white wine
½ tsp English mustard
6-8 slices gruyère cheese

for the béchamel sauce
2 onions, finely chopped
850ml (1½ pints) milk
70g (2½oz) butter
70g (2½oz) plain flour
150ml (5fl oz) cream
salt and pepper

1 For béchamel sauce, put 1 tbsp of chopped onions and milk in pan and bring to boil. Put to one side to infuse.
2 In another pan, melt butter and add flour, stirring. Cook over medium heat for a few minutes to make a roux.
3 Add a little milk mix to the roux, stirring. Repeat until all milk mix has been added. Cook on a low heat for 30 minutes, stirring. Stir in cream and

seasoning, then sieve.
4 Melt 25g butter in a pan, add oil and rest of onions and fry for 3-4 minutes without browning. Increase heat, add sliced mushrooms and fry for 2-3 minutes. Add leeks and fry for 2 minutes. Add wine and reduce until almost dry.
5 Stir onions, leeks and mushrooms into sauce. Add macaroni, mix well and warm through. Add mustard, salt and pepper. Spoon macaroni mix into a flameproof dish. Top with gruyère slices.
6 Place under a hot grill until cheese has melted and is golden, then serve.

why not try...

flavour boost
Spice up the macaroni cheese sauce with Tabasco or Worcestershire sauce. Replace half the cheddar with grated stilton for 'blue' macaroni. For a richer sauce, replace 150ml (5fl oz) of the milk with single cream.

quick macaroni cheese
Here's a great dish, made in minutes. Cook 350g (12oz) macaroni, following the instructions on the packet. Drain and put into a flameproof dish. Pre-heat grill to medium. For the sauce, mix 125ml (4fl oz) milk with 25g (1oz) cornflour. Bring 500ml (18fl oz) milk to boil. Whisk in cornflour mixture, a little at a time, to make a thick white sauce. Simmer for 5 minutes, stirring. Add 115g (4oz) grated mature cheddar cheese and 1 tsp Dijon or English mustard and stir until melted. Season, then pour over macaroni and stir in. Sprinkle with 55g (2oz) grated cheese. Finish under a hot grill until golden. Serve at once with crusty bread and a green salad, or with broccoli and roasted tomatoes. It makes enough for 4-6 people.

eats well with...

Serve the macaroni with cooked fish, cauliflower, broccoli or spinach.

vegetable crumbles

Seasonal vegetables are combined with lots of fresh herbs in a creamy sauce and topped with a tasty savoury crumble

A crumble is a mixture of flour or breadcrumbs, lightly bound together with butter. The best thing about such a mixture is that it's nice on its own, but is even more delicious pepped up with mustard, as here, or parsley, lemon zest, horseradish or herbs. The finished dish can be served on its own as a complete meal, or it can be an accompaniment to fish main courses.

Lovely layers
Three delicious elements make up the main crumble recipe – creamy, cheesy mashed potato forms the base, followed by a layer of lightly cooked leeks, then a mustard and herb crumble topping. While the crumble is baking, the cooking liquid from the leeks is reduced and blended with butter for a sauce.

The crumbles are assembled in individual 10cm (4in) rings. If you don't have rings, you can use individual tartlet tins or the more conventional large baking dish.

Italian flavour
For an Italian mood, fresh leaf spinach is mixed with a ricotta cheese sauce. Sautéed mushrooms are added, followed by a nutmeg-flavoured crumble.

Gary's special touch

I like to make my crumble mixtures with untoasted breadcrumbs, rather than the more usual mix of rubbed-in flour and fat. The fresh breadcrumbs give a looser texture, which sits lightly over the vegetables, and turn a lovely golden colour when baked. You can try it with wholemeal or granary bread as well as white.

making leek and mustard crumble

You will need

serves 6

preparation time *20 minutes*
cooking time *15 minutes*
pre-heat oven *180°C/350°F/gas 4*

for the cheesy potato mash
900g (2lb) potatoes, quartered
115g (4oz) butter
2 tbsp double cream or milk
115g (4oz) cheddar cheese, grated
salt and white pepper

for the leeks and sauce
115g (4oz) unsalted butter
2 onions, sliced
300ml (10fl oz) ready-made vegetable stock
675g (1lb 8oz) leeks, halved

lengthways and sliced
salt and white pepper

for the crumble
55g (2oz) unsalted butter
2 large shallots or ½ onion, finely chopped
8 slices white bread, crusts removed and made into crumbs
2 tsp chopped fresh parsley
2 tsp chopped fresh tarragon
2 tsp wholegrain mustard

equipment
6 x 10cm (4in) metal rings or deep-sided, loose-bottomed tartlet tins, buttered

| Put the buttered rings on a greased baking sheet. For the mash, boil the potatoes until tender. Drain, then mix in butter and cream or milk and mash until smooth. Stir in cheese, salt and pepper. Cover.

When preparing the breadcrumbs for the crumble mix, always go for bread that is a day or two old. Very fresh bread is difficult to crumb and tends to turn doughy.

Discard the bread crusts, then break the bread into small pieces and blitz briefly in a food processor or a liquidizer. Alternatively, grate the bread using a cheese grater.

Go for green

For a good colour, which contrasts well with the creamy potatoes that make the base of the vegetarian crumble, use the green parts of the leeks as well as the white parts. Halve the leeks lengthways, then slice thinly and cook for just 30 seconds in the boiling stock – they'll finish off cooking in the oven and turn out soft and silky. Drain very thoroughly after boiling in the stock.

Prepare ahead

You can prepare all the layers for the crumble up to a day in advance and assemble them before the meal. Keep everything in the fridge, well covered with plastic wrap. Bake for an extra 10 minutes to ensure that everything is heated through. When the crumble is ready, run a knife around the inside of the rings before removing them, so that they come away cleanly and retain their shape.

A choice of cheeses

A good strong, mature cheddar cheese is excellent for the cheesy mashed potatoes in this dish, but you could also try other hard cheeses. Smoked cheese tastes good – you can buy excellent smoked cheddar from delicatessen counters, for instance. Make sure to choose a hard cheese that grates easily.

Cook's notes

All the colours in this vegetarian dish are pale – the potatoes are creamy, the leeks are a soft green and the crumble topping is a pale gold. For this reason it's a good idea to use white pepper – not black – for the seasoning. Little black flecks would spoil the look of the sauce and the vegetables. Also the pungent taste of black pepper could very easily overwhelm the delicate flavours of the leek and potato. Save black pepper for more robust meats and fish – or for when you want freshly ground black pepper as a garnish.

2 While the potatoes boil, prepare the leeks. Melt 25g (1oz) butter in a pan. Add the onions and fry until soft. Add the stock and leeks and boil for 30 seconds. Strain and keep covered. Reduce liquid by half.

3 For the crumble, melt the butter with the shallots or onion. Fry gently until slightly softened, then cool a little. Gradually add the breadcrumbs to the shallots and butter, then stir in the herbs and mustard.

4 Divide the cheesy mash between the rings or tins and smooth to create an even layer. Spoon the leek mixture on top, then add the crumble. Bake for 20 minutes, or until golden and crispy.

5 Meanwhile, heat the leek liquid. Whisk in the rest of the butter with a hand-blender or balloon whisk until the sauce is very creamy. Season to taste.

6 Transfer the crumbles to plates, run a knife around the inside of the rings to loosen them, then carefully remove the rings. Pour the sauce around the side and serve with roasted cherry tomatoes.

Variations on a theme

spinach, ricotta and mushroom crumble

Spinach, ricotta and mushrooms under the conventional crumble mixture are mixed into a thick white sauce that loosens up as it bakes.

serves 6

preparation time
15 minutes

cooking time 30 minutes

pre-heat oven
200°C/400°F/gas 6

ingredients
55g (2oz) butter
3 tbsp plain flour
450ml (16fl oz) milk
salt and white pepper
250g (9oz) ricotta cheese
600g (1lb 5oz) spinach
350g (12oz) mushrooms, thinly sliced

for the crumble
225g (8oz) granary flour
125g (4½oz) unsalted butter, plus an extra knob
2 large shallots, chopped
85g (3oz) parmesan, grated
85g (3oz) walnuts, chopped
1 tsp grated nutmeg

equipment
1.7 litre (3 pint) ovenproof baking dish

1 Melt three-quarters of butter in pan. Add flour and stir over low heat with balloon whisk for 2 minutes. Stir in milk until mixture is smooth. Simmer for 5 minutes, stirring until thickened.

Season and add cheese.
2 Put spinach into large colander. Pour on boiling water to wilt leaves then drain well. Add spinach to sauce, then spoon into ovenproof dish.
3 Melt rest of butter in pan. Add mushrooms and fry for 2 minutes. Spoon over the spinach.
4 Make crumble by rubbing butter into flour. Melt knob of butter in pan, add shallots and fry gently to soften. Leave to cool. Add to crumble, then stir in parmesan, walnuts, nutmeg and seasoning. Spread over mushrooms.
5 Bake crumble for 30 minutes until golden.

why not try...

any bread
Use granary bread for more roughly textured crumble, or wholemeal bread if you prefer.

horseradish tang
Replace the mustard in the leek crumble, or the nutmeg in the spinach crumble, with horseradish sauce or grated fresh horseradish.

roasted winter vegetables
Toss 900g-1.3kg (2-3lb) prepared sliced winter vegetables, such as carrots, parsnips, baby onions, turnips or swede, in butter, salt and pepper. Roast in a hot oven for 30-40 minutes, turning occasionally, until tender and golden. Spoon into a baking dish. Cover with either of the crumble mixtures. Bake as before. Serve on its own or with salad.

three-cheese crumble
For an extra Italian flavour, replace half the ricotta cheese in the spinach and mushroom crumble with mascarpone.

eats well with...

These crumbles are particularly tasty served with fish, for example, herring.

veggie burgers

Moist and rich in flavour, veggie burgers are wonderfully satisfying and easy to make

You don't have to compromise on flavour or texture with veggie burgers – it's easy to make some that leave both meat eaters and vegetarians satisfied. Both of these burger recipes are packed with flavour that they will please even the most hardened of meat eaters.

Mix and match flavours

The secret (as with any burger) is to use good-quality ingredients. Classic veggie burger combinations use vegetables teamed with pulses, such as red or black beans (for Tex Mex style burgers) or chick peas (for Indian-inspired veggie burgers). Rice, millet, couscous or breadcrumbs are used to give the burgers substance.

Just as with meat burgers, the mixture is bound together with eggs. Cheeses, such as cottage cheese and ricotta or grated hard cheeses, also help stick the ingredients together.

Easy to please

The nut and cheese burgers are incredibly moreish – strongly flavoured cheddar, roasted nuts, wild mushrooms and plenty of fresh herbs give them a delicious taste and texture. Portobello mushroom burgers, in the variation recipe, are simple to make and marinating the mushrooms adds a special savoury flavour.

Gary's special touch

Despite being a great fan of meat, I'm also a true lover of well-made vegetarian dishes. These burgers are certainly very good. The combination of the different crunchy nuts, the soft mushrooms and the brown rice, plus the melted cheese gives them an irresistible texture and a wonderful savoury flavour.

making nut and cheese burgers

You will need

makes 8-10 burgers	1 tbsp chopped fresh parsley
preparation time 45 minutes, plus chilling	1 tsp chopped fresh thyme
	1 tsp chopped fresh marjoram
cooking time 45 minutes	1 tsp chopped fresh sage
pre-heat oven 180°C/350°F/gas 4	55g (2oz) brown rice, cooked and cooled
	2 eggs, beaten
ingredients	4 tbsp cottage cheese
85g (3oz) walnut halves	140g (5oz) gruyère or cheddar cheese, grated
85g (3oz) cashewnuts	
1 onion, finely chopped	freshly ground salt and pepper
25g (1oz) butter	semolina, for dredging
1 garlic clove, crushed	2 tbsp olive oil
115g (4oz) cup mushrooms, chopped	4-8 wholemeal or granary baps, relish and salad leaves, to serve
15-25g (½-1oz) dried porcini mushrooms, soaked and chopped	

1 Spread the cashews and walnuts on a baking tray and transfer to the oven. Toast for 15 minutes until golden brown but not burnt. Set aside to cool.

Start this recipe off by toasting the nuts – this helps to release their natural oils and flavours. After letting them cool for a while, put them in a food processor to chop them. Don't chop them up too finely – larger pieces of nut add interest to the burgers. You can do this by hand but the bits of nuts tend to fly everywhere.

Making the burger mix

The next stage is to fry the onions and mushrooms with the garlic and herbs. As the mushrooms cook, a fair amount of liquid comes out – be sure to cook them until all this liquid has completely evaporated. Once cooked, allow the mixture to cool slightly before adding the rice, nuts, eggs and cheeses.

All you need to do then is shape the mixture into burgers and it's simplest to do this with your hands. If you wet your hands first, you'll find it easier to handle and shape the burger mix. It's then a good idea to chill the burgers for about an hour. This will help them hold their shape better during cooking.

Into the fryer

When you're ready to cook the burgers, coat them lightly in semolina – just pour the semolina on to a plate and turn the burgers in it. This gives them a crisp coating once they are fried. To cook, just heat some oil and butter and fry the burgers – they'll take 8-10 minutes on each side. You'll probably have to work in batches – unless you have an big frying-pan – so keep the cooked burgers warm as you fry the rest.

The burgers are served in split baps with lots of salad leaves and plenty of relish. If you use large baps, you'll probably be able to get two burgers into each one. These burgers are very crumbly so handle with care.

5 Cover the burgers with plastic wrap and chill for 1 hour. Then put some semolina on a plate and turn the burgers in it to coat them.

2 Put the toasted nuts in a food processor and pulse until they are roughly chopped. Don't chop them too finely – there should be some larger pieces left.

3 Fry the onion in 15g (½oz) butter until soft. Add the garlic, mushrooms and herbs and fry until the liquid released by the mushrooms has evaporated. Set aside to cool.

4 Thoroughly mix the cooked mushroom mixture with the rice, nuts, eggs and cheeses; season to taste. With wet hands, form the mixture into burger shapes.

6 Heat the oil and remaining butter in a frying-pan and fry the burgers, in batches, over medium heat for 8-10 minutes on each side until browned.

7 To serve, split the baps in half and place some salad leaves on the base of each one. Top with 1 or 2 burgers and some relish. Place the top of the bap over the burgers and serve.

Variations on a theme

portobello burgers

serves 4

preparation time
25 minutes, plus marinating

cooking time *10 minutes*

for the burgers
4 fresh portobello mushrooms, about 115g (4oz) each
vegetable oil
4 sesame-seed burger buns
watercress, to serve

for the marinade
6 tbsp soy sauce

2 tbsp medium-dry sherry
3 tbsp rice vinegar
2cm (¾in) piece fresh ginger, finely chopped
2 tbsp caster sugar

for the coleslaw
2 tbsp mayonnaise
1 tsp sesame oil
½ tsp honey
1 tbsp cider vinegar
½ white cabbage, finely shredded
3 carrots, finely shredded
3 spring onions, finely shredded

1 Put the marinade ingredients in a small saucepan and bring to the boil. Simmer until syrupy in consistency and reduced by about half, then cool.
2 Put the mushrooms into a large plastic bag and pour in the marinade. Seal the bag and shake it to coat the mushrooms. Place the bag on a plate, making sure the mushrooms are sitting flat in the marinade and leave to marinate for 1 hour.
3 Meanwhile, make the coleslaw. Whisk together the mayonnaise, sesame oil, honey and cider vinegar in a large bowl.
4 Mix the shredded cabbage, carrot and spring onions with the mayonnaise mixture. Set aside in the fridge.
5 Pre-heat the grill to high. Put the mushrooms on to the grill pan and brush lightly with vegetable oil. Cook for 3-5 minutes on each side until tender.
6 Split the burger buns and lay some sprigs of watercress on the bottom half of the bun. Top with a cooked mushroom and then replace the top of the burger bun. Serve at once, accompanied by the coleslaw.

why not try...

vegan version
The portobello mushroom burgers are ideal for vegans, especially if the coleslaw is made with an egg-free mayonnaises available in health food and specialist shops.

un-marinated mushrooms
The portobello mushrooms can be cooked without being marinated first. Just grill the mushrooms and team with flavoured mayonnaise, mustard or horseradish, or top with a thin slice of cheddar for a more traditional burger.

eats well with...

The cheese and nut burgers taste delicious cold in a sandwich – the flavours develop wonderfully.

If you have marinated mushrooms left over, slice them and add them to a stir-fry – they'll give it a real flavour boost.

chapter three
desserts

sweet pancakes

Crispy-edged pancakes take on banoffee-pie style with a filling of chunky bananas and smooth toffee cream

Fun to make and very versatile, pancakes – or crêpes – are made from a simple batter of flour, egg and milk. A thin layer of the batter is briefly cooked on both sides in a pan to become a *pan cake*. Traditionally sweet pancakes are served with nothing more than a squeeze of lemon juice and a light dusting of caster sugar.

Banoffee-pie style
With a little imagination, simple pancakes can be turned into the most sophisticated dish. In the main recipe, fine, crispy-edged pancakes are filled with thick slices of ripe banana and a toffee cream, then served with a dusting of icing sugar and a little maple syrup to turn them into a stylish dessert.

Choosing a filling
Pancakes work well with a range of sweet stuffings. Try them filled with caramelized apples and spiked with apple brandy, or with sharp summer fruits and crème fraîche. Serve them with fresh fruit purée, or with a tangy sorbet for an exciting zing. Creamy custard, clotted or double cream or a dash of alcohol make nice additions.

Gary's special touch

I find making this toffee is very easy. All you do is put an unopened can of sweetened condensed milk into a saucepan of boiling water. Take it out 3 hours later, cool, open and hey presto! Luscious toffee. To make toffee cream just add cream, then spoon it on the pancakes.

making banana toffee pancakes

You will need

serves 4

preparation time
pancakes *5 minutes plus 30 minutes resting*
toffee cream *3 hours 5 minutes*
cooking time *20 minutes*

ingredients
4 bananas
a squeeze of lemon juice
1 quantity toffee cream (see Recipe Tip, below)
maple syrup (optional)
icing sugar, sifted
sprigs of fresh mint to decorate

for the pancake batter
(makes about 8 pancakes)
115g (4oz) plain flour
pinch of salt
1 egg
300ml (10fl oz) milk
25g (1oz) unsalted butter, melted
vegetable oil

equipment
25cm (10in) pancake pan or heavy frying-pan or a 20cm (8in) pan and reduce the quantities of batter used for each pancake (see below)

1 Sift flour and salt together, beat the egg into the milk and whisk into the flour. Rest batter for 30 minutes if you have time. Add melted butter.

The key to getting a perfect pancake lies in using just the right amount of batter and tilting the frying-pan to distribute a thin layer evenly over the base. You'll need 3 tbsp of the batter for a 25cm (10in) pan or 2 tbsp for a 20cm (8in) one.

Before you begin, pre-heat the pan and rub it lightly with oiled kitchen paper. Keep the pan on a steady medium heat and, when the edges begin to curl and the top bubbles, the pancake's ready for turning. If the pancake looks too dark, lower the heat; increase it if it's taking too long. Once the first one is right, all the rest can be cooked at the same heat.

Storing the pancakes

Once cooked, keep the pancakes warm in the bottom of the oven, or wrap them in a tea-towel and set them on a plate over a pan of simmering water. If making the pancakes in advance, separate them with sheets of greaseproof paper and keep in the fridge for a couple of days, or freeze. Gently reheat the pancakes in the oven or microwave.

Recipe tip

Toffee cream
ingredients

400g (14oz) can sweetened condensed milk
300ml (10fl oz) single cream

Put the unopened can into a large saucepan and completely cover with cold water. Bring water to the boil and simmer for 3 hours, topping up water when needed. Leave can to cool in the pan, then refrigerate. When ready to use, stir the toffee in a bowl to loosen, add 250ml (8fl oz) single cream and whisk. If you want the filling stiff, chill it for 30 minutes before use.

4 Cut bananas into thick diagonal slices and sprinkle with lemon juice to prevent discolouring. Put a pancake on a plate, and overlap a few banana slices on to one quarter.

2 Warm the pan well and rub lightly with kitchen paper dipped in oil. Put some batter in the pan (see Tip, right), and tilt the pan so that the mix covers the base in a thin layer.

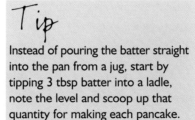

Tip

Instead of pouring the batter straight into the pan from a jug, start by tipping 3 tbsp batter into a ladle, note the level and scoop up that quantity for making each pancake.

3 Cook for 15-20 seconds until edges curl and the underside is golden. Flip and cook on the other side. Turn out and keep warm. Repeat until the batter is finished.

5 Spoon some toffee cream on top of the bananas. Fold the pancake in half, and then in half again to make a triangular wedge shape.

6 Drizzle with maple syrup, if using, and dust icing sugar around the plate. Garnish with fresh mint and serve with ice-cream.

Variations on a theme

apple pancakes

These apple pancakes are based on a traditional crêpe recipe from Normandy in France. For a bit of spice, add ½ tsp each of cinnamon and nutmeg to either the batter or to the apples when cooking. Sprinkle with sugar and glaze under a hot grill. Add fire with a dash of Calvados (Norman apple brandy), then serve with ice-cream, custard or cream.

serves 4

preparation time
pancakes *5 minutes plus 30 minutes resting*
apples *20-30 minutes*
cooking time *20 minutes*

ingredients
pancake batter, as before (see pages 186 and 187, steps 1-3)
7 ripe eating apples
55g (2oz) unsalted butter
55g (2oz) icing sugar

1 Make the pancakes (see pages 186 and 187, steps 1-3).
2 Peel, core and chop 2 of the apples and cook to a pulp in half the butter and half the sugar.
3 Peel and quarter 4 more apples, then cut each quarter into 4 or 5 slices. Cut the last apple into 8 thin rings. Melt the remaining butter in a pan and toss the slices and rings in it for a few minutes until just softening.
4 Remove the slices and add to the apple purée; warm through then remove from the heat. Leave the rings in the pan until they caramelize.
5 Allowing 2 pancakes per portion, divide the purée between the pancakes and fold the sides over the purée.
6 Sprinkle with the remaining icing sugar and glaze under a hot grill.
7 Serve with the caramelized apple rings and a dollop of cream, custard or ice cream, as desired.

why not try...

The traditional way to serve pancakes is with a sprinkling of sugar and a drizzle of lemon or orange juice. Simply roll them up and enjoy.

summer fruit pancakes
For a sharp fruity filling, use a fresh or frozen mixture of blackcurrants and redcurrants. Poach fresh fruit briefly in a few spoons of sugared water (85g/3oz of sugar to 350g/12oz fruit). If frozen, defrost first, then cook briefly and sweeten. Fill the pancakes with the fruit mixture and serve with crème fraîche and a dribble of crème de cassis.

peach melba pancakes
Halve some peaches and gently caramelize them in butter and brown sugar. Serve each pancake with a golden peach, a dollop of vanilla ice-cream and raspberry purée poured over.

eats well with...

Cream, crème fraîche and custard all go well.

Flavour bought custard with Calvados for apple pancakes, or with Cointreau if you want an orange taste.

A sharp sorbet is delicious with pancakes.

profiteroles

Simple, yet so delicious, sweet profiteroles are a happy marriage of light choux pastry, a creamy filling and luxurious topping

The name profiterole comes from the French *profit*, meaning a small gift. Traditionally filled with whipped cream and topped with hot chocolate sauce, this recipe replaces the usual chocolate with rich caramel sauce which perfectly matches the golden colouring of the little buns. A delicate piece of spun sugar provides an ultra-modern decoration on top and is made with the same type of caramel used for the sauce.

No rolling out
Without any rubbing-in or rolling out, choux pastry is one of the easiest pastries to prepare, and you don't need any special equipment.

Choux ring
For a stunning centrepiece, the raw choux paste is arranged in a circle on the baking tray, so it joins together to form a single ring when baked. After baking, the tops of the buns are sliced off and the ring is filled with an easy-to-make raspberry ice-cream. Luxuriously glossy chocolate sauce and a light dusting of icing sugar supply a wonderfully decadent finish.

Gary's special touch

As you know, I love working with sugar, and these profiteroles are the perfect foil for a rich caramel sauce. I make it by boiling a mixture of water and sugar to form a chestnut-brown caramel to which I add double cream. After cooling a bit, the luscious sauce is ready to pour over the little cream-filled choux buns.

making the caramel profiteroles

You will need

serves 4

preparation time 30 minutes
cooking time 20 minutes
pre-heat oven 200°C/400°F/gas 6

ingredients
75g (2½oz) plain or strong white
flour
pinch of salt
2 eggs, lightly beaten
55g (2oz) butter, finely diced
150ml (5fl oz) cold water
webs of spun sugar to decorate
(see Recipe tip)

for the filling
300ml (10fl oz) double or whipping
cream
2 tsp caster sugar

for the sauce
150ml (5fl oz) water
250g (9oz) caster sugar
250ml (10fl oz) double cream

equipment
large, non-stick baking tray, buttered
and dampened with cold water

Dampen the baking tray under the cold tap after greasing it – this creates steam and helps the buns to rise.

Chuting the flour
Before you sift the flour on to the greaseproof paper, fold the paper in half and unfold it to leave a crease. Then you can chute all the flour into the boiling water and butter at once and beat to a smooth dough.

Caramel care
For the sauce, gently heat the sugar and water until the sugar dissolves. When making caramel, it is important that all the sugar crystals are dissolved before the syrup comes to the boil.

Keep an eye on the syrup while it cooks, as it can easily burn. Simmer the syrup until it is a dark golden caramel or reads 158°C/325°F on a sugar thermometer. Cool for a few seconds, then slowly stir in the warm cream. Simmer gently for 5 minutes, then leave the sauce to cool and thicken up slightly before serving.

Recipe tip

Spinning a sugar garnish
Take great care when making or working with caramel. Remember that it's very hot burnt sugar – even a tiny splash can hurt you.

ingredients
150ml (5fl oz) water
250g (9oz) caster sugar

1 Dissolve the sugar in the water over a low heat, then simmer until the syrup is chestnut-brown or reads 158°C/325°F on a sugar thermometer. Whip the pan off the heat and plunge its base into iced water to stop the caramel browning further. Cool until syrupy.
2 Drizzle the thickened caramel into four swirly patterns on non-stick baking paper. Leave the caramel webs to cool and harden before decorating the profiteroles.

1 Sift the flour and salt on to greaseproof paper. Bring the butter and water to the boil. Add all the flour in one go and beat to a smooth dough over a low heat. Cool for 10 minutes.

5 Slit the sides of the cooked choux buns with a sharp knife. Leave to cool completely on a wire rack.

2 Gradually beat in the eggs with a wooden spoon until the paste is smooth and stands in peaks. Make sure each amount is fully blended before adding any more egg.

3 Spoon 16 teaspoonfuls of paste on to the tray. Bake for 20 minutes, until crisp and golden. If your oven is very hot, reduce the heat to 190°C/375°F/ gas 5 halfway through baking.

4 For the sauce, dissolve the sugar in the water, then simmer until brown. Remove from the heat. Warm the cream separately, then stir into the hot caramel. Simmer for 5 minutes.

Cook's notes

Split the choux buns as soon as you take them out of the oven. This lets any steam inside escape and keeps them crisp.

Although you can make the choux paste and caramel sauce up to a day in advance and whip the cream up to 4 hours ahead of serving, do not fill choux pastry cases more than 30 minutes before serving or the pastry will become soggy. When filling choux buns with ice-cream or topping them with a hot sauce, always serve them straight away.

6 For the filling, whip the cream and sugar in a bowl until stiff peaks form. Spoon into the buns, then arrange on dessert plates and serve with the warm sauce poured over the top.

Variations on a theme

raspberry choux ring with chocolate sauce

This chocolate-coated choux ring, filled with raspberry ice-cream, is inspired by the classic French dessert Paris Brest.

serves 4

preparation time
30 minutes

cooking time *30 minutes plus 4 hours freezing time*

pre-heat oven
200°C/400°F/gas 6

ingredients
1 quantity choux pastry (as before)

icing sugar to dust

for the filling
225g (8oz) raspberries
juice of ½ lemon
115g (4oz) icing sugar
425ml (15fl oz) double cream

for the sauce
225g (8oz) plain chocolate
4 tbsp cold water
25g (1oz) butter
4 tbsp golden syrup

1 For the filling, purée the raspberries, lemon juice and icing sugar, then sieve to remove pips.

2 Whip the cream until soft peaks form and fold into the purée. Freeze in a shallow container for 4 hours, stirring halfway through, until solid.

3 Using a plate to help you, draw a 19cm (7½in) circle on a sheet of non-stick baking paper. Turn over the paper, then use it to line a baking tray. Sprinkle the paper with water.

4 Spoon about 10 tablespoonfuls of the choux mixture around the circle outline so they just touch. Bake for 25-30 minutes, or until golden. Leave the pastry in the turned-off oven for 10 minutes to dry slightly.

5 Transfer the pastry ring to a wire rack, slice off the tops of the buns with a sharp knife and leave to cool completely. Place the bottom half of the ring on a large plate.

6 For the sauce, heat all the ingredients together in a pan and stir gently until smooth. Dip a tablespoon or ice-cream scoop into hot water to warm, then use to scoop balls of the ice cream into the bottom half of the choux ring.

7 Replace the tops of the buns, then spoon or pour the sauce on top. Dust the ring with icing sugar and serve at once.

why not try...

You can flavour the choux pastry before baking or serve the cooked buns with a host of tasty fillings.

flavouring the dough
Sweeten the choux paste by adding 1-2 tsp vanilla sugar after the flour. Add the grated zest of ½ orange or ½ tsp cinnamon for a hint of spice.

cut the fat
Instead of whipped cream, fill the profiteroles with low-fat crème fraîche or fromage frais, sweetened with a little icing sugar and flavoured with vanilla essence. You can also add grated citrus zest, a dash of brandy or orange-flower water.

custard style
Replace a quarter of the whipped cream in the main recipe with ready-made custard: just fold together.

coffee rush
For a mocha flavour, replace the water in the chocolate sauce with black coffee.

easy fillings
You can also fill choux buns with crème pâtissière (pastry cream) or mascarpone cheese. Or slip slices of banana or orange segments in with the cream.

quick toppings
You can top the buns with icing, fruit coulis, chocolate, coffee, butterscotch or toffee sauce.

fruit mousses

Tangy, fresh and light,
a fruit mousse lends
understated elegance
to any meal

Fruit mousses make delicious desserts, particularly welcome on a hot day or after a heavy meal. Simple to put together, they rely on whipped cream and beaten eggs to give them their bubbly texture, while gelatine helps them set. They look very pretty in a decorative bowl, adorned with piped cream and fresh fruit. Alternatively, serve mini mousses in individual ramekins or glass dishes.

Keep it light
The key to this scrumptious lemon mousse is to whisk maximum air into the eggs and cream and then to fold them together carefully, losing as little air as possible. This results in a beautiful, light, melt-in-the-mouth texture that complements the fresh citrus flavour.

Pink perfection
Mousse is a very versatile dessert that works well with lots of different fruits. Simply start with a purée made with whatever fruit is in season. Raspberries have bags of flavour and a beautiful rich colour so they create a dessert that's out of this world. For a true taste of summer, serve fresh raspberry mousse with whipped cream and shortbread.

Gary's special touch

I like to make the most of this light, airy dessert by building it up above the dish so it looks really dramatic. Simply spoon the mixture into a large soufflé **dish with a greaseproof paper collar and let it set in the fridge. Before serving, decorate the sides with chopped almonds or pistachios.**

making the lemon mousse

You will need

serves 8-10

preparation time
25 minutes plus 2-3 hours chilling

ingredients
6 eggs, separated
finely grated rind and juice of
6 lemons
175g (6oz) caster sugar
2 x 11.7g sachets
powdered gelatine

600ml (1 pint) whipping cream

for decoration
whipped cream
pistachio nuts, chopped and toasted
curls of lemon and lime zest

equipment
1.2 litre (2 pint) soufflé dish,
wrapped with greaseproof paper

For a really delicious lemon mousse, choose the best quality fruit you can find. Lemons and many other citrus fruits are coated with carnauba wax or shellac after harvesting to prevent moisture loss. For a recipe that actually uses the zest of the fruit, like this one, it's important to choose unwaxed lemons (these are available in most supermarkets and clearly labelled). An even better option is organic lemons. Not only are these free of waxes and pesticides, they have the added benefits of superior flavour and more juice.

Temperature control

Follow a few basic rules and you can be sure of making a wonderful mousse. For maximum volume, make sure the cream is well chilled before you start whipping it. The egg whites, on the other hand, will respond best if they are at room temperature when you beat them. Don't do this until the last minute because the beaten egg whites will lose height if left to stand.

For successful results, make sure all your ingredients are at about the same temperature before you actually combine them. Allow very cold things, like the whipped cream, to get to room temperature and make sure hot ingredients, like the dissolved gelatine, cool down. Adding hot gelatine to a cold mixture will make it set quickly and unevenly, producing lumps rather than a smooth texture. Very hot liquids can cook the eggs in the mousse, causing it to curdle. To keep the mixture aerated, fold the whipped ingredients together carefully using a large metal spoon.

Safety first

As with any dish that uses uncooked eggs, it's best to avoid serving mousse to very young children, the elderly or pregnant women.

Tip

Keep fruit mousses refrigerated and don't store them for more than a couple of days. They quickly lose their fresh flavour and bubbly texture.

Place the egg yolks, lemon rind and sugar in a large mixing bowl and whisk them until pale, creamy and doubled in volume.

Cook's notes

For extra height, wrap a double thickness of greaseproof paper around a soufflé dish so that it sits 5-7cm (2-3in) higher than the lip of the dish. Secure it with string. Pour in the mixture to the top of the paper and smooth the surface. Chill the mousse for 2-3 hours, then remove the paper carefully.

2 Sprinkle the gelatine into 150ml (5fl oz) lemon juice. Soak for 2-3 minutes. Sit the mix over simmering water until the gelatine has dissolved.

3 Allow the gelatine to cool then stir it into the whisked egg mixture. Leave to stand until the mixture thickens and shows signs of setting.

4 Whip the cream lightly until it just holds its shape then fold it carefully into the thickened egg, lemon and gelatine mixture.

5 Whisk the egg whites until they form soft peaks. Stir a spoonful of the beaten egg white into the lemon and cream mixture to loosen it, then gently fold in the rest with a large metal spoon.

6 Spoon the mousse into the prepared soufflé dish and smooth the surface. Chill the mousse for 2-3 hours until set. Decorate with chopped nuts, whipped cream and lemon and lime zest.

Variations on a theme

raspberry mousse

Fruit mousses can be made with egg whites alone, rather than whole eggs, which gives them a firmer texture. This delicious raspberry version contains cream cheese as well, which makes it particularly rich and velvety.

serves 6

preparation time
25 minutes plus 2-3 hours chilling

ingredients
450g (1lb) raspberries
1 x 11.7g sachet powdered gelatine
4 tbsp cold water
115g (4oz) cream cheese
55g (2oz) caster sugar
150ml (5fl oz) whipping cream
2 egg whites

for decoration
whipped cream
fresh raspberries
sprigs of mint

equipment
6 small glass dishes

1 Press the fresh raspberries through a sieve to make a smooth purée and set this aside.
2 Sprinkle the gelatine on to the water in a small bowl. Soak for 2-3 minutes then place the bowl over a saucepan of simmering water and stir until the gelatine has dissolved. Make sure the mixture does not boil.
3 Beat the cream cheese and sugar together until very smooth then stir in the raspberry purée.
4 Pour the dissolved gelatine slowly into the cream cheese and raspberry mixture, whisking all the time. Leave to stand until the mixture thickens and shows signs of setting.
5 Whip the cream until it forms soft peaks. Then whisk the egg whites until they form stiff peaks.
6 Lightly fold the whipped cream into the raspberry mixture, followed by the beaten egg whites.
7 Pour the mousse into the glass dishes and chill until set.
8 Before serving, decorate the mousses with fresh raspberries, whipped cream and sprigs of mint.

why not try...

fruit medley
You can choose from a vast array of fruits to make a mousse – gooseberries or blackberry and apple work well. If you use seeded fruits, push the purée through a sieve to remove all the pips.

honey sweet
Make a honey mousse by following the lemon recipe, replacing the sugar with 125ml (4fl oz) of honey and using less lemon. Serve with fresh ripe figs.

liqueur mousse
A generous dash of Grand Marnier liqueur makes a really good addition to an orange mousse, boosting the flavour and lending it a touch of sophistication.

fresh tang
Any citrus fruit makes a great mousse – clementines and limes work especially well.

eats well with...

Serve mousse with a fruit coulis. Make one by puréeing brightly coloured fruits like raspberries or apricots, passing the purée through a sieve and sweetening it with sifted icing sugar. Add a splash of liqueur for good measure.

Creamy mousses are great served with light biscuits such as tuiles or ratafias.

caramelized fruit

Delicious slivers of golden fruit with a crisp, sweet caramelized crust make a perfect autumn dessert

Caramelized fruit always looks good. It retains its shape and colour while being softened and sweetened with a hot coating of molten sugar.

In this dish, pumpkin wedges are grilled until slightly charred then given a deep sugar glaze, creating a bittersweet finish. The whole thing is rounded off with a cool spoonful of lemon sherbet.

A small, ridged, cast-iron grill pan is perfect for caramelizing fruit. If you don't have one, simply pan-fry and glaze the pumpkin and you'll still be satisfied with the result.

Flavour match
Pumpkin, a member of the squash family, is strictly a vegetable fruit but its sweet flavour, bright colour and beautiful shape make it ideal for desserts. It remains firm and golden when cooked and can support a bubbling crust of sugar without collapsing.

Traditional fruits
Apple is a fruit that caramelizes wonderfully too. Serve it hot with a scoop of rich blackberry ice-cream. This is a great way to combine traditional flavours in a deliciously different manner.

Gary's special touch
The caramel crust on these glorious pumpkin wedges is simply burnt sugar. I use icing sugar to create the caramel because the fine grains melt quickly under the grill and allow me to build up crisp, delicate layers in very little time. If you have a kitchen gas gun, use this rather than a grill to melt the sugar – it's even faster.

grilled pumpkin with lemon sherbet

You will need

serves 4	**for the sherbet**
preparation time *20 minutes*	*115g (4oz) caster sugar*
freezing time *1½ hours for*	*150ml (5fl oz) water*
the sherbet	*grated zest and juice of 3 lemons*
cooking time *25 minutes*	*85ml (3fl oz) milk*
	1 egg white
for the pumpkin slices	
small pumpkin weighing 450-750g	**equipment**
(1-1lb 7oz)	*plastic freezerproof container;*
25g (1oz) butter, melted	*griddle pan; large baking tray,*
4 tbsp icing sugar, sifted	*buttered*

It's essential to use very high temperatures when caramelizing fruit. The aim is to get the sugar to begin burning without cooking the fruit underneath. Don't be nervous about turning the grill up as high as it will go – just keep a careful eye on the fruit while it caramelizes.

Two layers of icing sugar ensure that these pumpkin wedges develop a lovely brittle, crunchy coating. Add a third dusting of icing sugar and grill again to create an even crispier topping. If time is short, you can omit the sugar altogether and trickle golden syrup or honey over the grilled pumpkin.

Sherbet dab

Sherbets are very similar to sorbets except that they include milk and whisked egg white, which makes them a little creamier. In this case, the zing of lemon in the sherbet is an ideal foil to the sweet pumpkin.

You can make the sherbet in advance. Freeze it, then transfer to the fridge 30 minutes before serving to soften, ready to be scooped out as the hot, crisp pumpkin wedges are served fresh from the grill. Home-made

sherbet really is unbeatable and if you have an ice-cream maker you can make some very easily. The first step is to boil a basic sugar syrup to which you add lemon juice, zest and milk. This mixture is then frozen but, just before the sherbet is set, fluffy whipped egg white is stirred in to lift and lighten it.

Citrus twist

If you don't have time to make your own sherbet, you can use sherbet, sorbet or ice-cream bought from the supermarket. If you can't find lemon sherbet, try a sorbet flavoured with lime, which also goes very well with pumpkin.

Tip

When shopping for this dish, look for a small, heavy, highly coloured pumpkin. These signs all indicate good flavour – large pumpkins with fibrous flesh won't taste as good and may collapse during the grilling and glazing process.

1 To make sherbet, dissolve sugar in water, bring to boil and simmer for 8 minutes. Add lemon juice and zest, return to boil then remove from heat. Add milk and leave to cool.

5 Lay the grilled pumpkin slices on the buttered baking tray and dust heavily with icing sugar. Put the tray under a very hot grill until the sugar caramelizes.

2 Once cool, put mix in a plastic container. Freeze, stirring every 15 minutes, until thick and creamy. Alternatively, churn in an ice-cream maker for 20-25 minutes.

3 Just before sherbet is ready, whisk the egg white until it forms stiff peaks. Mix it into the sherbet and leave in the freezer to firm up while you prepare the pumpkin.

4 Cut the pumpkin into 8-12 wedges. Remove the seeds and skin. Brush each slice with butter and place on a hot grill or griddle pan. Grill for 7-8 minutes on each side.

6 Once the sugar begins to bubble, remove the tray, dust again with icing sugar and place back under the grill. This time, the sugar will colour and begin to form a crust.

7 Once golden and crisp, the pumpkin wedges are ready to eat. Arrange them on plates (2-3 slices per person) with a large scoop of the lemon sherbet. Add a spoonful of thick whipped cream for extra indulgence.

Variations on a theme

golden apples with blackberry ice-cream

Make this delicious dessert with well-flavoured, firm-fleshed dessert apples such as Braeburn, Cox's or Granny Smith's.

serves 4

preparation time
1 hour

freezing time
1½ hours for the ice-cream

cooking time
25 minutes

ingredients
4 medium-sized apples
25g (1oz) butter
4 tbsp icing sugar, sifted
dash of lemon juice

for the ice-cream
225g (8oz) blackberries
55g (2oz) icing sugar, sifted
150ml (5fl oz) water
85g (3oz) caster sugar
2-3 tbsp crème fraîche

equipment
plastic freezerproof container; frying-pan

1 Set aside a few blackberries for decoration. To make the ice-cream, blitz the remaining blackberries and icing sugar in a food processor then push through a sieve.
2 Dissolve the caster sugar in the water, bring gently to the boil and simmer for 2-3 minutes to make a syrup. Cool.
3 Mix the blackberry purée with the crème fraîche and the syrup. Taste the mix – if it's too sharp, add more sifted icing sugar. Freeze in a plastic container, stirring every 10-15 minutes, until set. Or, churn in an ice-cream maker for 15-20 minutes.
4 Core the apples and slice them in half (don't peel them). Place in a bowl of water laced with lemon juice to stop them turning brown.
5 Heat a frying-pan and add the butter. Pat the apples dry and place them, cut side down, in the pan. Fry for 5-6 minutes until golden brown but still firm. Turn and fry the other side.
6 Sift icing sugar over the apples in the pan and place under a very hot grill until the sugar melts and caramelizes.
7 Remove from the grill, sprinkle with fresh icing sugar and grill again. Serve the hot apples with blackberry ice-cream and fresh berries.

why not try...

sweet sensation
Many firm-fleshed fruits caramelize well. Try peaches, bananas or plums, and serve them with appropriate accompaniments. Caramelized peaches with raspberry sorbet, for instance, are a delicious variation on the classic peach Melba idea.

cream dreams
Hot caramelized fruit works well when partnered with a cold, creamy dessert. Don't stop at sherbet – try sorbet, ice-cream, custard, parfait or frozen yoghurt. For a quick fix, mix up a simple fruit cream by combining chopped fruit or cold fruit purée with crème fraîche, fromage frais or whipped cream.

Italian style
Caramelized fruit tastes wonderful when served on a piece of toasted pannetone or sweet focaccia. Pour any remaining caramelized fruit juice over the top and finish with a scoop of vanilla ice-cream.

barbecue treat
For an alfresco dessert, griddle fruit on the barbecue. When cooked, sprinkle with sugar and blast with a gas gun or grill. Alternatively, just leave the sugar to melt on the hot fruit.

crumble tarts

For a fruit dessert that's deliciously different, combine crisp buttery pastry with the crunch of a nutty crumble

A crumble tart is simple to prepare and makes the perfect end to a family meal. It can be served warm or cold with ice-cream or custard and you can alter the fruit filling according to the season.

Texture contrast

The crunchy, sugary texture of a crumble topping marries perfectly with soft, tender fruit. A more sophisticated version of the classic fruit crumble, this elegant tart has a sweet, shortcrust pastry base filled with colourful pumpkin, raisins and mixed peel and crowned with a nutty crumble topping. The pastry case is baked blind so that it's crisp when the fruit is added. Along with the crumble topping, it forms a crunchy, buttery envelope for the velvety filling.

Crisp crumbs

A 'betty' is similar to a crumble except that it's topped with breadcrumbs instead of pastry-like nuggets. When made with wholewheat bread it has a wholesome quality which complements sweet ingredients such as bananas. Baked in elegant miniature tartlets, a golden fruit betty is a real winner.

Gary's special touch

I put chopped nuts in my crumble topping to provide extra crunch – they really make a difference. Use almonds, pecans, hazelnuts or walnuts. If possible, buy nuts whole and chop them by hand or in a processor just before you need them. This ensures a better flavour.

pumpkin and raisin crumble tart

You will need

serves 8
pre-heat oven *200°C/400°F/gas 6*
preparation time *1 hour*
cooking time *40-45 minutes*

for the pastry
225g (8oz) plain flour
55g (2oz) icing sugar
150g (5½oz) chilled, unsalted butter, chopped
1 egg, beaten

for the filling
1 small, firm pumpkin
85g (3oz) raisins

25g (1oz) candied mixed peel
85g (3oz) soft light brown sugar
25g (1oz) butter, melted
1 tsp ground mixed spice

for the crumble topping
225g (8oz) plain flour
115g (4oz) butter, diced
115g (4oz) demerara sugar
115g (4oz) chopped nuts

equipment
25cm (10in) loose-based tart tin, at least 3cm (1¼in) deep, buttered

Pumpkin is a very versatile member of the squash family which works equally well in sweet or savoury dishes. Choose a small, firm pumpkin (see Tip on page 198). To prepare it, use a sharp, heavy knife to cut it into segments. Scoop out the seeds and fibres with a small spoon, then remove the skin with a small knife or vegetable peeler and cut the flesh into cubes.

Touch of brandy
If you'd like to add a dash more sophistication to the tart filling, soak the raisins and peel overnight in a few tablespoons of brandy. Mix them with the other filling ingredients, discarding any remaining liqueur.

Perfect pastry
Uncooked pastry can become sticky at the best of times but when it has sugar added, this is even more likely to be the case. To combat the problem, handle the pastry as little as possible, bringing it together with the egg quickly and lightly. Chill it for 20 minutes before use and roll it out on a cool, floured surface – a marble slab is ideal.

Cook's notes

Crumble crunch
Don't make the crumble topping too fine and uniform. A mixture with a slightly lumpy texture bakes into a deliciously crispy topping. Rub the fat into the flour as lightly as possible, lifting your hands high over the bowl to aerate the mix. Shake the bowl from time to time to bring large lumps to the top of the mixture so you can work them in. Then stir in the sugar and chopped nuts.

1 To make the pastry for the base, sift the flour and icing sugar into a bowl. Lightly rub in the butter with your fingertips until the mixture resembles coarse breadcrumbs.

5 Mix with the other filling ingredients and 1 tbsp water. Cook gently for 5-10 minutes until the pumpkin is soft but still holds its shape. Pack into the pastry case.

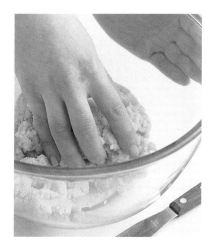

2 Add the egg and mix into the crumbs with a round-bladed knife until they start to bind. Gather the mix into a soft ball, cover with plastic wrap and chill for 20 minutes.

3 Line the tin with pastry, without trimming it. Line with greaseproof paper and baking beans. Bake for 20-25 minutes. Remove the paper and trim the pastry.

4 Cut the pumpkin into segments. Scoop out the seeds and fibres, remove the skin and cut the flesh into 1-2cm (½-¾in) cubes.

6 To make the crumble topping, sift the flour into a bowl and rub the butter into it lightly to form coarse crumbs. Then stir in the sugar and chopped nuts.

7 Spoon the crumble mixture on top of the pumpkin and bake the tart for 40-45 minutes until the top is golden and crisp and the filling soft.

Variations on a theme

banana betty tartlets

Buttery breadcrumbs and oats bake to a gorgeous crispness in the oven, making them an ideal alternative to traditional crumble topping.

serves 6

pre-heat oven
200°C/400°F/gas 6

preparation time
50 minutes

cooking time *15 minutes*

ingredients
225g (8oz) sweet shortcrust pastry (see pages 202-203, steps 1-2)
6 medium-sized bananas
85g (3oz) caster sugar
juice and zest of 1 orange
115g (4oz) unsalted

butter
55g (2oz) fresh wholewheat breadcrumbs
40g (1½oz) rolled oats
55g (2oz) soft brown sugar
1 tsp ground cinnamon

equipment
large frying-pan; 6 tartlet tins, buttered; baking tray, buttered

1 Roll out the pastry and line the tartlet tins. Line them with greaseproof and baking beans. Bake for 10-15 minutes.
2 Cut the bananas into 3cm (1¼in) chunks.
3 Put the caster sugar, orange juice and 40g (1½oz) butter in the

frying-pan. Cook over a medium heat for 3-4 minutes, until the mixture is a light caramel colour. Stir in the banana. Remove from the heat.
4 Put the breadcrumbs, oats, brown sugar, cinnamon, 1 tsp orange zest and remaining butter in a bowl and combine with your fingers until the mix is crumbly. Spread on the baking tray and bake for 10-15 minutes.
5 Spoon the banana mix into the tartlet cases. Scatter the breadcrumb mix over the top.
6 Place the tartlets on a baking tray and bake for 15 minutes or until the topping is golden.

why not try...

tipsy plums
Cook up a rich, alcoholic filling of plums, cinnamon and cognac to make a deliciously indulgent pudding for cool days. This is perfect with a scoop of vanilla ice-cream.

apple idea
You can't go wrong with a classic apple filling for a crumble tart, spiced up with cinnamon and sultanas. Make sure the apple mixture is not too wet or you risk making the pastry base soggy.

tea-time treat
Use apricots – fresh, tinned or dried – to create an elegant crumble tart that can be served cold with afternoon tea. Include almonds in the topping.

festive fare
At Christmas, make a crumble tart with rich mincemeat and apple. Serve with custard or brandy butter.

tasty toppings
To add more crunch to crumbly toppings, mix in oatmeal, sunflower seeds or desiccated coconut. For an even richer flavour, make the crumble with wholemeal flour and throw in some mixed spice.

biscuit puddings

Inspired by classic tea-time treats, these desserts are fun to make and delicious to eat

These individual puddings are a tribute to the traditional biscuits which consist of a creamy filling sandwiched between crisp outer layers. By replacing the basic components of the biscuit with pudding ingredients, you can make a rich and sumptuous dessert.

Chocolate flavour
The Bourbon biscuit puddings in the main recipe are a treat for dinner guests who enjoy the taste of chocolate. Buttery biscuit layers enclose a gorgeous chocolate ganache and delicious brownie sponge. The brownie is cooked very briefly so that it stays moist and it lends texture, flavour and more chocolate to the basic Bourbon biscuit. To counteract the sweetness of so much chocolate, there is a hint of coffee in the brownie sponge. The pudding eats very well with a trickle of rich coffee syrup.

Jam delights
You can continue the biscuit theme by creating a pudding based on traditional jammy dodger biscuits. In the variation recipe, buttery biscuit discs sandwich a delicious strawberry sauce and a layer of rich vanilla ice-cream.

Gary's special touch

To get the look of these Bourbon puddings right, I cut the biscuits using a card template with rounded corners. This gives an impressive finish and ensures that all of the biscuits are the same size and shape. As a final touch, I make holes in the biscuits with a skewer before baking them.

making the chocolate puddings

You will need

serves 8	115g (4oz) cocoa powder
pre-heat oven 180°C/350°F/gas 4	3 eggs
preparation time 1 hour	350g (12oz) caster sugar
cooking time 20 minutes	115g (4oz) plain flour
	2 tsp vanilla essence
for the biscuits	2 tbsp strong coffee
115g (4oz) butter	
115g (4oz) caster sugar, plus extra	**for the ganache**
for sprinkling	225g (8oz) good-quality plain
1 egg, beaten	chocolate, chopped
275g (9½oz) self-raising flour	250ml (9fl oz) double cream
pinch of salt	2 egg yolks
8 tbsp cocoa powder	25g (1oz) caster sugar
6-8 tsp milk	
	equipment
for the brownies	1 large baking tray with a slight lip,
175g (6oz) butter	buttered

1 Cream the butter and sugar for the biscuits. Add the egg and sieve in the flour, salt and cocoa. Mix, softening with milk to form a soft dough. Refrigerate for 20 minutes.

These biscuit puddings are served cold, so you can make the different layers in advance and bring them all together to make the biscuit shape just before you serve them.

You will need a baking tray with a slight lip so that the brownie mixture can be baked in a thin layer. When the brownies are cooked, clean the tray and butter it again for the biscuits.

Mix and match

One of the great pleasures of these wonderful desserts is the contrast in texture between the soft, silky centres and the crunchy biscuits. In order to make the biscuits particularly crisp, roll them very thinly and, when baked, cool them on a wire tray. They can be stored in an airtight container for approximately 24 hours but do not keep them any longer.

Creamy dream

Ganache is cream and melted chocolate, blended to a thick, flexible paste and often enriched with butter and eggs. It is a useful recipe which can be used for a number of desserts. Its richness and deep chocolate flavour make it ideal for icing, decorating and filling. Here, it provides a foil to the crisp biscuit and sticky brownie.

Recipe tip

To make a rich coffee syrup to complement these puddings, dissolve 150g (5oz) caster sugar in 300ml (10fl oz) strong coffee (fresh or instant). Boil until the liquid is reduced by half. For a liqueur coffee sauce, add a dash of Tia Maria.

5 For ganache, melt chocolate with half the cream over a pan of simmering water. Whisk yolks with sugar, add chocolate, whisk again. Lightly whip remaining cream and add.

2 Meanwhile, make the brownies. Melt the butter and mix with the cocoa powder. Whisk the eggs and caster sugar until fluffy and add the cocoa mixture.

3 Mix in all the remaining ingredients and pour the mixture into the baking tray in a 5mm-1cm (¼-½in) layer. Bake for 7 minutes, turn out and leave to cool.

4 Roll the refrigerated dough to 3mm (⅛in) thickness and cut 16 rectangles, about 6 x 10cm (2½ x 4in). Place on the baking tray and make holes. Bake for 10 minutes and cool.

6 Cut the brownies slightly smaller than the biscuits. Spread ganache on a biscuit. Add a brownie, a thick ganache layer, another brownie, more ganache and a second biscuit.

7 Sprinkle the Bourbons with caster sugar and serve on a plate drizzled with coffee syrup (see Recipe tip, opposite).

Variations on a theme

jammy dodgers

These biscuit puddings are filled with a layer of rich vanilla ice-cream. Serve them surrounded by extra syrup and dusted with icing sugar.

serves 8

pre-heat oven
180°C/350°F/gas 4

preparation time
1 hour

cooking time
10 minutes

freezing time
2-3 hours for ice-cream

for the ice-cream filling
1 tsp vanilla essence
1 x 425g carton custard
150ml (5fl oz) double cream
icing sugar to taste

for the biscuits
115g (4oz) butter
115g (4oz) caster sugar
1 egg, beaten
275g (9½oz) self-raising flour
pinch of salt
6-8 tsp milk

for strawberry syrup
450g (1lb) ripe strawberries
175ml (6fl oz) water
115g (4oz) caster sugar

equipment
shallow, freezerproof container; round 7.5cm (3in) cookie cutter; baking sheet, buttered

1 To make ice-cream, mix vanilla and custard. Whip cream then fold into custard. Add icing sugar to taste. Pour into freezerproof container. Freeze for 2-3 hours until firm.
2 To make biscuits, cream butter and sugar, add egg and sieve in flour and salt. Beat, softening with milk to form dough. Chill for 20 minutes.
3 Roll out dough to 3mm (⅛in). Cut 16 circles with cookie cutter. Cut small circles from the centre of half the biscuits. Bake for 10 minutes then cool.
4 Simmer syrup ingredients until strawberries are tender. Remove from heat, cover and cool.
5 Push strawberry mix through sieve. Return to heat and boil until reduced to a very thick syrup. Cool completely.
6 Remove ice-cream from fridge and allow to soften slightly. Spread a layer on a whole biscuit, spread syrup over ice-cream, top with a biscuit with a hole. Leave in freezer for 5-10 minutes.

why not try...

lemon puffs
Create lemon puff puddings by sandwiching a lemon-flavoured ice-cream filling between two layers of crisp puff pastry.

custard creams
Using the basic biscuit pastry (without cocoa), bake rectangular biscuits and sandwich with ice-cream or custard set with gelatine. Add a little strawberry syrup for colour and contrast.

coffee creams
Follow the custard cream adaption above but fill with ice-cream flavoured with 1-2 tbsp very strong coffee. Serve with the coffee syrup from the main recipe.

ginger nuts
Add ½ tsp ground ginger to the basic biscuit pastry and bake in rounds. Sandwich with ice-cream and serve with a caramel sauce.

any left?

These puddings won't keep well because the filling soon makes the biscuits soggy. Make only as many as you require or, if you want to make more later, store the layers separately.

Arctic roll

A play on two popular desserts, this luxurious sweet makes the most of favourite ingredients

Black Forest gâteau and Arctic ice-cream roll are combined to make an impressive dessert. Black Forest gâteau is famous for three main elements: chocolate sponge, black cherries and cream. In this frosty adaptation, the sponge and cherries are retained, but the cream is replaced with vanilla ice-cream and all three are frozen as an Arctic-type roll.

Adapting the traditional
To prepare the Arctic roll, chocolate Swiss roll is spread with cherry jam, then wrapped around a log of cherry and vanilla ice-cream. The roll is frozen again until firm, then sliced and served with extra cherries in a jammy sauce and clotted cream.

To achieve a neat roll shape, you'll need a cylinder in which to freeze the ice-cream. Use a foil-lined tube – you can use a container which holds potato crisps – this is ideal, as long as you empty the crumbs and trim it to length first.

Pastel perfection
For another take on a favourite tea-time cake you can make a Battenberg iced sponge. An almond-flavoured sponge is carefully wrapped around a chequered block of vanilla and strawberry ice-cream to imitate the look of this distinctive cake.

Gary's special touch

I love the idea of throwing a new slant on popular recipes. This time, I've combined the best bits of a Black Forest gâteau with an ice-cream centre which can be frozen in advance, then wrapped in sponge just before serving. Although Arctic roll is usually just served to children, this recipe is sophisticated enough for adults.

making Black Forest Arctic roll

You will need

serves 6	for the chocolate sponge
preparation time *45 minutes*	*3 eggs*
freezing time *overnight for the ice-cream, 30 minutes for the filled roll*	*75g (2¾oz) caster sugar*
	50g (1¾oz) plain flour
cooking time *10-15 minutes*	*1 tbsp cornflour*
pre-heat oven *180°C/350°F/gas 4*	*2 tbsp cocoa*

for the filling and sauce	to serve
225g (8oz) stoned bottled, canned or fresh cherries	*clotted cream, chocolate flakes (see page 214), mint sprigs and icing sugar*
600ml (1 pint) vanilla ice-cream	
150ml (5fl oz) water	
100g (3½oz) caster sugar	**equipment**
7 tbsp black cherry jam	*15cm (6in) long foil-lined tube;*
a dash of Kirsch (optional)	*33 x 22cm (13 x 8½in) Swiss roll tin, lined with non-stick baking paper*

1 Dry half the cherries with kitchen paper. If you are using ready-made ice-cream, take it out of the freezer to soften, then transfer to a bowl.

A range of techniques is used to create this special dessert, but they can be done in stages so you don't have to do too many things at once.

For the ice-cream, you can use a good ready-made vanilla ice-cream, or make your own in advance.

Making ice-cream

Pour 300ml (10fl oz) double cream and 300ml (10fl oz) milk into a pan. Add 1 drop of vanilla essence and bring to the boil. Whisk 6 egg yolks and 175g (6oz) caster sugar together until pale. Slowly pour in the hot milk and whisk well. Stir occasionally until cool. Then strain into a plastic container, add the cherries and freeze. Stir every 15 minutes until it starts to solidify.

Working with cherries

Bottled or canned cherries work well in this dessert, but you can use fresh cherries when available (see

Cook's notes, below). Dry the cherries before adding to the ice-cream, or they will discolour it and turn it streaky.

Making the chocolate sponge

Bake the sponge for 10-15 minutes, or until it is just set. When cooked, take it out of the oven and cover with a clean, damp cloth to prevent it drying out. Leave to cool completely in the tin, then turn out on to greaseproof paper. Trim off the crusty edges with a sharp knife.

Cook's notes

Stone fresh cherries and simmer for 2 minutes in a syrup made from the water and sugar. Drain, cool and dry half the cherries and add to the ice-cream. Save the syrup for making the sauce.

5 Uncover the sponge and turn out on to a sheet of greaseproof paper. Peel off the lining paper and trim the edges. Brush the remaining jam evenly over the surface.

2 Gently stir the dry cherries into the ice-cream until evenly distributed. Pack the mixture firmly into the tube. Freeze overnight or until the ice-cream is firm.

3 Pre-heat the oven. For the sponge, whisk the eggs and sugar until tripled in volume. Sift the flours and cocoa, then fold in gently. Pour into the tin and bake for 10-15 minutes.

4 Cover the sponge with a damp cloth and let it cool. For the sauce, boil water and sugar until slightly syrupy. Add 3 tbsp jam (and Kirsch). Strain and mix with remaining cherries.

6 Unwind the cardboard of the tube from around the ice-cream. Lay the ice-cream along one short end of the sponge and roll up using the paper to help. Cover in plastic wrap and freeze for 30 minutes.

7 Unwrap the Arctic roll and trim the excess sponge from the ends with a sharp knife. Cut into slices, then serve with the sauce, clotted cream, chocolate flakes and mint sprigs.

Variations on a theme

Battenberg iced sponge

Vanilla and strawberry ice-cream are stacked in a checked pattern, then wrapped in sponge. Buy the ice-cream in a long block or plastic tub.

serves 8

preparation time
30 minutes

freezing time
45 minutes

cooking time *10 minutes*

pre-heat oven
190°C/375°F/gas 5

ingredients
3 eggs
75g (2¾oz) caster sugar
3 drops almond essence
85g (3oz) plain flour
1 tbsp cornflour

for the filling
2 litre (3½ pint) block or tub vanilla ice-cream
2 litre (3½ pint) block or tub strawberry ice-cream
3-4 tbsp strawberry jam

for the coulis
225g (8oz) strawberries
1 tbsp icing sugar, plus extra to dust
1-2 tbsp water
strawberries and mint
sprigs to decorate

equipment
33 x 22cm (13 x 8½in) Swiss roll tin, lined with non-stick baking paper

1 Whisk the eggs and sugar until tripled in volume. Whisk in the almond essence. Sift the flours, then fold in. Pour into the tin and bake for 10 minutes, or until set. Cover and cool.
2 Turn out the ice-cream on to greaseproof paper. Cut 2 long blocks from each flavour, measuring 19cm (7½in) long and 3cm (1½in) wide. Stack the 4 blocks in a checked pattern. Freeze until firm.
3 Turn out the sponge on to greaseproof paper. Remove the lining paper. Spread the jam on top.
4 Unwrap ice-cream and sit across the sponge, just past the centre. Trim the long sides of the sponge up to the ends of the ice-cream block.
5 Score sponge along the long sides of the ice-cream. Bring up sponge to enclose side of the block. Repeat to enclose entire block. Trim and freeze for 30 minutes.
6 Purée the coulis ingredients, then sieve. Slice sponge and serve with coulis, strawberries, mint sprigs and icing sugar.

why not try...

You can use different flavoured ice-creams for both desserts. For the variation recipe, it is best to choose flavours with contrasting colours, such as chocolate and vanilla, and coffee with rum and raisin.

Christmas log
Make the Black Forest Arctic roll but spread the sponge with chocolate spread and fill with chocolate ice-cream, mixed with the cherries. Cover the roll with whipped chocolate cream, then top with chocolate flakes and a dusting of icing sugar.

rippled cappuccino
Make the Black Forest Arctic roll, but pack the tube with alternating spoonfuls of coffee and vanilla ice-cream. Spread the sponge with apricot jam. Serve with chocolate sauce.

banoffee treat
Make the sponge as for the Battenberg variation, but replace the almond essence with vanilla. Spread 2 bananas, mashed with 2 tsp lemon juice, over the sponge and use a combination of vanilla and toffee ice-cream to make the checkered block. Serve with piped whipped cream and crushed praline or chocolate-coated nuts.

frozen torte

A melt-in-the-mouth frozen mousse cake makes a luscious dessert

Frozen tortes are iced mousse cakes by another name. *Torte* is the German word for gâteau and is often used to describe large cakes with deep, rich mousse-like fillings. A frozen torte is really two delightful desserts in one – it's more impressive and more durable than the average mousse yet it's less trouble to make than ice-cream.

Everyone's favourite flavour

A dreamily rich chocolate mousse is the perfect candidate for freezing. Not only is it universally popular, but it also freezes incredibly smoothly and its fabulous richness survives the sub-zero temperatures unscathed. The chocolate mousse mixture is frozen on a crisp chocolate biscuit base, which makes an exciting contrast to its creamy texture.

Fruity freshness

The frozen-mousse idea works well for fruit-flavoured mousses too – especially when you freeze them on a base of soft sponge. The lemon mousse variation is sharply refreshing.

An iced torte makes an excellent dinner party dessert as you have to make it in advance to freeze it, leaving you with plenty of time to concentrate on other courses. Decorate it with crumbled flakes of chocolate.

Gary's special touch

Is it a mousse? Is it an ice-cream? Is it a torte? When you taste this amazing frozen chocolate torte, I bet you'll agree that it's the best of all three worlds! Certainly I think the combination of the super-light, ice-cold chocolate mousse on the crunchy biscuit base looks and tastes sublime.

making frozen chocolate torte

Baking a made-to-measure biscuit base for the torte gives the mousse a neat crunchy plinth to sit on. There's no need to worry about rolling out the dough – you simply press it into the base of the cake tin with the back of your fingers.

Whisked sponge base

For a totally different effect, you can sit the mousse on a soft sponge base instead (see page 216). Always use a light whisked fatless sponge rather than a creamed cake mixture which freezes rather firmly. A whisked sponge does not become too hard so you can cut and eat the cake quite easily while it's still frozen.

Airy and light

The success of any mousse depends on beating lots of air into the egg whites and the cream. Remember to check that your whisks and bowl are absolutely grease-free for the egg whites. Beat the eggs and cream carefully and check the consistency as

you go – it's all too easy to overwhip them, which makes it difficult to fold them into the mixture smoothly.

Chocolate flakes and curls

Make chocolate flakes by rubbing a slab of chilled chocolate against the medium-coarse grade of a grater. Alternatively, use a potato peeler to shave ribbon-like curls from chocolate left at warm room temperature. Experiment with both white and dark chocolate for the ultimate finishing touch.

Watchpoint!

Raw eggs!
The eggs in a frozen torte are not cooked so it's best not to serve it to the elderly, pregnant or very young children. Also, always make sure you put any remaining torte straight back in the freezer after serving.

1 For the base, cream the butter and sugar until fluffy. Sift the flour and cocoa together and stir in. Press the dough into the base of the tin and bake for 10 minutes. Leave to cool.

5 In a clean bowl, whisk the egg whites until stiff. Gradually add the rest of the sugar, spoonful by spoonful, whisking after each addition to form stiff peaks.

2 To make the mousse, break the chocolate into a bowl and add the cold coffee. Set the bowl over a pan of simmering water to melt the chocolate. Stir occasionally.

3 Meanwhile, whisk the egg yolks with half the caster sugar until the mixture is fluffy. (To maximize the volume, whisk over warm water.) Gently stir in the melted chocolate.

4 Whip the cream by hand with a balloon whisk until it holds soft swirls. If you prefer to use a hand-held electric whisk, be careful not to whip the cream too firmly.

6 Fold the cream into the chocolate mixture, then fold in the egg whites. Pour the mousse on to the cool biscuit base, cover and freeze for at least 4 hours or overnight.

7 Take the torte out of the freezer and remove the sides of the tin. Leave to stand for 15 minutes, then decorate with piped whipped cream, chocolate flakes and a dusting of cocoa powder.

Variations on a theme

frozen lemon mousse torte

In this fresh light frozen dessert with a sharp citrus tang, the lemon mousse sits on a base of whisked sponge.

serves 8
preparation time
15 minutes for the sponge; 10 minutes plus overnight freezing for the mousse
cooking time
25-30 minutes for the sponge
pre-heat oven
180°C/350°F/gas 4
equipment
20cm (8in) springform cake tin, base-lined

for the sponge base
3 eggs
85g (3oz) caster sugar
85g (3oz) plain flour, sifted
25g (1oz) butter, melted

for the mousse
3 eggs, separated
115g (4oz) caster sugar
finely grated zest of 3 medium-sized lemons and the juice of 2
142ml carton whipping cream
whipped cream, lemon zest and nuts to decorate

1 To make the sponge, whisk the eggs and sugar in a bowl over hot water until trebled in volume. Take off the heat and whisk until cool, and trails from the whisk hold their shape for at least 5 seconds.
2 Gently fold a little flour into the mixture with a metal spoon.
3 Lightly fold in a little melted butter. Repeat folding in butter and flour alternately until smoothly incorporated.
4 Pour the mixture into the prepared tin and bake for 25-30 minutes until a fine skewer inserted into the centre comes out cleanly. Cool for 10 minutes then transfer to a wire rack.
5 For the mousse, beat the yolks and sugar together in a bowl until pale, then stir in the lemon juice and zest.
6 In another bowl, whisk the egg whites until stiff, then gradually fold into the lemon mixture with a metal spoon.
7 Whip the cream and fold into the lemon mix.
8 Cut the sponge in half horizontally, and put one half in the bottom of the cake tin. Pour the mousse on top, cover with plastic wrap and freeze overnight.
9 Release the torte and decorate the top with cream, finely shredded lemon zest and nuts.

why not try...

crushed biscuits
Rather than baking a biscuit base, you can use crushed biscuits instead. Blitz the biscuits to a fine crumb, mix with melted butter and press into the bottom of the tin. Then chill this base in the fridge to firm it up.

lemon and ginger
A crumbled gingernut base under the lemon mousse makes a delicious option.

top and bottom
To create more of an iced-gâteau effect, you can lay the other disc of sponge, cut side down, on top of the mousse before freezing.

surprise fruit
Arrange a layer of fresh fruit – whole strawberries or raspberries are ideal – on top of the base before you pour in the mousse. This works well with the chocolate or fruit mousses.

any left?

Simply cover the leftover torte with plastic wrap and put it back into the freezer straightaway so it stays frozen.

Freeze the leftover half of the sponge for making a second torte or a trifle on another day.

dacquoise

A simple yet elegant gâteau, this dacquoise is made of layers of meringue sandwiched with cream and pecans

A dacquoise is a meringue gâteau that originates from south-west France – a *dacquoise* is a female inhabitant of Dax, a major town in the region.

The gâteau normally consists of discs of meringue, made with ground almonds or hazelnuts, sandwiched together with flavoured whipped cream or butter cream. Often fresh fruit is added as well. This rich, sweet gâteau is served as a cake for a special tea party or as a dessert at the end of an otherwise light meal.

Pecan and maple syrup
Here, the main dacquoise is made up of three pecan-nut meringues with layers of whipped cream and more chopped pecans in between. For good measure, the cream is lightly flavoured with maple syrup and rum. An extra drizzle of maple syrup and some pecan halves are all you need to decorate the gâteau.

An icy alternative
The variation recipe is a frozen dacquoise with fruity sorbets spread between the meringues. The whole gâteau is frozen before being decorated with fresh raspberries and served with a raspberry coulis.

Gary's special touch

For the freshest nutty flavour you want to use just-shelled nuts, so I usually buy pecans still in their shells and then shell them myself when I need them.

I also try to buy the best maple syrup available – look out for American or Canadian brands in your supermarket for an authentic flavour.

making pecan dacquoise

You will need

serves 8

preparation time *45 minutes, plus 4 hours chilling*

cooking time *1½ hours*

pre-heat oven *140°C/275°F/gas 1*

ingredients

5 egg whites

225g (8oz) golden caster sugar

175g (6oz) pecan nuts

600ml (1 pint) double cream

100ml (3½fl oz) maple syrup

3 tbsp rum

equipment

2 baking trays lined with non-stick baking parchment

Before you begin making this dessert, you will need to prepare templates to ensure that the three meringue rounds are the same size. These are simply three circles drawn on to the baking parchment that is used to line the baking trays.

All you need to do then is spread the meringue mixture evenly within the outlines of the circles. Don't worry if the surfaces of the meringues aren't perfectly smooth. A little bit of roughness just makes a more interesting finish.

A golden addition

The meringue mixture is made in the usual way by whipping egg whites and then adding sugar. This recipe uses golden caster sugar to give the meringues slightly more flavour. Chopped pecans are folded in at the last minute before the meringue mix is transferred to the baking trays.

The meringues do take quite a long time to cook – 1¼ hours – and the assembling and chilling of the finished dacquoise adds even more to the preparation time. However, you can make the meringue rounds the day before and then assemble

the dacquoise the next morning. Just wrap the cooled meringue rounds in baking parchment and store in a cool dry cupboard.

Making up is easy

The meringue rounds are layered with chopped pecans and whipped cream – the cream is flavoured by whipping it with maple syrup and rum. Once the layers are sandwiched together, the finished dacquoise is chilled in the fridge for at least 4 hours. This helps the cream filling to firm up and the meringue to soften slightly, making it easier to cut.

Cook's notes

Individual dacquoises

For a special dessert you can make individual dacquoises. Draw six 7.5cm (3in) circles on each piece of baking parchment and spread the meringue in the 12 circles. To assemble, sandwich together just 2 meringue discs for each serving and pipe some whipped cream on top.

1 Line 2 baking sheets with non-stick baking parchment. Using a 20cm (8in) bowl or plate as a guide draw 2 circles on one piece of parchment and 1 circle on the other.

5 Meanwhile, chop 55g (2oz) pecans and set aside. Whip the cream with 4 tbsp maple syrup and the rum until it forms soft peaks.

2 Put the egg whites in a bowl and whisk until they form soft peaks. Sprinkle in the sugar, a spoonful at a time, whisking well after each addition.

3 Grind 55g (2oz) pecan nuts and fold into the whisked egg whites. Spread the meringue mixture roughly in the circles drawn on the baking sheets.

4 Bake for 1¼ hours until the meringues are crisp. When cooked, leave for 10 minutes then peel off the baking parchment and transfer to a wire rack to cool completely.

6 Spread a 2cm (¾in) thick layer of whipped cream on 1 meringue and sprinkle with the chopped pecans. Cover with another meringue.

7 Spread on another layer of cream and chopped nuts and top with the last meringue. Chill for 4 hours. Decorate with the remaining whole nuts and drizzle with the rest of the maple syrup.

Variations on a theme

iced dacquoise with raspberry coulis

serves 8

preparation time
45 minutes, plus 4½ hours freezing

cooking time
1¼ hours

pre-heat oven
140°C/275°F/gas 1

ingredients
5 egg whites
225g (8oz) vanilla caster sugar
500ml (18fl oz) raspberry sorbet
500ml (18fl oz) apple or gooseberry sorbet
280g (10oz) raspberries
55g (2oz) icing sugar
142ml (5fl oz) carton single cream

equipment
as before (see page 218)

1 Using a 20cm (8in) plate as a guide, draw 3 circles on the sheets of baking parchment.
2 Whisk the egg whites into soft peaks. Add the sugar, a spoonful at a time, whisking well after each addition.
3 Divide the mixture between the circles and spread it out evenly.
4 Bake for 1¼ hours until

crisp. Leave for 10 minutes then transfer to a rack to cool.
5 About 30 minutes before making up the dacquoise, transfer the raspberry sorbet to the fridge to soften a little. Place 1 meringue on a freezer-proof plate and spread on the softened sorbet. Cover with another meringue round and freeze for about 30 minutes until firm.
6 Transfer the apple sorbet to the fridge while the raspberry meringue is in the freezer to soften. Then spread it on top of the raspberry meringue sandwich. Top with the last meringue and freeze for at least 4 hours.
7 To make the coulis, purée 225g (8oz) raspberries and push through a sieve. Stir in the icing sugar and chill until needed.
8 To serve, leave the dacquoise at room temperature for 10 minutes. Drizzle a little coulis over the top and decorate with the remaining raspberries.
9 Cut into slices. Pour some coulis around each portion. Using a teaspoon, pour drops of cream into the coulis. Drag a skewer through the drops of cream to create heart shapes.

why not try...

fruit fool filling
Instead of using the whipped cream or sorbet to sandwich the meringues together, why not use a fruit fool? Simply make a purée of the fruit of your choice and fold it into whipped cream; chill to firm before spreading on the meringues. Good fruits to use are gooseberries (cooked with elderflower syrup), rhubarb (sweetened and then flavoured with a pinch of ground ginger) or blackberries.

iced coffee dacquoise
Make your meringues for this version with some ground walnuts. Mix some chopped walnuts with some softened coffee ice-cream and use to sandwich the meringues together in the same way as you would the sorbet. Decorate with walnut halves. Make a coffee syrup by dissolving 150g (5oz) caster sugar in 300ml (10fl oz) strong fresh coffee. Boil until reduced by half. Cool to room temperature and then serve with the dacquoise.

chocolate-chip filling
Sandwich the meringues together with softened chocolate-chip ice-cream. Then re-freeze until the ice-cream is firm again before slicing. Serve with chocolate sauce drizzled over and around each slice.

acknowledgements

Photographs:
Eaglemoss Publications (Karl Adamson) 4, 9, 10, 11(bl), 41(t,b), 42, 43(br), 44(t), 56(tr,br), 57, 66(tl), 67(t,b), 68, 70(l), 74(t), 87(b), 88(r), 89, 145(b), 147(t,b), 148, 149, 158(t), 183(t,b), 184, 186(t), (Chris Alack) 28(tl), 36(tl), 94(tl), 126(tl), 130(tl), 208(tl), (Edward J Allwright) 5(c), 51, 87(tr), 90(tl), (St John Asprey) 5(t), 17, 102(t), 115, 123(tr,b), 124, 163, 183(br), 193, 217, 218(b), 219, 220, (Iain Bagwell) 49(br), 118(tl), 151, 167, 196(tl), 200(tl), (Steve Baxter) 8, (Ken Field) 25, 45, 49(tl), 59(tr,bc), 60(tl,tc,br), 62(tl),

63, 75(t,b), 76, 78(t), 108(tr,br), 109, 110(t,c), 111, 119, 131, 143(t), 144, 146(t), 155(t,b), 156(tr,bl,br), 157, 170(tl), 183(tr), 201, (Ian Garlick) 103, (Amanda Heywood) 11(tr), 29, 33, 37, 38, 39, 40(t), 49(tr), 55(tr,bc), 58(tl), 71(t,b), 72(t,b), 73, 83(tr,bc), 84(tr), 85, 86(tl), 143(b), 175, 183(tl), 189(t,bc), 190, 191, 192(t), 209(t,b), 210(b), (Sian Irvine) 107(bc), 110(tl), (Nigel James) 91, 171, (Graham Kirk) 154(tl), 183(bl), 212(tl), 216(tl), (William Lingwood) 159(tr,bc), 160(tr,br), 161, 162(tl), (Thomas Odulate) 32(l), 82(t), 150(t), 174(tl), 178(tl),

(Juliet Piddington) 60(bl), (William Reavell) 98(tl), (Howard Shooter) 11(tl), 16(tl), 20(tl), 127, 166(tl), (Simon Smith) 11(br), 24(tl), 48(tl), 67(b), 95, 107(tr), 114(tl), 182(tl), 204(tl), 205, 213, (Andrew Sydenham) 21, 49(bl), 99, 139, 179, (Jon Whitaker) 5(b), 13, 106(tl), 134(tl), 197, 218(t), (Philip Wilkins) 79(tr,bc), 80(tr,br), 81.

Illustrations:
Robert Hook 3, 4, Coral Mula 109(r), 145(r).